Ronald Burrell
1981

Boston Priests, 1848–1910

A Study of Social and Intellectual Change

BOSTON PRIESTS, 1848–1910

A Study of Social and Intellectual Change

Donna Merwick

Harvard University Press
Cambridge, Massachusetts
1973

To My Mother

Contents

Preface

For those who advert to it at all, Boston Catholicism has been wholly identified with "Irish Catholicism." It has been regarded as the creation of the immigrants. As such, it has been seen as a set of values which had and still has no existence apart from the Irish or Irish-American mentality. Similarly Boston clergymen have been typed as Irish priests. They have been looked upon as men who resisted cultural and intellectual pressures, preferring to remain responsive only to some Catholic social philosophy learned either in Ireland or in Irish-American homes. These beliefs extended beyond strictly theological matters and embraced wider social, political, and cultural concerns. If they showed any sign of change, the alteration was only toward a greater intensification of the original beliefs. The acculturation of the priests, it has also been presumed, was nothing more than the clerical equivalent of the Irish migrants' adjustment to Protestant America.

Yet three successive generations of Catholic clergymen lived in Boston in the last half of the nineteenth century. Contrary to popular opinion, their lives and their ways of thinking were significantly affected by the surrounding Yankee culture. Their assumptions, values, traditions, and talents were repeatedly tested against those of the prevailing society. This was the case in the

1840's when native Protestants were the majority, or in the 1850's when every Boston citizen was adjusting to the dislocations created by the immigrants, or in the 1890's when the Catholic population had reached almost 750,000. As a result, each generation of diocesan clergymen to one degree or another parted with a given configuration of ideas as it assessed, responded to, and reshaped New England's society. Essentially, then, the thinking of the Catholic priests of Boston was not static. A surprising intellectual diversity was in fact dictated by the particular circumstances of Boston.

Throughout the entire period, the Roman Catholic Church was intellectually a house divided. Independence of thinking manifested itself on matters ranging from the European revolutions of 1848 to the parochial school issue of the 1870's and 1880's. Several factors account for this. Most important, the administration of the diocese in the nineteenth century never fell wholly into the hands of Irish or Irish-American priests connected with the immigration from Ireland after 1845. The diocese was administered largely by Yankee-Catholic clergymen until 1907. Quite apart from what this suggests regarding a sympathetic rapport with Yankee Protestants and the traditional Boston culture, this factor suggests as well the presence of at least two traditions within the church. The tradition rooted in Boston was dominant among the churchmen of the first and in part the second generations. They were born between 1820 and 1860; one of them, John J. Williams, was archbishop of the diocese from 1866 to 1907. These priests were especially conscious of their separation from the immigrant clergy and were intent upon constricting their influence. The other tradition was Catholicism brought over from Ireland. It was European, Jansenistic, tied to a village way of life, nationalistic, and militantly anti-Protestant. It was represented by most clergymen of the second generation, that is, by men born between 1840 and 1860 either in Ireland or in Irish-American homes in Boston. Fewer of that generation were born, educated, and trained for the priesthood in Ireland than has been supposed. For example, in

1894 there were ninety-seven pastors of English-speaking parishes in the Boston area. Of these priests, only thirty-nine were born in Ireland and only seven men ordained there. The important point is that, as a tradition, Irish Catholicism in the last half of the nineteenth century met steady opposition in Boston. It had to contest with an established Yankee–Catholic tradition which proposed a set of values laid in the earlier, more pluralistic society of Boston. Later it had to contend with a second sort of ideological opposition, one which arose while the influential vestiges of Yankee Catholicism were still about. This was the brand of Catholicism introduced into the archdiocese in 1907 by Williams' successor, William Henry O'Connell. It was representative of the third generation of clergymen and was, in its own way, a rejection of both previous traditions.

To speak of "the Roman Catholic Church of Boston" suggests some sophisticated institutional structure. Yet the organization which the archbishop supervised during the nineteenth century was at first small—inconsequential in the 1840's—and later chaotic. This again made for intellectual diversity. But Boston Catholicism was also flexible in the nineteenth century because Williams exploited those circumstances in Europe which kept the papacy weak and distracted throughout most of the century. In the 1890's these conditions changed when a stronger man than Pius ix and better days than the 1850's returned to the Vatican. Nevertheless by that time many Boston clergymen were accustomed to the same freedom of thought and operation that the Massachusetts Bay colonists cherished during Cromwell's rule in England. No less cunningly did they maneuver for its perpetuation. Williams again was the key figure. He encouraged the growth of "Americanism" in Catholic thought, registering no feelings of disloyalty although this "heresy" was condemned by Pope Leo xiii in an encyclical in 1898. He brought a relative autonomy to the diocese, keeping at bay Roman churchmen as well as Irish clerics. The result was a pluralism within Catholic culture, at least for the duration of his administration.

This study ends in 1910, three years after the consecration

of William Henry O'Connell. He was a man two generations younger than Williams and one who finally achieved for Rome its imperial designs in the Boston archdiocese. He had been trained in the Vatican's bureaucracy as rector of the North American College in Rome, a residence for American seminarians. From 1895 to 1901 he had discovered a sophisticated Catholic way of life in the Vatican court and the rich Italian villas surrounding it. This matched and, to his mind, bettered the gentility of Brahmin Boston. O'Connell took Rome as the font of culture, the rule of theological interpretation, and the exemplar of organization. As a result, he introduced two levels of Catholic culture to the Boston archdiocese, neither one of which was to be a hybrid with American Protestantism. For the wealthy and well-educated Catholics, he allowed a permissive set of values. His expectation was that Catholic leaders like the Bellamy Storers would recreate in Boston the elite social circles to which many American Catholic *émigrés* belonged in the Edwardian days in Italy. The masses of Irish-Americans, on the other hand, needed prepackaged ideas. To implement this indoctrination, he, for example, converted *The Pilot,* previously independent, into an official diocesan newspaper within thirteen months of his consecration. Each pastor was made personally (and financially) responsible for placing it in every Catholic home.

O'Connell organized the archdiocese with a zeal for centralization matched by others of his generation, like Theodore Roosevelt, J. P. Morgan, and other efficient managers of "the progressive era." While he and his appointees took leadership, the clergymen of the generation before O'Connell remained a generation squeezed between an earlier group of priests attuned to the city's older values and this younger generation which had incorporated American ways and found Irish-Americanisms decidedly embarrassing. Under O'Connell, they were subjected to institutionalization, not the least part of which was a kind of intellectual martial law which discouraged—and punished—nonconformity. If it is ever valid to compare Roman Catholic thought in Boston to a monolith, it is from that point on.

I want to express my deepest gratitude to those members of the history department at the University of Wisconsin who have assisted me in this work. I am especially appreciative of the encouragement and guidance of Professors Merle Curti and William R. Taylor. They deepened my understanding of the responsibility of writing history and made this undertaking a rewarding one. I owe thanks to Professor Taylor also for reading the manuscript in its early stages and offering important suggestions.

I am greatly indebted to the Danforth Foundation which supported me financially as a Kent Fellow from 1965 to 1968. I am grateful to the University of Melbourne for financial support in bringing this work to publication.

I wish to thank those who made archival materials available to me: Monsignor Matthew P. Stapleton, former rector of St. John's Seminary (Brighton) and Reverend Robert J. Banks, presently rector of the seminary; Monsignor Timothy J. Shea, vice-chancellor of the archdiocese of Boston; Monsignor Vincent Tatarczuk, vice-chancellor of the archdiocese of Portland, Maine; Miss Katherine Haywood and Mr. Daniel I. Cronin of the Society of St. Vincent De Paul in Boston; Reverend Joseph J. Shea, S.J., and Mr. James M. Mahoney of the College of the Holy Cross, Worcester, Massachusetts. To my husband, whose encouragement made the book possible, no adequate amount of gratitude can be expressed.

Boston Priests, 1848–1910
A Study of Social and Intellectual Change

Introduction
1866 as Vantage Point

By the 1860's native Bostonians were fairly sure they had drawn the black lot. Religiously the precarious balance of Unitarian-Transcendentalist Boston was giving way. At least some Bostonians had also lost pride in their own capitalistic ventures and feared that the incredible prosperity that had overtaken the country in the 1850's would "deprave the national character," not to say their own. And then too had come the endless immigrants. But here the salient held. For the New Englander was always able to make the distinction between himself as "the practical Anglo-Saxon" and the Irishman as "the imaginative, gay Celt who lacked the capacity to create or sustain successful political institutions." Clearly the immigrant lacked a great deal more than political acumen, and that realization also underpinned the Bostonian's sense of time-honored superiority.[1]

Yankee antagonism toward the Irish-Catholic immigrant in the 1860's was willful and bitter. Yet it did not encompass the Brahmins' relationships with or attitudes toward all Catholics in Boston. In fact, Boston society of the last half of the nineteenth century was not simply bifurcated into Protestant Yankees and Catholic Irish-Americans. For the Catholic clergymen of Boston, to isolate one group, were not exclusively "Irish." In fact the prominent Roman Catholic clergymen until the mid-1880's were neither Irish immigrants nor the sons of the "Famine Irish." Rather they were men like John J. Williams. He was born "of Boston stock" in 1822, educated by a New England schoolmistress, and served as vicar-general from 1857 to 1866 when he was installed as bishop. William Blenkinsop and James Fitton were both missionaries functioning in the diocese long before the 1848 migrations. The irascible Hilary Tucker and the two young Healy brothers, Sherwood and James, were priests taken into the diocese from the midwest and the south, and given key positions at the procathedral. They too were of Irish ancestry but in no way connected with the massive immigration of the 1840's. Father John Roddan, who was prominent as a novelist and editor of *The Pilot* from 1848 to 1858, was born in Boston and worked in a piano factory before studying for the priesthood. George Haskins was also a leader in diocesan affairs. He was graduated from Harvard, ordained as an Episcopal minister, and later converted to Catholicism. Working with him was Joshua Bodfish, a sinewy New Englander who was the son of the Episcopal minister at Falmouth. Williams appointed Bodfish chancellor of the archdiocese in 1881, a position he held until 1886.

The ideas and sympathies of these Yankee Catholics were as significant as the prominence which they enjoyed. In the years after 1866 and until 1907, Williams as bishop set official policy for the Catholic church in Boston. He was forced to tread a narrow lane between Yankee Catholics and Irish-American Catholics, and his adoption of an increasingly aloof position toward the latter had wide consequences. John B. Fitzpatrick, who was bishop of Boston from 1846 to 1866, had also been forced to walk with care during the 1850's. Yet much as he was annoyed at "having to be on our sharps," he faced none of the decisions which Williams would have to make. In the process of making those decisions over the years, Williams chose to disqualify himself for real leadership rather than destroy a world that he hoped might yet somehow survive. For Williams was a legatee of Boston as "the pedestrian city," a small commercial port rich in person-to-person contacts and a sense of individual self-reliance. He never fully realized that a special type of solidarity was needed by the Irish immigrants. There was only one society available to his imagination and it was the compact, nervous society that eddied around the streets east of Tremont Street. Smallness was a category with which he could take hold of this society, and tightness made it temperamentally comfortable. So persuasive was this way of thinking that in 1898 when the Irish migrants and their children had changed Boston into "a conglomeration of villages and suburbs inhabited by nearly a million people . . . [with] the neighboring towns . . . growing up to the very walls of the city," Williams refused the offer of becoming the United States' second cardinal lest the dignity for the Boston archdiocese highlight a kingdom within a kingdom or, more exactly, a totally new realm. In fact, he had even failed to develop such bureaucratic machinery as would have been to the advantage of the city as well as Catholic interests. During the last quarter of the nineteenth century when the Catholic population reached nearly a half-million, he clung to a utopian desire for Catholic insignificance. He appeared to assume that if it were strictly observed, this invisibility might prolong the hospitable consensus of earlier days, and Boston gentility might be widely absorbed. But the raw truth was that while Williams cherished "the unknown American future" as much as did James Russell Lowell or Charles Eliot Norton, the future of Boston even in the 1860's already belonged to the Irish.[2]

By 1866, Catholics had resided in small numbers in Boston for over seventy-five years. In 1792, there were four priests residing in Boston and serving both its single congregation and outlying mission territories. Three priests were French, one was Irish. They were shortly joined by Jean Cheverus who was appointed bishop in 1808 when the diocese of Boston was created.

It would never have occurred to the gracious and charming Jean Cheverus, first Catholic bishop of Boston, that Roman Catholics of the city would one day consider the Massachusetts government and Boston culture dangerous to their interests. Williams had to face the reality of this hostility. But to Cheverus, who resided in Boston from 1796 to 1823, life in the Yankee city was a series of experiences shared with citizens like his lifelong friend Josiah Quincy. His handsome Church of the Holy Cross had been designed by Bulfinch and erected with funds raised through a subscription list headed by John Adams with a gift of $100. One-fifth of the total cost of the church came from local Protestants with sums added by John Quincy Adams, James and Thomas Handasyd Perkins, John Lowell, Harrison Grey Otis, Joseph Coolidge, David Sears, Theodore Lyman, and other prominent Bostonians. In Salem the Unitarian minister, Reverend William Bentley, assisted in obtaining contributions from merchants like Joseph Peabody, William Gray, Nathaniel West, and George Crowninshield. Cheverus ardently immersed himself in the needs of his congregation and his city. "When a load of firewood that [Bishop Cheverus] . . . had sent to a poor sick woman in Water Street remained unsawed by her neighbors," the story was told, "the bishop quite simply got up before daybreak, shouldered his own sawhorse, walked to the woman's house and did the job himself." He was similarly present when fortifications were being constructed at South Boston during the War of 1812 and was observed "trundling a wheelbarrow, with two hundred and fifty of his congregation." Personal fulfillment required there be as few social barriers as possible. So it was neither pomposity nor subterfuge that prompted 226 Protestant citizens of Boston—"almost every prominent citizen of Boston at the time from Daniel Webster to Harrison Grey Otis down"— to appeal against the French government's decision to appoint Cheverus to a home diocese. They wrote the French government in 1823 begging fruitlessly that the bishop be left in Boston. "We hold him," the letter read, "to be a blessing and a treasure in our social community, which we cannot part with and which, without any injustice to any man, we may affirm, if withdrawn from us, can never be replaced. . . . In no place, nor under any circumstances, can Bishop Cheverus be situated where his influence, whether spiritual, moral or social, can be so extensive as where he is now." Nor was it empty formality that directed Cheverus' words back to Mayor Quincy in 1826 from Montauban, France, where he had taken up his duties. "If, as you have the goodness to assure me, I am not forgotten in Boston, I can say, with truth, that I do not forget Boston. So dear and familiar is the name of the beloved city," he wrote, "that even in conversation I say Boston instead of Montauban, and this often. And then I am told," he concluded ingenuously, "you love Boston better than Montauban."[3]

The Catholic church in the Boston diocese in the first half of the nineteenth century had its lean and fat years. There were periods when a head count of Catholics registered rapid growth, and alternate years when Catholics were scattered and few. There were periods when Yankees and Catholics lived in peace, and years when there was open hostility. In 1820, Catholics in the entire Boston diocese numbered 3,500. So poorly did this compare with the 30,000 then in the city of Philadelphia or the 24,000 in the city of New York that four years later when there was no noticeable numerical progress it was twice suggested to Rome that the see of Boston be reunited with New York. In 1825 when Benedict Fenwick became bishop only 385 persons were baptized at the single strong parish in the diocese, the cathedral parish of Boston. In the same year the bishop had only five priests. Yet between 1827 and 1838 large-scale immigration occurred; halted by the panic of 1837, it nonetheless rose again in 1842 to continue, with minor fluctuations, until the Famine migrations overshadowed all previous figures. Baptisms in the metropolitan area increased from 524 in 1830 to approximately 2,483 in 1846 when John B. Fitzpatrick became bishop. The Catholic population of Boston in 1846 was "at least 32,000" according to the *Boston Recorder*.[4]

Bishop Fenwick's administration was marked by more frequent explosions of "No Popery" than Fitzpatrick's. The evangelists of "the second Great Awakening" intermittently attacked Romanism from 1828 to 1834. In that year and as a result of the religious antagonisms aroused, mobs burned an Ursuline convent at Charlestown, natives fought with Irish immigrants in the Broad Street riots, and the Antimasonic Party kept up its assault upon Catholics. It is impossible to estimate the number of Protestants who deplored such behavior. Yet the official historians of the diocese contend that "in reality . . . the intellectual climate of the age was by no means so unfavorable to Catholicism as it might at first sight appear." Certainly it was not unfavorable after 1846 when Fitzpatrick, unlike Fenwick, sought association with non-Catholics, "was welcomed into the more prominent circles of Boston," joined the eminently liberal Thursday Evening Club, kept up his friendship with the Cabot family, and was, as Henry Cabot Lodge wrote, respected by Boston Protestants and Catholics alike as "Bishop John."[5]

In the 1850's, when Williams was in his early thirties and was swimming at Holy Cross College with fellow priests and sledding there with Bishop Fitzpatrick, Catholicism was still organizationally small-time. "Bishop Fitzpatrick, the kindly chief of the little cathedral staff of which Williams was a member," wrote a journalist of the 1890's, "was the last Roman Catholic bishop to be seen in ordinary society. He lived in South Street, among old Boston neighbors, and might have been met at several dinner-tables which he frequented." In fact it seems clear that Fitzpatrick and Williams were not uneasy at the relatively unaggressive place of Catholicism in Boston. It was an accepted and comfortable state of affairs. In such a style, the Catholic church of the 1850's and 1860's was thriving as much as Fitzpatrick and Williams wished. It had merchant connections like Joseph Iasigi, converts among the illustrious Tuckerman family and the respect of the Citizens' Association. It was pleasing that "altar boy" and other Catholic phenomena still carried a certain kind of awe and appeal. Charles Fairbanks, Jr., Joseph Coolidge Shaw, and George Haskins—all of Boston's good families— moved painlessly into Catholicism and into personal friendship with the bishop, though within just a generation this could not be so. In short, the "second spring" moved along under an easygoing momentum.[6]

In this context, there was little consolation for a man like Williams in Phillips Brooks' insistence at mid-century that materialism or Romanism were the only live alternatives to the present infidelity. Rather, this was frightful in the confrontation which it suggested. For Williams inherited from Cheverus and then Fitzpatrick a nonviolent stance regarding civil and religious rights for Catholics. Following their example, he held that a bishop was seriously responsible for his personal social relationships and for forming his own social conscience. But the stabilizing of the democracy in the city and the nation was to be left to the more intelligent and prosperous classes. It was a task for liberal-minded men like Nathaniel Bowditch who, if they disagreed on religious matters, were still personal friends. Later priest-writers like William Henry O'Connell were quite incorrect (as some well realized) in insisting that Protestants and Catholics in Boston had always carried on a bitter war of attrition. There was not always the organized religious or cultural hatred of later psychotic proportions. If after 1848 and the Irish emigration mutual respect and self-respect dismally disintegrated, it too was gradual. Haskins repeatedly insisted in the 1860's on the existence of amiable relations between Protestants and Catholics of the city, and this opinion was substantiated by such courtesies as the closing of the Boylston school district for the funeral of Bishop Fitzpatrick in 1866. Similarly the burning of the Irish shanties in the North End in 1859 greatly chagrined the Protestant population and seems generally to have been the outcome of an irrational fear of somehow descending to the imagined barbarism of the Irish.[7]

The official Roman Catholic policy toward the ill-suited Irish immigrants in the last half of the nineteenth century was that they be slipped into Boston society like a soiled handkerchief into the back pocket. They were to be manipulated as much into the provincialism of mid-century Boston as they would later be manipulated by Cardinal O'Connell into social patterns acceptable to the upper-class society of Rome in the 1890's. Those who could not conform—either through ignorance, open dissent, or noticeable breaking of the peace—were to be hushed up. In Williams' time, this was the job of the local pastors, operating individually or meeting in synod. In O'Connell's time, it was accomplished by demanding utter obedience to himself through the bureaucracy created immediately on his accession in 1907. As for Irish-American nationalism, Fitzpatrick and Williams looked forward to its demise but were wise enough to suffer the existence of it in such institutions as Patrick Donahoe's *The Pilot*. In this weekly newspaper, articles insisted on strong ties with the "Auld Country." Both Fitzpatrick and Williams allowed a harmless outspokenness on Irish issues in *The Pilot*. For this assuaged the deeper hurt and guilt of a group whose Irish patriotism was too quickly slipping away under the burden of its own bewildered submission to Boston traditions, not the least of which was the nonimmigrant Roman Catholic Church.[8]

Acceptable neither to the Yankee nor the Yankee-Catholic population, the Irish immigrants after 1850 were squeezed into an incomprehensible conformity by the very persons from whom they might have expected leadership and direction. They lived the madness of having to see things through the veils at once of two customs, two educations, two environments. And by the 1860's Bishop Bacon of Portland, Maine, had already typed the "Irish parish priest" with disdain.[9]

Meanwhile Yankee-Catholic priests, many of them converts like Theodore Metcalf, Joshua Bodfish, and George Haskins, continued to hold what few key positions there were in the diocese. At the same time local priests—chiefly Irish or Irish-American—were establishing parishes despite disappointments and hardships. Within twenty-five years of Williams' installation as bishop, the non-Yankee Irish population which they represented would become the irrepressible force in Boston. One effect would be the forceful challenge for leadership of the local Irish-American clergy, men whose lives were largely shaped by these same parishioners.

But all of this is to highlight lines of conflict and to make a theoretician of Williams, whereas in reality, like the Brahmins, he was just losing out. Meanwhile and until he lost out both to the Irish and to Rome, he cheerfully allowed the shape of the diocese to be determined largely by geographic and other environmental conditions. This in itself kept Catholicism unpretentious in its ambitions and highly experimental. For example, outside Boston and yet still within a diocese that in 1866 comprised all of the Commonwealth of Massachusetts, the priests of Williams' generation were encountering experiences which no manual of clerical behavior could have anticipated. Father Edward Turpin was living in a boardinghouse where young and bothersome girls resided; he had no rectory yet. Many priests had to be out alone at night, yet for those who were Jesuits this was an accommodation they had to make against their Rule. Others were frequently boarding in individual homes while on begging tours. In Pembroke, Massachusetts, these were days when Mass was celebrated in stores and shops. In Sandwich, Massachusetts, as elsewhere, laymen functioned as elders "deliberating on the best method of disposing of their old church" and instructing that "herewith Your Lordship [Fitzpatrick] may authorize Father Batoldi to dispose," and so forth. Throughout the diocese and even in Boston, much of the preaching had a discernibly evangelical tone and was accompanied by all the appropriate revivalistic techniques. In East Boston, James Fitton had returned to the city through whose paths he drove cows as a child, a kind of gentle Lorenzo Dow come home to rest after missionary journeys for fifty years in six New England states.[10]

At the procathedral on Franklin Street, the tidy landscape and homey neighborhood surroundings offered to the imagination nothing of bureaucracy or institutional structures. Until 1863 when Hilary Tucker began worrying about her noises, a cow was part of the cathedral rectory "family." With a folksiness which one of his own priests captured in a novel, "Bishop John" formulated with the priests living in the rectory such day-to-day policies as the diocese required. He, and Williams after him, conceived of himself primarily as rector of the procathedral parish rather than bishop, and not unreasonably so. "Bishop" connoted a responsible administrative role. But the circumstances in which it was enacted in the United States were so colonial, as Tucker's diary points out, that the term also signified men who were simply financial beggars *extraordinaire*. Besides, apart from clerical appointments, there was tangibly little to administer. There was no seminary. For Williams' generation, the bishop's house was a tutorial school for young men with priestly vocations. And Williams perpetuated this bit of very human, if unsystematic, medieval clerical experience. He attempted to maintain this highly personalized approach to seminary studies and ordination even at the large seminary which he founded in 1884, though, predictably, chaos was the result. There was no ecclesiastical court, no system of parish reports, no semiannual diocesan examinations of young, newly ordained priests. Few priests had a knowledge of Canon Law. Often they disregarded laws pertaining to marriage cases either out of ignorance or willfulness. But whether rooted in stupidity or knavery, much had to be tolerated because of the dearth of native priests. Incardination was a chancy but necessary game of avoiding "whiskey priests," runaways from Europe, or men otherwise unworthy. Finally, there was no parochial school system and little desire for it. Fitzpatrick was educated in the Boston Latin School of Messrs. Leverett and Parker on Boylston Street, and despite every pressure to do so, Williams never conceded that the Boston schools could be bettered.[11]

If Williams found congenial the inbred ways of Boston, he was equally fond of his autonomy of Rome. European events of the mid-nineteenth century had made it impossible for the papacy to assert centralization. So the situation of the Boston diocese was a free one, much like that of the Massachusetts Bay Colony before 1686 when James II determined to rule the colony more rigidly. Williams cherished his isolation from the papal throne throughout his administration no less gleefully than an earlier Boston citizen, John Winthrop, treasured his remoteness from Stuart England. On the eve of Williams' administration there was not even an apostolic delegate in the country, and the demands of the nuncio were easy to ignore. Besides, in the Boston area before 1870, before the definition of papal infallibility, it was not uncommon to hear the pope referred to as the bishop of Rome, as one among others in the college of bishops.[12]

The process, then, by which the Boston Catholic community would gain or be manipulated into cohesion and into oneness with Rome was to go on for several generations among individuals only partly conscious of the changes in their own ideas and attitudes and needs. O'Connell's authoritarianism in Boston and obeisance to Rome would make it complete.

Chapter I
1848 to 1866:
"Varieties of Religious
Experience"

Too many writers have distorted the early history of Catholicism in Boston. Like Louis S. Walsh, a priest who wrote *Origins of the Catholic Church in Salem* in 1890, they have so externalized the history as to obscure the real if somber story of inner experience. Walsh and other Catholics buried in saccharine rhetoric such cranky old men as Father Patrick Strain of Lynn and Father Jeremiah J. Healy of Gloucester. They interred with them, more unfortunately, the real milieu to which these men were responding. Most of the internments took place at the turn of the century, at a time when parishes had come of silver jubilee age. This called forth crocheted memorials and the printed reminiscences of revered old ladies of the parishes.[1] Such turgid editions are seldom the quarry of revisionists. Consequently, a host of clergymen and layfolk, all of angelic dimensions, are still hailed as representative of nineteenth-century Catholicism in Boston. Each parish priest is presented as a kindly and, it is assumed, Irish-American *soggarth-aroon*. Similarly, every local Catholic is presented as in agreement with James Joyce's Aunt Dante in her dogmatizing that "if we are a priest-ridden race, we ought to be proud of it. They are the apple of God's eye . . . Right! Right! They were always right! God and morality and religion come first." As a consequence, no essential distinctions are drawn among three successive generations of clergymen who assumed leadership between 1850 and 1910. Yet the fact is that beyond the basic acceptance of Catholic creed, the thinking of the priests of Williams' generation was no more like that of O'Connell's (two generations later) than was Charles Francis Adams' like his grandson's. Especially among Williams' priest-contemporaries, there was a conspicuous and persistent intellectual individuality. But again such novelty has been totally submerged.[2]

The dialectic between reflection and experience was a noticeable characteristic in the lives of the priests who watched Williams' consecration in 1866. They were freed from uniformity by such factors as sheer geographical dispersement, the casualness with which Fitzpatrick administered the diocese, and the sickness-unto-death in Rome. Their ways of thinking were accordingly disparate. Although second-rate thinkers, they were nonetheless able to be individually responsive to social and intellectual pressures; in a world where contingency ruled rather than, as later, the dictates of Cardinal O'Connell, they faced the necessity of ordering their own existences. By 1866, however, most of their exciting thinking was over. The most articulate priests of Williams' generation were off the stage by the late 1850's: John T. Roddan died in 1858; Nicholas O'Brien was out of the diocese after 1855; James Fitton wrote nothing substantial after 1863; and John Boyce wrote the last of his three novels in 1860. Their ideas had been shaped in a fireworks of speculative interchange from 1848 to the mid-1850's. After that, these men seemed spent and willing to let others contend with the residues of Know-Nothingism, the antics of Fenians, and the tragedy of the Civil War and its aftermath.

THE PHILOSOPHER-KINGS

In the 1840's Europe was a world notoriously in political collapse. And in the same decade, John B. Fitzpatrick, John J. Williams, George Haskins, and Nicholas O'Brien were at the Grande Seminaire of St. Sulpice near Paris advancing toward

ordination for Boston. John T. Roddan, the first Boston boy sent
to the College of Propaganda in Rome, was ordained there for
Boston in 1848. John Boyce, one of the genuinely bright graduates of Maynooth, left Ireland for the Boston diocese in 1845.
But Europe did not teach these young men to be reactionaries
or defiant defenders of the European status quo. On the contrary, Roddan returned to Boston as a young rebel. Even Williams, if he retained a lifelong regard for the Sulpician Fathers,
never suffered tears for the hypochondriasis which persisted on
the Throne of Peter even through the reign of Leo XIII in the
late nineteenth century.

These men did recognize a world in metaphysical collapse,
one where the political upheavals were but symptomatic of more
fundamental social anxieties. In response, they advanced ro-
tund theories on those transcendental human values which
would, they were certain, triumph and remain normative for
universal order. In these efforts, they operated as the typical
nineteenth-century philosopher-kings. They became self-styled
pontiffs on matters of science, aesthetics, theology, history, and
philosophy. Small wonder that they assumed this role. For Fitzpatrick put no barriers in their way; publications such as O'Connell would later censor reached as many as 50,000 people in the
case of Roddan's writings. And these priests were single-handed
system-builders for a more powerful reason. They felt no community about them. Moreover, they felt this lack of community
because philosophy and theology had not yet made person-to-
person relationships—horizontal relationships—central. The only
community which these Catholic clergymen seemed able to call
upon was one: the Roman Catholic Church of the past. They
could reach backward and use the weight of the ancient church
against European liberals, Cardinal Manning, or William Ellery
Channing. Yet at the same time, they were not able to sense a
community of co-workers in the field. Even John Boyce, who
was one of Fitzpatrick's own band of young priests in Boston,
spoke of this isolation in 1853 in his novel *The Spaewife*. "And
what," he asked, "would we be without a past? Nothing but isolated beings." Many priests *were* geographically isolated, dis-

persed across the New England states and living alone. But more important than distance, they were isolated in terms of mutual concern.[3] The result of this monism was a series of highly individualized, self-contained treatises on the faith. Each attack was sovereign and all-encompassing, as though the writer could not be sure but that his was the only defensive effort being made. "O'Callaghan on Heresies," done by a mean-minded priest of Burlington, Vermont, was only the most ludicrous of these productions, if not the most pathetic in its implications.[4]

Orestes Brownson was pied piper to a remarkably large number of these clergymen. Brownson had resided in Chelsea since 1836. In 1844 he had become an enthusiastic Catholic and self-styled seer of what was best for the church. His conversion was in several respects one of the great disasters to befall Boston Catholicism. For his blistering apologetics, heartily admired yet pointed toward defense of the faith rather than any sort of Christian unity, drove further underground Cheverus' open approach to Protestants. His stereotypes of Catholics and Protestants began to make the ways and days of Cheverus both quaint and unbelievable. It was only in Worcester that a Catholic literature other than bitter apologetics was kept alive by Father Boyce and Charles Bullard Fairbanks, Jr., a young convert. This sort of literature as well as an interest in Boyce and Fairbanks as writers would not dominate in Boston until the 1880's and particularly the 1890's. Then Bostonians like John Boyle O'Reilly, Jeff Roche, Louise I. Guiney, Alice Brown, and Henry Austin Adams would engage in writing fresh literature out of their American Catholic experiences. But for the present—from the late 1840's until he left Boston in 1855—Brownson was allowed to be the *defensor fedei* by Fitzpatrick. During that time, Catholic intellectual growth in the Boston area was dominated by him. He was the eye of the needle through which a priest had to pass to "get published." For he controlled Patrick Donahoe whose publishing house was long the most influential in Boston Catholicism; he dominated *The Catholic Observer,* a publication which collapsed in 1849 but was edited by priests who admired him; and he published *Brownson's Quarterly Review.* Eventually, Brownson's ideas also came to dominate *The Pilot* after he captured the intellectual allegiance of its young editor, Father Roddan. Brownson knew Father George Haskins well enough to assess his talents quickly and request him to write an article in 1848 on the Albigensians for the *Review*. At the same time, he worked closely with Father Nicholas O'Brien and knew him sufficiently well to make personal comments on the priest's slipshod ways of editing the *Observer*.[5]

The trouble for Brownson's would-be imitators—and through them, for the Catholic community—was that his vision of truth changed with his experiences. In "the Argument of '45," for example, he held that faith was impossible without an infallible witness and interpreter, namely, the Roman Catholic Church. He concluded that non-Catholics could not place an act of faith. From 1849 and until the mid-1860's, he continued to hold that Protestantism was practical atheism. Yet at one point and when attracted by the communionism of Laroux, he argued that all men *could* be elevated to the supernatural life by communion with the "providential men" of whom Jesus was but one. Later the concept of Christ as sole mediator replaced this wider interpretation.[6] His apologetics were riddled with weaknesses—not that it mattered. His style was admired nonetheless and, as indicated above, suited the New England priests. In his writings, he was the single-handed warrior doing combat with evil ideas. He solicited articles for the *Review* but, in fact, the quarterly was his voice alone. "In Brownson's next review [sic]," wrote Haskins to James Roosevelt Bayley, "you will perhaps see an article by me." "Try and see if you can pick it out," he urged Bayley, for authors' names were never cited in the quarterly. In "Conversations of Our Club" in the *Review* of 1858, Brownson presented three figures who were meant to be paradigms of the Irish-American prelate, the German Catholic idealist, and the Yankee convert. As the fourth conversationalist, Brownson introduced "Father John," a sort of demi-god who was clearly Brownson's persona. No real conversation actually unfolded. Rather the conversation was a series of long arguments, a string of individual monologues which never moved into any real dialogue. The procedure was to enter into combat solely with the opponent's ideas and use them as mere ploys while disregarding the person of the opponent altogether. Arguments became dangerously oversized and overpersonalized in all of this ("O'Callaghan on Heresies" followed by "O'Callaghan on the Church"). As a further result and because one had so surely identified himself with his treatise, one admitted error only with the greatest reluctance. "Don't answer at all," Fitzpatrick advised Brownson in 1852 when the British *Tablet* attacked Brownson in his on-going controversy with John Henry Newman. In encouraging this, Fitzpatrick summed up the spirit of the age more aptly than he would have supposed.[7]

Among the Boston diocesan clergy, however, Brownson dealt with priests of considerably smaller mental caliber than Newman. Yet there was no clergyman so ignorant but that Brownson would instruct him in the tactics of apologetics. Such a pupil was Father Charles McCallion. Little is known of him except that he was collecting funds in 1846 in Boston to pay a $500 debt on his church in the Cincinnati diocese and that he was given to writing his bishop such pledges of future integrity as mark the consciously weak man. "I spend some of my evenings," he wrote Bishop Purcell of Cincinnati, "reviewing my Theology under Professor Orestes A. Brownson." McCallion "guesses" that "the Baltimore Cath. Mag. has been making a fool of itself in defending Newman's development [theology]. Would you write me your opinion of Newman's book, Brownson's article and the article in the magazine." But then he reckoned he "could guess at it" also and concluded, "On the development principle we have much to find out yet."[8]

McCallion was doing here a noticeable double-checking on Brownson's theological position. This was a maneuver which was typical of the intellectual cat-and-mouse game which for many priests was the only way of treating with Brownson. Father Haskins, for example, was a Harvard graduate of 1826 and a man who wanted to write on public issues as a priest just as he had earlier when an Episcopal minister in Boston. He used Brownson's *Review* in 1846 as the best available outlet for a

Catholic. At the same time, he was quite frank about his reservations regarding Brownson's editorial skills. Yet a full decade later, he turned to Brownson rather than Fitzpatrick for information on obtaining lecturer's privileges in the diocese of New York. Even Brownson and Fitzpatrick played cat-and-mouse, though for the philosopher and the bishop the results were at best disappointing. Fitzpatrick never succeeded in whittling Brownson into a tuneful mouthpiece; one local priest's novels picked up without any difficulty how essentially ill-suited the instrument was to the musician. And Brownson left Boston in 1855 brooding over a blunted ego.[9]

It was not that priests were rejecting the theological structures of Brownson wholesale. They simply stopped concerning themselves about "old Brownson"—as even he knew the younger clergy referred to him. To their minds, Brownson's hopes for intellectual camaraderie among the Catholic clergy were a secondary consideration. Their efforts were given primarily to answering the demands of the Irish newcomers upon their lives. Even Roddan, who probably enjoyed living on the speculative level more than any other Boston clergyman, put the responsibility of his parish first. Nicholas O'Brien who bore the respected title of editor of the *Observer* and who participated with Roddan, Haskins, Thomas D'Arcy McGee, and Brownson on the lecture circuit was another young man who for the same reason would never develop into a worthy disciple. "Mr. O'Brien, as good a soul as ever lived, a man one must quarrel with every day and yet love with all his heart," wrote Brownson to Father J. W. Commings in 1847, "has no editorial tact. I doubt," he continued, "if he has read more than two articles in my *Review* for as many months. He probably saw the lecture [on law by Commings], saw who it was from, said to himself—all's straight, and being in a hurry, sent it to the printer, and thought no more about it." Haskins found genuine friendship in Bishop James Roosevelt Bayley, not Brownson; his real satisfaction was in working with delinquent boys, not in writing controversial articles. Even Fitzpatrick, as Lord Acton commented, had "made good studies . . . [but was] not a great theologian." In fact, Acton wisely chose to appraise Fitzpatrick as an administrator. "He was called out," Acton wrote, commenting on their interview, "at least twenty times by poor people who wish to see him. This goes on all day . . ." Between interruptions, they fell to talking of what Fitzpatrick recognized as the plaguing double concern of his career, the problem "of the Irish and of American public men."[10]

This same plague descended also on Brownson. Earlier Brownson's theological concern was an epistemological one. Put simply, if reason did not lead to God, then it was unreasonable to be religious. So Brownson's single-handed fight had been to establish the rational bases of Catholic dogma. But after 1848 his living in Boston meant gagging as the city filled up with, like it or not, coreligionists of a brutish and nasty immigrant type whose every action shouted irrationality. Only when the same Catholic populace would come to show signs of social maturity and knowledge would the reasonableness of religion be saved. So by 1858 Brownson had moved away from concentrating on the intellectual dimensions of man's experience and appropriately interested himself in respectability. He agreed now that religion earned its livelihood by offering a useful moral code. He knew he needed subtlety in discussing the intellectual and social limitations of the Irish-Americans for he was already highly unpopular on this account. He nevertheless plunged in since his career and self-image rested so squarely on the dignified deportment of other Catholics. In a "Conversations of Our Club" article, he worked toward his point from an analysis of the 1856 Treaty of Paris. He could argue that this agreement of the European powers bartered away the rights of Western Christendom and its religious institutions and that therefore "every Catholic layman has *to be* his church now in his own sphere" [my italics]. He asked his readers to recall that "the age is a fast one and is sure to outrun Catholics." As a result, these Catholics— carefully generalized—"must recover and take the lead of the age, and do so by their real superiority in mental and moral activity."[11]

In the next issue of the *Review*, Brownson directed the plea for respectability and learning specifically to Catholic New Englanders. He courted his audience there by calling their bishops "venerable," whereas by 1858 both Fitzpatrick and Hughes were in reality his enemies. He also assured his readers that their clergy could "make the faithful people here a model people." He concluded that the respectability on which he relied rested on intelligence and virtue. "Our Catholic population," he half-hoped, "is not yet clean gone; it still has a conscience and is able to appreciate moral respectability . . . tho' living in obscurity and clothed with rags."[12]

To Brownson, Catholicism was first a metaphysical abstraction then a policy of social control. His new disciple Roddan drove it down the same tracks, ultimately granting science a sphere of influence over knowledge, and religion a sharply separated sphere of influence over feeling and will. Brownson had satisfied himself by the 1860's that "where the rabble drinks too, all wells are poisoned." Yet ironically, it was in imitating Brownson that Roddan became part of "the writing-rabble."

FATHER JOHN T. RODDAN

From 1848 to 1850, no local clergyman tilted so capably with Brownson as John T. Roddan. Trained for the priesthood at the College of Propaganda in Rome, he edited *The Pilot* for Patrick Donahoe on his return to Boston in 1848 and remained in that capacity until his death at thirty-nine in 1858. Sixty years later under Cardinal O'Connell, everything about Roddan's career as a young priest would have been an impossibility. First, in 1848 his youth was an asset—seniority as a factor of preference and power in the diocese was still in the future. Also the fresh theological insights which he as a young scholar would bring to the diocese from afar were eagerly awaited by Fitzpatrick. Roddan also lived in a time when the Church in Boston was less afraid of heterodoxy from within. There was no official diocesan censor. The young priests themselves censored one another in publications. Roddan in *The Pilot* fiercely debated with Nicholas O'Brien, editor of *The Catholic Observer*. One entered the public lists ready to take a drubbing as artist or theologian from Brownson, O'Brien, or Father Joseph Finotti, literary editor of *The Pilot* in the late 1850's. Under such circumstances and especially in his first three years, Roddan published editorials that O'Connell would have quashed in a week. The breadth and courage of his early speculations are easily more vibrant than the mannered classical forms which later generations of Boston clergymen learned from the Jesuits at Boston College and Holy Cross College.[13]

Such brilliance and range were to be expected of Roddan. He was born in Boston three years before Williams. His early life was marked by poverty but also by an intellectual inquisitiveness. This drew him away from a series of unsuccessful "mechanical pursuits" and into what was one of the most dynamic areas of speculation before the Civil War, religion.

Nothing is known of Roddan's early desire for the priesthood except that it became a goal only after he had financed his own studies to enter college. He used the priesthood as a roadway toward theorizing on social issues rather than, as before, being practically involved as a worker. In this respect, Roddan wrote a remarkable autobiographical article in 1850 on "Political Priests." Here he prided himself on his many years as a layman and artisan, explaining jauntily, "I was not born a priest, as the saying is . . . I was a qualified voter some years before I thought of becoming a priest. I lived in the world—I saw how it wagged and I wagged with it." He admitted to a renewed conviction that priests must be active in secular affairs, and he evaluated an earlier passing opposition to this as stubbornness growing out of his own impressionable nature, a trait which did in fact seem to mar his character. In the same article, he was already overly serious about ideas. He cited as "principles," for example, those notions which were clearly the opinions of a young man still in his early twenties. "I know now," he confessed, "that the principles which I had picked up were heretical and atheistical. Yet I would have been shocked if any man had shown it to me. I thought that I was a *nice* Catholic, while I held statements which would be well received at any lodge of Illuminati in

France . . ." He was penetrating, optimistic and worldly-wise. Characteristically, he absorbed everything he could of Italian affairs while a seminarian in Rome. At the time, the cultured Boston convert, Joseph Coolidge Shaw, S.J., wrote of him to Fitzpatrick: "You will have in him a most faithful and excellent priest and a good theologian."[14]

Soon after his return to Boston, Roddan began to do battle with Brownson. In spring of 1848 he made himself known in an editorial which struck directly at the central misconception toward which Brownson had been heading throughout the 1840's. It was an antireformist eccentricity that could be reduced to one premise: the temporal miseries of this life should be of little concern as it is only the place man gains in heaven that matters. "Ventura's Oration and Brownson's Review" was Roddan's calculated attack upon that premise. What he had determined to assault in the editorial was not only the unwillingness of Brownson to allow man the rightful pursuit of secular duties as well as religious, but he felt he was also exposing a provincial mentality that lodged itself in the precise and uncluttered cubicle of logic and from that removed inner-office rejected such political movements as the European revolutions of 1848. Further, Brownson's rejection was founded not on the basis of evidence but on the strength of a priori propositions. Roddan defended the revolutions, arguing for withholding judgment at least. In rebuttal and within ten weeks, *The Catholic Observer* had dissected Roddan's editorial and "located" propositions of a "heretical" nature. These it printed together with a defense of Brownson and a request for retraction.

It was not Roddan's open defense of the European revolutions which disturbed the *Observer*. Rather it was the way he used them, namely, to build a case for relativism. What rankled the *Observer*'s editors was Roddan's insistence that "human knowledge must always give different ideas to different minds," and that "there is no cause so bad but *something* may be said in its favor." Pure falsehood, he held, was impossible and no mind could conceive it since it could not be an object of the mind. Man simply could not know all the answers.[15] The relativist implications of this kind of logic were not overlooked by the *Observer*. It culled no less than five heretical propositions out of the editorial. Two of the paraphrased propositions restated Roddan's "heresies" exactly. Did he not maintain that "the final purpose of the earthly [duties of man] is unknown to us"?[16]

The content of the controversial article itself was simple enough. Gioacchino Ventura was a politically liberal Italian Theatine priest who had made a name for himself by insisting that given the posture of affairs in Europe in 1848, the wise policy of the Church would be to abandon the despised governments, appeal to the people, and form an alliance between religion and liberty. Brownson, with what Roddan judged to be a logician's wantonness, had refused to confront Ventura's position but rather had reduced his statements to meaningless word analysis. Roddan, however, found the position eminently defensible. He not only left its contentions intact but argued further that popular institutions were as much the "innumerable evidences of omniscient design" as traditional monarchies. Popular uprisings were therefore valid as "means of protecting the people against oppression and securing their social well-being." To justify this argument, he took Hegel's approach—as did Thomas D'Arcy McGee and countless other contemporary thinkers to varied purposes—reading history his own way and then divinizing it. "God's hand," he explained, "leads generation after generation, like wheel after wheel, to the fulfillment of some inscrutable, unconceivable destiny." Not only were revolutions divinely purposive but the new arts and biological sciences were also providential blessings. One had only to understand what history was about, wrote Roddan, and then "science reveals exhaustless wonders, and art ministers her delights; the passions and vicissitudes of life bring forth poetry and eloquence and philosophy and romance." Meanwhile, Roddan had dismissed Brownson as a narrow-minded pedant, an "enthusiast who mistakes his pious whims for cardinal virtues." His apologetics were "flippant" and "unsound."[17]

In a vacuum Roddan could have carried this internecine warfare off. As he did in the Ventura article, he could have called

for "a crusade against the governments of Europe" and criticized those Catholic fellow-theologians whose "manner of reasoning" would not let them entertain the possibility of its justice.
In Boston, however, the sectarian enemy without was fast pre-
cluding an enemy within; and Roddan who called Brownson's
style "bizarre" could expect to be considered exactly that throughout the next century by vote of the Catholic clergy. As a start
and in the summer of 1848, other Boston priests, specifically
O'Brien and Haskins, debated his position. They did so not as
clerics with necessarily opposite views of liberty and revolution but as logicians whose style had been attacked by a ro-
manticist.[18]

In the course of the next two years, Roddan's *metanoia* took
place. It was a period of honest bewilderment in which he
changed from being an open-minded, humane seeker to a dogmatist. He wrote revealingly during this period that metaphysicians were subject to bewilderment more than most men
"because they have a juster notion of the difficulties . . . We
really know many facts, but these very facts suggest impenetra-
ble mysteries." When this bewilderment lifted for him, it left
him, rather grotesquely, a disciple of Brownson.[19]

Roddan thoroughly enjoyed the role of metaphysician and
The Pilot continued to provide an outlet for his speculations.
But even in his writings his most frequent metaphor during the
late 1840's and 1850's came to be simply "the house." For as the
Irish moved in and settled, house-raising was his daily experience. These were years when his wide mission district along the
South Shore included Hingham, Cohasset, Randolph, Quincy,
and North Bridgewater, all places that were filling up with Irish
Catholics. It was a time when zealous young priest-friends like
Boyce, O'Brien, Williams, and Haskins joined together in accul-
turating the Irish by taking up something of a new genre, the
lecture series. And lecturing was exhilarating for them. Sometimes, as Roddan wrote of a lecture in Cohasset, they were "saying things to the Irish they don't want to hear." But at the same
time he could also report that "the principal [Protestant] men of

the place came to listen. A gentleman told me that it would have been quite otherwise a year ago." With a young person's delight at having won acceptance, he explained in *The Pilot* that the lecture series gave non-Catholics an opportunity "that most of them had never had before, of seeing a live Catholic priest. Some had nerved themselves for horns and tails. But they went away saying that the priest looks just like other people—that his sermon sounded like good doctrine, after all." These were days before prosperity seemed devilish and before pastors would feel compelled to stereotype it as a lesson learned from the Yankees. On the contrary, the Irish Catholics, Roddan encouraged, "ought to show that the immigrant can build up his worldly house without destroying that habitation that was made for him in a better world."[20]

As such concrete considerations of life in Boston began to touch Roddan's life, they also began to give shape to his thinking and writing. As editor of *The Pilot* he continued to print foreign correspondence which applauded popular causes in Europe. It was commonplace to read that "the stupid and cold-hearted rulers of every nation of Europe are following in the old paths . . . They forget that the intelligence of the age will seal their doom." Roddan put *The Pilot* on record as accepting a republic in Rome. Pius could harmlessly devote "his whole time to the Church of Christendom and its members." But Boston was gradually drawing Roddan into its own nexus. Its immediate problems were cajoling him away from the cautiousness for which he ordinarily contended. In its place he yielded to many more blustering, if honest and independent, overstatements. In July of 1849 he felt the need to answer *The Boston Daily Times*' contention that Irish-Americans should not be sending funds to aid the beleaguered pope. His first remarks were timid ones, reflecting the plea for hesitancy which was ordinarily his approach. "We *really* believe and *time may shortly tell*," he counselled, "that these allies [Radetsky and Ferdinand of Naples] are struggling for their own interests, and that the Pope is lapsing away, beyond the circle of their bloody intervention" [my italics]. But this was no hearty rebuttal, so he inserted a seconding appositive. "If we wish to put the Pope—an old Chief of our Church whom our traditions have taught us to respect greatly—as men respect Washington and so forth, on his old seat, and wish to buy him swords and guns, for the purpose, what of that, either?" And so it went, until the American Republic—whose Republicanism Roddan formerly used admiringly for illustration when arguing for European republics—was attacked for ignoring the plight of Hungary and Rome, for going ahead "in the pursuit of dollars with a 'fat, contented' neutrality."[21]

Two months later, Roddan felt obliged to support the Boston Journeymen Tailors' Society in its fight against forty-one master-tailors of the city. Typically, he was reluctant to judge the causes of the rift and suggested reflectively that *"perhaps . . . the hard dealings of the employers . . . were necessary to force this change"* [my italics]. At the same time he recognized that these were circumstances where the indecision of the metaphysician had to be abandoned for the outspokenness of the propagandist. "In a republic like this," he had decided, "the press must naturally side with labor." "Labor," he went on, "is the basis of all society and all things are tending to this consummation." Yet Roddan knew this was socialism and therefore immediately leapt to his own defense in the next sentence. More important, he was aware of a community of Catholics and Protestants to whose rejection of such premises he had to accommodate. He had two defenses, both of which he used here. First he insisted that his brand of socialism came out of his reading of the Bible. "This is not socialism: it is the decree of God—registered somewhere in the second chapter of Genesis . . ." Secondly, he reminded his readers that he was not the Church speaking. He was, he argued, a professional journalist. Workingmen's rights was a secular affair, and he spoke as a citizen. He did not draw the Church into the affair but appealed to "the press and the public" to "give the workers a fair opportunity for effecting a revolution of their own." Yet both defenses crumbled within the year and with them his revolutionary ideas.[22]

Roddan's method of reasoning was failing and his ideas falling apart as a house of cards. The fight he put up to retain his liberal social principles and to stay outside the antireformist and religiously intolerant circle of Brownson was a solid one but he was caught from the outset. He was clearly captivated by the concept of mystery as creatively filling the world rather than making it irrational. Yet this set him apart from Brownson, Haskins, and O'Brien. On the other hand, as a man of faith, he had no real place with the radicals either. He could use metaphysics to argue brilliantly for the rights of trade-unions. But too much of this and one was caught in the merely rationalistic methodology of Brownson. Yet to present a justification for the rights of trade unionists from scripture was more entangling. He had, for example, supported the demands of workers on the strength of the second chapter of Genesis. Yet these were the very years when the historical relevance of the Bible, and especially Genesis, was being subjected to scientific criticisms. To support the first meant to reject the other; or given Roddan's position, to be socially revolutionary meant to be a reactionary biblicist. Such was his position in "The Appeal of Modern Science from God's Account of His Own Creation," an 1850 lecture appearing in three successive front page spreads of *The Pilot*.

The editorial was originally delivered before a popular audience at the Melodeon in mid-winter and contained just enough oversimplification to distort Descartes, Macaulay, and Hume into popular intelligibility. Still "The Appeal of Modern Science" was not the work of an amateur philosopher or hedge-row orator. Nor was it contemptuous. In fact as a critic of Robert Chambers' account of man's evolution, Roddan was at times tentative and altogether too friendly toward the religious radicals in general. Similarly, he was altogether too hopeful that "modern sciences, when they are rightly studied, lead to Christianity." Chambers' book, *Vestiges of the Natural History of Creation*, was supposed to be his target in the lecture. However, the real enemy, as it developed, was not the skeptic Robert Chambers. It was the system-builder, any scholar who, like this popular follower of Laplace, would "magnetize truth" until it followed his mind and was captured. Such men, as he put it, did not want to share the house of which revealed religion had been in possession for ages. They wanted to dispossess the owners and replace time-honored conclusions with guesses. He suggested that those skeptical of revelation should present what could be proved "with the most absolute certainty, to be facts, and you [the iconoclasts] will be welcome because *then* we need not vacate the house for you, both parties can enjoy it together." It was all wishful thinking, as Roddan well knew. For he remarked further in the same article that facts would only suggest further mysteries. He was already referring to the critics of a Catholic absolutist position as "our enemies."[23]

Roddan's thinking was at a dead-end. He dodged about in the lecture, suggesting that Catholics bide their time: wait, and animal magnetism might prove itself beneficial; wait, until one can say "precisely what electricity is"; wait, before ridiculing the artificial creation of human life. He was evolutionist enough to recognize the validity of the new scientific findings. He could appreciate that even the long-waged debate on the body-soul relationship and "things which were always discussed by metaphysicians" were now among the objects of psychological investigation. But wherever the theories of biological evolution were taking others, they led Roddan to raise the question not of the possible evolutionary nature of man, but of God. His rejection was qualified. "We must," he warned, "distinguish between science and its trumpeteers; the wind may be good while the trumpet is cracked." But his statements were increasingly more cautious. He was already talking like an absolutist and at the same time indicating the direction in which he would go. "One is not really a man of faith," he wrote, "who has no fixed standard by which he can measure the value of everything else . . . What agrees with it is true, what clashes with it is false. The immediate effect of this is a feeling of perfect security."[24]

Back in 1849, Roddan had suggested that the theories of European socialists might solve the disputes of Boston journeymen tailors with their masters. His editorial was idealistic; it was a blend of the socialists' dogma and his own confidence in their answers. Gradually, however, he reversed this methodology, suiting what ought to be done to what could be done. He was particularly eyeing the problems of the Irish as these people filled all the interstices of the social structure of Boston. He began writing out of the context of individual lives, immigrants coming to him looking for advice regarding employment. "They have come to me," he wrote sympathetically, "looking like bruised images of giant despair." As Roddan became more intimately involved in their needs, he was less and less the distanced professional journalist. He was increasingly the parish priest, then the champion, then the combination of the two. He still combined an eager if misplaced optimism for their future with a genuine admiration for prevailing American values. So while he was progressively outspoken, he did not become a nag as would later priest-writers. In further contrast to later clergymen, he remained utterly honest in depicting the humble origins and bumbling, nonadaptive ways of the Irish immigrants. He encouraged them to request immediate American citizenship, arguing that "in this country your religion is not a matter commonly meddled with by law-makers; the labor of your hands is protected, the well of knowledge lies open to every comer . . . If he [the Irish immigrant] hurts his soul attending to his mortal and physical welfare, it is not the fault of the government . . ."[25]

Here again was the problem that had nagged Roddan from the first, the question of the extent to which the immediate preoccupations and needs of an individual or a society must be regulated by an intrusive supernatural world. He was not yet ready in mid-1850 to capitulate to the notion that all decisions must be made only after the supernatural soundings had been taken. So he made nimble combinations like "God has given the world freedom . . . Humanity contains in itself all that is necessary to make it blessed, and if it is diseased, it works its own cure." But this was vacuous. He wrote that he could not accept Lamartine's perfectionism because it embraced a radical error, namely, "an utter denial of the supernatural order or its utter separation from the natural world." Yet he was no Manichean. To Carlyle's despair for the world he answered, "The earth is good enough, if we would behave in it like Christians."[26]

In 1850 Patrick Donahoe published Roddan's novel, *John O'Brien, or The Orphan of Boston: A Tale of Real Life*. The novel gives evidence of some narrative skill as John O'Brien pursues his picaresque adventures in and out of Massachusetts and Connecticut after he is orphaned by the death of his father. The fiction is thoroughly held under by Roddan's intermittent sermons, catechism lessons, and Socratic dialogues between John and (all) other characters. Most actors are non-Catholics through whom, as one commentator has aptly remarked, "John amiably disputes his way." The novel also gives evidence of how directly and totally Boston had closed in on Roddan. On the one hand, he alludes to the "literary gentlemen and ladies who are Catholic . . . those who have always been wealthy and happy." There are still Protestant Bostonians who are tolerant, who may even enjoy his book, and who do not live a morality that is "legal" and "forensic." There are even Catholic children who are taken to hear "The Creation" and are allowed to read *A Pilgrim's Progress*. Yet on the other hand, Boston was becoming for Roddan the city of "those Catholics who move in what are sometimes called the middle and lower ranks of society." It was the place of "Catholic parents who neglect their children" and of "Catholic children who are running wild in the streets." For these Catholics, a mixed society like Boston was dangerous.[27]

Roddan made John O'Brien into a disputant like himself. There are charming passages like John's query to his father, " 'Where is France? I know that Bishop Cheverus has gone there and I thought it was across the Charles River, near Cambridge.' " But generally John is, as his father chided him, "a logician" and remains so. Roddan's views about Catholic-Protestant relations were hardening. As he speaks through John, he rejects "mixed schools," "latitudinarian Catholics and Protestants," "liberal or homeopathic Christianity," and shallow Protestant theology. Some of his former tolerance is there and much of the reluctance to stereotype the Protestant community. He declares that "there is no salvation out of the one true Church," yet he must then give himself several pages to argue that he does not mean this unequivocally. He excoriates those Protestants who ridicule Catholics, yet he separates from them the "Friends and Fathers [of public institutions]" and "pious old and young ladies." As one of Roddan's critics wrote in 1968, "[John O'Brien] does not hate Protestants, as we suspect Father Roddan did not." Nor did he. Yet the children of the poor in and around Boston were "in danger of losing their faith." Many were being sent without a worry to "Calvinistic" and Unitarian Sunday Schools while others were working in the homes of Protestants who either disregarded their religion or discouraged loyalty to it. Contact with "twenty persons in and around Boston" supplied "the facts" behind the novel. Obviously Roddan's witnessing of the tangled and pained Protestant-Catholic relationships was giving new shape to his theology.[28]

By late summer of 1850 Roddan was especially distrustful of any set of notions that endorsed mob violence. It would have been difficult for Roddan to endorse precipitous action under *any* circumstances given his natural irresolution and his continued hope for the peaceful coexistence of the Yankees and the Irish Catholics in Boston. In *John O'Brien,* for example, his only unrestrained tirade was against "the Protestant mobs." But now he became psychotic on mobs wherever they appeared, whether Irish or socialist or Yankee. Understandably then, one of the first indications of a change in the whole galaxy of his ideas appears in an 1850 editorial on "Foreign Anarchists in America." "The socialists, red-republicans and mob" in New York affronted Roddan not with their ideology but with their misconduct on the city streets. And, a step inward, they confronted him with the cost of his own impressionable nature, specifically, his earlier outspoken support of the 1848 European revolutions. "We behaved like simpletons," he wrote, drawing in his readers but actually beating his own breast. "We did not observe that the inmates of every house were the best judges of their own affairs . . . [We] very foolishly believed that they [the rioting European socialists] fought for a republic, that the republics they wished to establish were like our own." But gold differs from brass, and "so does our conservative American republicanism differ from the wild, red image set up in the streets of Rome, Paris, Vienna, Berlin."[29]

Roddan conjured up European chaos chiefly as preventive medicine for Boston's social ills. It was nearby violence that was on his mind: Garibaldi's supporters in New York, Irish nationalists in Boston advocating "physical force," labor disturbances, and the anarchy in the American-Catholic newspaper business. The same recognition of proximate violence drove him to an irrational condemnation of Theodore Parker's oration on behalf of fugitive slaves. He saw Parker as a "pawn" of the rabid congregation that hired him. It was a demonic group, and Parker was insane with violence in maintaining that a fugitive could kill a cruel master in good conscience with as little compunction as one would have in driving a mosquito from one's face. This kind of thinking told Roddan that "the men who mobbed Garrison some years ago were justified, as their conscience told them that such a man ought not to be suffered within the city." For the first time and apparently unconsciously, he found it useful here to recall to his readers that most useful of all later Boston Irish-Catholic polemicists' horror stories, the mob's assault on the Ursuline convent of Charlestown.[30]

In March of 1851, Roddan warned American Catholics that the entire country was sinking to the immoral level of the mob. Society was "torturing" chemistry to bring in new knowledge; phrenologists, biologists and Mesmerists were up to "horrendous doings." "Tolerance" and "religious liberty," he indicated in May of 1852, had lost their meaning. Protestantism had succumbed to nominalism and had introduced the anarchy of double-meanings even into the stock of words used for theological discourse. "Mischievous" confusions were abroad even within Catholicism. From England came Newman's arguments that those outside the Roman Church could be saved. Fortunately, Brownson seemed to have answers to Newman, and by early spring of 1851 Roddan was repeating these. He began imitating Brownson's style and incorporating his thought in *Pilot* editorials. For the next eight years he persistently denounced reformers, settled the Roman Church as the sole repository of the virtues, be-littled the reputation of Newman, ridiculed Catholic liberals and insisted "there is no salvation out of the church." Whereas he had written in 1848 that "human knowledge must always give different ideas to different minds," he was now writing on May 3, 1851, that "we are suspicious of any new light such men [as Newman] can throw upon the mysteries of faith." Now Brown-son was no longer an eccentric old man of "pious whims," de-spite Roddan's own earlier admission that it was "a common charge." He defended Brownson as a theologian of remarkable consistency. Still copying Brownson, he shifted from scurrility to temperateness in religious and political matters in 1858 when the master's thinking moved in a new direction that same year.[31]

Along with Brownson, Roddan had also found anarchy seep-ing into the most dangerous place, into institutions. Both he and Brownson saw society as being a composite of structures. And of these they wrote continually, magnifying some groups to the size of their fears (Parker's congregation, neurologists) or to the size of their needs (the Roman Church in Boston). Only certain institutional "orders" by maintaining themselves in cor-rect balance could secure the rights of the individual—or re-strain the unruly individual. Yet Roddan felt he was watching the rampaging of one institution against another, the shattering of this balance. The world looked to be a fragile vessel holding forces that were now in multiplication pell-mell. This dread of irreversible multiplying conditions was not unusual in 1853. In that year, such a fear characterized Nathaniel Bowditch's de-fense of Father McElroy's right to purchase the "jail lands" for a church. Bowditch's argument was that

the evil [the incursion of the Irish into the Leverett Street area] is al-ready upon them [the Yankees]. For this there is no remedy or pre-vention. No, Mr. Mayor and Gentlemen—a great principle is involved in this question. If there is an objection to a *Catholic* church in Lev-erett Street, why may there not be a like objection to it in every other part of the city? The question today is merely whether a *Catho-lic* church is a nuisance. Tomorrow the like question may be asked of any other church. Where can the line be drawn? If we refuse to the Catholics, in this their day of weakness, the permission now asked, how can we object to their doing the like by ourselves should they acquire—and they very probably may in a few years—the numerical ascendancy over all the other religious societies in our city?

In the same month, Roddan began a series of eight editorials on workers' strikes specifically because such demonstrations were becoming "a veritable epidemic."[32]

Workingmen's strikes merely symbolized that the whole "secular order" was running wild and that since 1848 "the spiritual order" had been mercilessly subordinated to it. Elsewhere Napoleon III was using religion as an instrument of the state. In the Treaty of Paris with its generous terms for Turkey the states of Europe had shattered the balance of Church and State. Only after these events and in 1858 did Brownson and Roddan reluctantly look to the individual to save the institutions. Religion was no longer free in its own right but "only in the right of the citizen or subject, as included in the number of his private or personal rights," therefore effort should be made to defend religion as an individual's right rather than as a necessary social institution. Also a reversal toward Protestantism was in order since secularism was rampant and, as Brownson put it in 1858, "we are no longer in the same world." So in 1858 Roddan condescended to accept Protestantism as an ally, insisting at the same time that "imperfect and erroneous as the teaching of Protestantism is [in Boston]—it is better than no teaching at all."[33]

Within a year of Brownson's reversal, Roddan was dead. The importance of his career is that it testifies not to a preconceived plan of what Catholic thought and life should be in Boston but to the haphazard thinking-out of social and religious solutions which mid-century conditions forced upon a Boston priest. Roddan's seminary studies in Rome clearly did very little to deflect either the impact of socialism upon his thinking or later that of the conservatism of Brownson. Though his thinking from 1848 to 1858 ran from radical to reactionary to moderate, it did so without the interference of Fitzpatrick, probably without his real concern. Roddan died in the bishop's own house.

Solutions to problems, then, emerged from local circumstances. These were generally solutions either unconnected with theology or for which so-called unalterable theological propositions were in fact often changed. Roddan had carefully argued in 1849 for the rights of laborers. At the same time he consciously used the rhetoric of socialism and endorsed its optimistic view of human nature. Yet four years later the futility of hoping for a sense of neighborliness on the part of the Yankees *or* the Irish in Boston, the denial by "the haves" of real economic opportunities for the Irish, and the evidence that profit-sharing association meant wealth only to him who "made it . . . serve him" had driven Roddan to the un-Catholic (but currently Brownsonian) position of man as depraved. Again, when there was little religious divisiveness in Boston in 1849, Roddan had reason to believe that employer-employee relations could be settled without religious considerations. But by 1853 circumstances had brought him to make a religious issue of labor relations, scolding the workers, hit-or-miss, for ever having deviated from the Church's regulations on labor and pointing out that "Protestant society" always asks the laborer to give an unequal amount of labor to the capitalist.[34]

Local circumstances also determined Roddan's attitude toward reformers and philanthropists. In 1848 he held that "religion does not forbid or grudge the patriot or the philanthropist their labor and their glory." But this was when Brownson, to Roddan's mind, was exasperatingly preaching against all reform and he, on the other hand, still hoped that his own reforming zeal would not cost him the respect of the community. However in the following decade he experienced the excesses of reformers like Theodore Parker, "Fathers and Friends" in *John O'Brien*, Henry Ward Beecher, the "native party," and Irish revolutionaries like Thomas Francis Meagher. He reacted to these efforts in crude, bumptious blasts which grudged them the least recognition. Yet again by 1858 when his political foes were discernibly "losing their influence" and a newly secularized

Europe seemed to demand an ecumenical crusade against world-liness, he was ready to accept the efforts of all Christians. At this point he acknowledged again the existence of "liberal and fair-minded Protestants," men and women whom he had excluded from the pages of *The Pilot* since 1851.[35]

Roddan changed his stand on fundamental theological issues according to the intensification of collisions between Bostonians and Irish immigrants. In 1849 when he was confident that even priests would soon be accepted in Boston society and that they would really be judged on what they did, his theology of redemption was generous and liberal. In March of 1850 just after wide sympathy had apparently been stirred by the shipwreck of an immigrant ship off the coast of Cohasset, he hoped for community harmony, writing that "sometimes a mountain of prejudice is like an old ruin, remove one stone and the whole comes tumbling down." Though he could not know it, Henry David Thoreau was present at the disaster and afterward recorded his sympathy with the overworked waves rather than with the grieving relatives. What Roddan did know by 1852 was that the mentality of "the so-called native party" had gained ascendancy over the "very many Protestant ministers who . . . [were] too high-minded, too loyal to endorse the conduct of the Parkers and Beechers who are exciting the good people to deeds of violence." In retaliation he denounced "the separated brethren" as well as any Catholic who "under the pressure of a contemptible toleration . . . is inclined to think that any man may be saved in any religion." This very harshness, however, was again reversed when Roddan defended the evangelical Protestant revivals in 1858. He understood the revivals to be a result of the "late economic crisis" and warned Catholics against treating "those who differ from us in matters of opinion as if their dissent constituted a minor species of heresy."[36]

In the same way Roddan's approach to the question of Church and State was without blueprint. At first he was convinced that immigrants had nothing to fear from law-givers in Massachusetts. He had encouraged the Irishman that his religion was "not a matter commonly meddled with . . ." By 1853, however, Roddan expressed his certainty that the powers of government were being used against the immigrants. In that year, one Boston newspaper put faith in an allegation that a delegation of priests had petitioned Mayor Benjamin Seaver (a Democrat) for permission to visit Deer Island and catechize the boys there. In retaliation, the *Traveler* suggested that Charlestown, Chelsea, Cambridge, and Roxbury incorporate into Boston to shift voting majorities away from the Democrats who made mayors like Seaver possible. Roddan was not a Democrat and had in fact made *The Pilot* an organ of Whiggism. But in the facts surrounding this dispute he read a real attack. He also read conspiracy into the *Times*' suggestion on the same incident that the priests be *granted* the permission because "the education the boys receive will tend to open their eyes to the [real] truth." Five years later and after tempers had subsided, Roddan handled a similar case with mildness, gratuitously admiring the Protestants' "sense of fair play."[37]

Nor were the solutions at which Roddan arrived during the decade from 1848 to 1858 those of an Irish priest or of a priest who wanted to recreate in Boston some idealized value system of Catholic Europe, some continuous *ecclesia* with European markings. His solutions were those of a Bostonian of the 1850's. To him no less than to others, the escalation of religious and social conflicts throughout the decade was a regrettable and bewildering melee of disharmony whose outcome could only be guessed at. After 1849 he coped with this uneasiness by creating in his writings those patterns and solid structures which he could not find in reality. To give security to his own epistemology, he adopted Brownson's apologetics. He looked to Jaime Balmes for the historical arguments favoring Catholicism over Protestantism. He needed to find *order* in the religious behavior of 1858 and so contended that "a [Protestant] religious revival is just as certain to follow a general monetary panic as a high sea to succeed a gale of wind on the Atlantic. Human nature is the same everywhere." Determinist or dogmatist, Roddan was patterning things for himself, protecting himself. In December of 1853 his personal fear of secret societies resulted in a severe condemnation of them in *The Pilot*. It was a stand taken without Fitzpatrick's authorization or that of the American bishops. Yet the article was written—and is now taken to have been written—as though it had all the force of the episcopacy behind it.[38]

Still more important, Roddan also invented in language a sturdiness for Roman Catholicism in Boston which did not in fact exist. Looking at the decade between 1848 and 1858, it is apparent that he was one of only thirty priests in Boston who did not know what real hierarchical leadership was, who had never experienced a diocesan synod, and who, if they desired it, could make an annual Retreat at Holy Cross College with the other clergymen but would then return to enormous parishes almost Congregational in their individuality. Yet *The Pilot* editorials give the impression of the ancient Catholic Church transferred in all its power to Boston. The same impression of stability is conveyed in Roddan's editorials. For though he was only in his mid-thirties when writing, his tone is elderly, seeming to speak for a venerable "establishment." Actually his thinking was aged only because of his deliberate estrangement from "Young America," his opting for Brownson as opposed to "the first American Left" of which Walt Whitman and the Paulist priest Isaac Hecker were a part.[39]

The Catholic Church had no venerableness, no definable shape in the 1850's. Nor was the Catholic population as cohesive in its thinking as Roddan would have had it appear in *The Pilot*. He in fact negated his own assertion in 1852 about Catholic audiences not welcoming "liberal Catholics" during the lecture season by admitting fifteen days later that writers and speakers were still "flattering our separated brethren . . . [expressing] frequently the charitable hope that *some* out of the Church will be saved."[40] Such ambivalences run through his writings.

Roddan, Boyce, Tucker, and Fitzpatrick once saw studies as the fulfillment in whole or in part of their personal ambitions. In Roddan's case this carried over into his editorials where he admonished the immigrants to see "mental improvement" as a "sacred debt" to America, and to realize that in America a man's prosperity could "almost always be measured by the amount of what he knows." He promised them that their children would "sit side by side [in school] with the children of the great ones of the land." This had been Roddan's experience. He had been able to make a successful career as a theologian and then as a popularizer of ideas. He had his years of independent brilliancy, even though this thinned out as he increasingly took Brownson as the provisioner of knowledge. Yet at the end of it all, even his trust in the intellect was shaken. By 1858 he had pathetically adopted as his rule-of-thumb a statement thanking God "that while He has given me an intellect that is fallible, He has endowed me with an instinct that is sure." He was disillusioned about the possibility of ever achieving harmony by pointing out the truth year after year. "We only flatter our self-love," he wrote, "by meditating on the great powers of the human intellect." As for the people, he no longer believed in "the necessity of introducing all classes of people in the relations of faith to the prevailing errors and tendencies of the age." Rather he judged that Catholics would do better to minimize metaphysical speculation and employ themselves literally "in saying their beads or imitating the active virtues of the saints."[41]

The Catholics in Boston in these years did not constitute a "church militant, conscious of its mission in the United States, vigorous and active in proselytizing and the search for converts." Its leaders were uncertain men like Roddan who, despite themselves, needed Brownson, vacillated on the matter of Protestant worship services, destroyed Newman's reputation in 1852 only to set him up for the people's admiration half a decade later, and did not know how to fit philosophy and practical religion together. The Church was timid not militant, groping its way toward answers and security. Roddan deliberately reran the opposite picture over and over, presenting the Catholic Church not only as militant but as one more uncontrollable force in the city. Yet closer to the truth was his mild protest in 1858 against Protestants taking bands of Irish delinquents and orphans from the public institutions and sending them to the West for evangelization. "The Catholic Church," he relented, "is not so transient an affair that she cannot afford to wait."[42]

FATHER JOHN BOYCE

It might be expected that the novels of John Boyce, a young Ulster priest who "came out" to the Boston diocese with the '45 exiles, would explode in stirring defenses of his peasant countrymen. This might be especially anticipated since his novels centered on the troubled, haunting past which was the Irish writer's legacy. But such an analysis incorrectly presumes that the Irish immigrants of the 1840's were all and without differentiation a "mass of transplanted peasants." It further regards them all as Catholic, all anti-English, and all mindlessly reverential on the subject of Irishmen. Clearly they were not all ignorant peasants. Boyce certainly was not. Nor did he feel the need to glorify the Irish peasant as would the next two generations of Boston Catholic clergymen.[43] In fact, he had a middle-class view of society like the Young Ireland group, the Protestant nationalists who made a formidable bid to bring about repeal of the 1801 Act of Union and win complete independence from Great Britain after 1840. "Eager and moralistic" like them, Boyce also shared their distrust of the peasantry.[44] His fictional characters like Colonel Templeton (the Anglican landowner), Kate Petersham (a high-spirited young gentlewoman whose Protestantism Boyce defends), and Ephraim Weeks (a Yankee huckster by trade and Unitarian by conviction) were members of the lesser gentry or middle class. They were far more important to the culture he wanted to preserve both in Ireland and in New England. Boyce wanted a pluralistic society. Forty years before they were officially condemned in the papal encyclical of 1893 *Testem Benevolentiam,* Boyce had ideas about how Catholicism should adapt itself to and cooperate with the predominantly Protestant American culture. He was the first of a line of Catholic writers in the Boston area to strive for a personal kind of self-expression that had wider aims than institutional religion and its polemics. Eventually these writers were rendered all but inaudible and driven into virtual hiding by the pre-eminence of Brownson and the spate of small-minded, untalented apologists who followed him. Yet this occurred only after Boyce had described and denounced Brownson in both *The Spaewife* in 1853 and *Mary Lee* in 1860. For Brownson was insisting that neither faith nor art nor virtue could exist outside the Catholic faith. Boyce was convinced on the contrary that there were many roles to be filled in society by people who had lived through a variety of religious experiences. In common with William James and opposed to Brownson, Boyce had a studied regard for the contribution to religious knowledge made by "the muddiness and accidentality of the world of sensible things." Peculiarly all of this was Boyce's because he never forgot the pluralist and strongly nationalist Irish world into which he had been born in 1810.[45]

Boyce was a native of Donegal, a town of notoriously tough-minded and fractious Catholics. His father was a wealthy and respected citizen, proprietor of the principal hotel, one of the magistrates of the county, and listed as "a moderate upholder of the British administration." Boyce then was not born into the world of the cabins, the treacherous and narrow world of the Celtic peasantry. He was socially advantaged, "a lad of parts, an athlete." As a child he was adept in running, jumping, swimming, riding the steeplechase, and handling a boat. At ten, he was writing poetry, and there is still something charming about his verses in *Shandy McGuire*, his first novel. Education for the priesthood acquainted him with the classics, but he was equally well-read in the Scottish reviews, Mrs. Trollope, Lady Morgan and other contemporary Irish writers.[46]

At some point in the late 1820's Boyce made the journey from northwest Ireland down to Navan, an important market town situated twenty-six miles northwest of Dublin at the juncture of the Boyne and Blackwater rivers. Here he attended St. Finian's Catholic Academy, a school founded in 1802 to prepare middle-class boys for the priesthood and learned professions. He won honors in rhetoric and philosophy. From this trading center where Black Castle looked down on the town's monthly fairs, Boyce went to nearby Maynooth. Here close by St. Patrick's College lay the ruins of Maynooth Castle, remains of the stronghold of the Earls of Kildare. These walls and towers were held responsible for beckoning the students toward that revolutionary political agitation which the faculty of the seminary then feared. This weird juxtaposition of the ruined castle of the Fitzgeralds with the dwellings of the French *émigré* priests who distrusted any sort of revolution introduced Boyce to a set of ambivalences that existed at Maynooth in the 1820's and 1830's. Several decades had elapsed since the prosperous Whigs under Henry Grattan had tried in vain to bring about lasting independence from England. Grattan had united Catholics and Protestants alike in efforts that closely paralleled the American Revolution. In 1782 these land-owners and middle-class proprietors had gained home rule but only for eighteen years. British rule was reintroduced in 1801. The transforming event in Ireland since that time had become the emergence of the Catholic peasantry mobilized by Daniel O'Connell in the interests of emancipation. Irish society, already sharply divided between the peasants and the gentlemen, was now all the more painfully torn in two. While Boyce was nearby at Maynooth, Lady Morgan "received" at Kildare Street in Dublin the members of United Ireland, now scattered and dispirited.[47]

In all of this Maynooth was not solving the problem of where young middle-class priests with the aspirations and the education of gentlemen should fit themselves into Ireland's revolution, as mastery of it fell progressively to their social inferiors. This was one of the central problems of Boyce's life. It was slight, however, compared to a later variant of the same question: where does the priest, still educated and still trained for a gentleman's place in society, fit into New England life where one's only contacts are substantially these same social inferiors?

Meanwhile Maynooth was sending its young men into a diocesan system in which, to use the cushioned words of Paul Cullen, archbishop of Dublin from 1852 to 1878, "discipline . . . [did] not greatly prevail." Maynooth was decidedly teaching its own brand of Gallicanism and contributing to every sort of ecclesiastical laxity. Its graduates, pleased to keep Rome at a distance, perpetuated in episcopal offices such men as would pamper the local clergymen. Boyce was ordained into this situation in 1837.[48]

In 1845 Boyce left Ireland and an inconsequential role as contributor to Young Ireland's *The Nation*. Three years after his arrival in America, and when settled at the age of thirty-four as pastor at Eastport, Maine, he gave the public a picture of his previous eight years in the Irish missions of Ulster. For in 1848 he accepted Bishop Fitzpatrick's request to make into a novel his light-hearted serial then running in *The Pilot* under the title of *Shandy McGuire* and published, as were all of his works, under the pseudonym of Paul Peppergrass. He retained the delightful nonchalance of a scribbled story concerning Irish peasants but also inserted Father Domnick as the dominant figure. He gave to this character all the traits of Reverend Daniel Murray, a man who was educated at Salamanca, served admirably as president of Maynooth, became coadjutor bishop of Dublin from 1809 to 1823, and finally was appointed archbishop of Dublin while Boyce would have been at Maynooth.[49] But essentially Father Domnick is an autobiographical character. In this respect, he reveals Boyce's attitudes toward society before and after his experiences in Boston as well as his encounters with Brownson and Fitzpatrick.

Like William Carleton and John Banim who were Irish novelists of his own generation, Boyce wrote in *Shandy McGuire* of the swift and confusing political changes in Ireland when O'Connell was calling to life its slumbering passions. "Prophecy-men were walking the roads of Ireland, selling chapbooks which proclaimed that 'twenty-five is the year.' Beggars were on the roads in their tens of thousands, families thrown out upon the road by clearings and evictions. In the Valley of the Black Pig in Ulster not a farm remained standing."[50] *Shandy McGuire* is a record of this peasant society in the 1820's on the eve of its disintegration.

Boyce quickly achieves the effect of a brooding fatalism in
Shandy McGuire by taking the "gentle reader" immediately into
a ravine sided by mountains rising "dark and jarred" and along
a "dreary road—bleak, darksome, and dispiriting to the way-
farer." Swiftly the reader is made to know Lough Devnish where
the atmosphere is "cold, foggy and disagreeable . . . the haunt of
the smuggler, or private distiller, [from] time immemorial." In
such a way are the peasants introduced: rapacious haters of the
law, then brighter and happier tricksters, then again the treacherous and most brutalized peasantry in Europe.[51]

Boyce, as in each of his novels, is superb as though by instinct
at painting in the peasants. He moves without effort from the
sardonic to the tragic. So he describes one tenant's children
with controlled understatement, isolating for narration "the in-
convenience they must have felt from the long pointed tatters of
their dress, that now, saturated with the bog-water through which
they passed occasionally, flapped heavily against their legs and
sides." With equal intelligence he introduces Colonel Templeton,
treating the overseer too fancifully for hatred, too understand-
ingly for contempt. In fact Templeton, though a Protestant and
presently vexed beyond endurance at his tenantry, is carefully
removed from any taint of charlatanry. It is the proprietor and
the priest Father Domnick who will ultimately face each other
regarding Ireland's future. For these gentry represent the learning of the upper classes. Whether Protestant or Catholic,
whether in Ireland or later in New England, they alone have
society's answers. But for now Templeton is riding to the shack
of Kathleen Kennedy "carrying with him the hated tracts: 'Anti-
Christ Exposed; Romanism Defeated; The Man of Sin Cloven
Down by Five Blows of the Holy Bible; Papist Idolatry; Daisies
of Piety; Primroses of Devotion; Dahlias of Faith,' etc., etc. . . ."
And Templeton is nodding complacently, whispering to himself
that the Bible "might be regarded as the seed, and the pam-
phlets the little watering-pots of religion."[52]

The village world which comes alive through the gaiety of
Boyce is, of course, a divided one. It is one of Protestants and
Catholics who are unable to think problems through in terms

other than "nation" and "religion." Yet in writing of Baxter Cantwell the Anglican rector, Ebenezer Goodsoul the Methodist Bible reader, or the Committee of Orange Lodge #516, Boyce is writing of familiar figures, men whom he understands to be victims of their own injustices to the villagers. He allows something likeable to emerge in the act of introducing Cantwell, a minister who, during his wife's philippic regarding his supine attitude toward Father Domnick, patiently opens *The Saints' Everlasting Rest*. Goodsoul too is fabricated as a sincere figure, though comic in his evangelical intensities. He is presented, for example, as one who misses the humor of his own nomination of the squalid, useless Irish village as "Babylon" and its uncomprehending peasants as "Amorites." So with gentle satire Boyce explores the hated New Reformation Society.[53]

Among the Catholic inhabitants there is a further dichotomy. The sharp division between the lower classes and the gentry is at once apparent. Boyce's gentlemen lack, as did John Banim's, the physical vigor of the peasants. But they are capable of heroic virtue on the intellectual level or, better, the level of decision making for society. As such they become increasingly Boyce's concern. His portrayal of the peasant tricksters is the most appealing aspect of his writing as well as the most suitable way of capturing the genius of Ireland, its "barbarism."[54] And later *The Spaewife* is largely a failure because minstrels and *seanachies* are mere roadside figures, deliberately undeveloped while attention is given to portraying gentlemen like Sir Geoffrey Wentworth. Yet only these landowners and clergymen could debate the issues disturbing Boyce. The issues haunting *Shandy McGuire* and later novels were two. The first was that of the priest whose social and intellectual leadership was threatened in a society where fixed and necessary social structures were being bartered away for egalitarianism. Boyce had watched this happening in Ireland in his last years there and it was a developing feature of New England society. Secondly he was concerned for societies like New England where religious extremists like Brownson were dividing the community by their use of apologetics and dogmatic oversimplifications.

Only when Boyce has the gentry, the priest and the peasant riff-raff of the village on the scene at once in *Shandy McGuire* can one see how desperately he counted on a deferential society to insure his role as priest and thereby his self-image. In his mind, the composite of social prominence, intellect, and virtue was so real that a peasant who proclaimed himself intelligent had to be a charlatan. So Boyce is quick to show the reader that Shandy's reputation for his "leanin' to p'lite lithr'thur" is harmlessly but quite fundamentally fraudulent. Father Domnick, however, is a man of intellect whose single precious possession is his library. Only the needs of his people draw him from it. When the library is burned out by the local Orangemen, it is taken by the old priest as a sign that his usefulness in Ireland is ended. Yet the violence of the Catholic or Protestant peasantry will never bring stability to society. If there is to be social and religious reconciliation, it will be effected by the gentry, and particularly the gentlewomen. By marriages such as that in *Shandy McGuire* between the Catholic gentlewoman Ellen O'Donnell and the Protestant Roderick O'Brien, the wider and absolutely necessary union of Protestants and Catholics will be achieved and independence gained. The peasants will again behold how "Catholic and Protestant join hands in friendship and fealty, forgetting all sectarian animosity, and animated by the same noble, generous spirit, swear . . . to fight like children of the same father for the freedom of their native land . . ."[55]

Between the writing of *Shandy McGuire* and Boyce's next novel, *The Spaewife,* the young priest took up a life in the Boston diocese which offered many personal satisfactions. He was close to Fitzpatrick, Williams, Roddan, and the Jesuits at Holy Cross College. He was held in general esteem by them and, more important, together they constituted a noticed and respected coterie around Boston. Writing of them at a dedication of a Newburyport church where "a large number of Catholics and Protestants attended," the Boston *Union* paused in admiration to describe Fitzpatrick and sixteen of his clergymen. "They were a fine looking set of men, young or in the prime of life . . .

The Bishop is about 45 years of age and has a noble appearance . . . The sermon was by John Boyce . . . a native of the north of Ireland." And Boyce must have been aware that, as here, such sermons were unexceptionally reported as delivered with "power and eloquence."[56]

His work at St. Joseph's in Eastport, Maine, and then in Worcester gave him a rolling-stone kind of life, first "strewing Washington County with mission stations" and then after 1847 working out of Worcester to places like Milford, Hopkinton, Clinton, West Boylston, and Southbridge. He was already a favorite among the boys at Holy Cross in Worcester, laughing with them on the train to Boston and playing ball with them and Williams back at the college. Nevertheless it was a hard life. From 1848 to 1850 the pew rent of St. John's church in Worcester netted only $60.04. And it was a life with which he was not coping altogether successfully. There were arguments about finances with the co-pastor, and he was obviously drinking. Only *The Spaewife* and *Mary Lee* betrayed his progressive frustration and "sense of . . . isolation." The problems of Irish nationalism continued to be with him but this would not have set him to writing again. Brownson did.[57]

The Spaewife is a miserable failure by any literary standards. It is two fumbling volumes of intriguing Elizabethans, Scotsmen, and women—with all of whom Boyce is at his worst. Yet he worked hard at it and, like his public, must have counted on it being a success. For it was dedicated to Fitzpatrick and accepted by printers in both London and Baltimore. It is clear from the outset that the spectacle he wished to put before the public was that of a mere "scribbler" come to court against the Goliath, Brownson. Roddan's negative view of the novel in *The Pilot* caught this mischief immediately. His first specific complaint was that "the old Knight [Brownson] . . . is represented at one stage as too imbecilic for the spirit and energy he betrays at another." Yet Boyce was determined. In the preface he mockingly lifted a toast to ahistorical storytelling. He insisted that the novel was "neither religious nor controversial" but fetched from "presumptive evidence." "And I am not sorry for it," he wrote gaily, "for I think, in all conscience, that we've had enough of *that* class." He intended his story for "plain, simple people, [and it was] not in the least dangerous to faith and morals." So saying, he based his narrative on a bit of historical data about Queen Elizabeth from Lingard—Lingard, whose skill Brownson was to denounce as un-Catholic later in the year.[58]

Boyce begins his assault on Brownson when the Protestant gentleman Plimpton introduces the reader to "an old man of great learning and eccentric habits . . . an inveterate enemy of the Anglican Church." Such is Sir Geoffrey Wentworth, a man whose Catholic excesses Boyce never ceases to satirize. The first appearance of Wentworth is as a ludicrous hedge-master rather than a knight. "As he advanced, the light fell upon a massive, antique gold crucifix, that appeared within the folds of his open doublet. Behind his right ear, he carried a pen, the feather of which lay against his glossy temple . . ." This man, not Queen Elizabeth, is the villain of the novel. As the tale progresses—or tries to progress—he emerges as a bigot and a pompous intellectual who would sacrifice his daughter's happiness rather than display a minimum of religious tolerance. Father Peter is the opposite of this vain, icy scholar so readily given to inane soliloquies on St. Thomas or St. Bernard. The priest (transparently Fitzpatrick) does put his life in jeopardy for Wentworth's daughter, Alice. Moreover under his tutelage, she comes to see the justification for respecting many different religious needs. "She saw her [the Catholic Church] making herself all to all that she might gain all to God. She saw her studying human nature in all its lesser qualities as well as in its prominent characteristics and making, for every need and every want, an appropriate and salutary provision." Alice had come to understand that it is through the senses and through experience that man is either turned from religion or to use Boyce's term "satisfied" by it. Nor should she fear Anglicans like the queen. Elizabeth's defection is after all one of the heart. The dangerous persons are extremists like Sir Geoffrey, those sterile scholars who refuse to accept experience as the deepest source of religious conviction. They substitute for it those theological and philosophical formulas that are "the translations," as William James would have it, "of a text into another language."[59]

Mary Lee, Or the Yankee in Ireland returns to the dark coast of northwest Ireland, to the timeless squalor of the Gaelic folk and the musty decadence of the gentry. Again Boyce has determined that at the risk of losing spriteliness the folk will serve only as a distraction from the drama of decision making going on wherever the gentry and clergy meet. Even the Yankee Ephraim Weeks, who is clearly intended to be the main character, comes out as another Malvolio. He is delightful but not central. That he is charming at all is curious. For he is a speculator come to Ireland with underhanded designs and even dishonorable intentions toward Mary Lee! Yet Boyce is typically both scornful and affectionate toward Weeks. He is also careful to preserve a place in society for this huckster, this Unitarian whose creed is one clipped phrase, namely, "the existence of a first cause and the perfectibility of man."[60]

Orestes Brownson is again the central figure. In the 1860 edition of *Mary Lee,* he appears as "David Henshaw," a lawyer and contributor to *The Edinburgh Review.* Actually the 600-acre farm of the Henshaws in Worcester County in the 1850's would have been well known to Boyce. The name was a byword for political opportunism in the 1850's. To make very sure of this libel, Boyce prejudges "David Henshaw" further. The narrator cites him as "a very despot in religion, [a man] without the least pity for those who had grown up in the midst of hereditary prejudices against Catholicity, or comprehension for those who would have willingly embraced it . . . [Rather] he consigned all beyond the pale of the church—all, without exception—to unutterable destruction." With Henshaw as foil, it is clearly Boyce's intention to uphold once again the place of religious pluralism. He does this in subsequent pages of debate between Henshaw and Father John. (Again Father John is a copy of Fitzpatrick. Here he is presented under a name which Brownson had formerly appropriated to himself in "Conversations" in his *Review*). In these theological exchanges, the priest calmly accuses Henshaw of being a dangerous man. He warns him of the danger to himself and to the church if he continues to operate as the anointed spokesman. There is danger to the church, he emphasizes, "lest your non-Catholic readers might mistake your productions for fair specimens of the true tone and spirit of Catholicity."[61]

Kate Petersham gives flesh and blood to Father John's warning. She is an intelligent, widely read and tolerant young Anglican whom Henshaw condemns both for her appreciation of Jonathan Swift and her obstinate refusal to denounce Protestantism. Father John however accepts Kate's religious beliefs with patience, confident that "the grace of God and the influence of example" will in time bring Kate to Catholicism. How this comes about is somehow all-important to Boyce, for it is through the saccharine example of Mary Lee. Yet it is also not important. For Kate is portrayed as an Irish woman of remarkable qualities *before* her conversion; she is already a wise and satisfied young lady. The Protestant characters of later Boston Catholic stories are far different. They are tales of semiheathens who *have to* have defects or basic dissatisfactions which conversion to Catholicism will speedily clear away.[62]

Boyce created Ephraim Weeks in order to speak about basic religious differences in New England. And Weeks is created sympathetically enough to evoke confidence in his analysis of how religion functions there. In America, as Weeks explains, religion is functional. Unlike Ireland, it does not lay on the heart like a legend. Claims for the religiosity of the New Englanders are necessarily few. "Well, it's just like this," he offers. "One class of our people does the praying, and the other does the trading—kind of makes it easy, you know, on both; so that, take them on the hull, they're a very religious people." Weeks also comments on Catholicism in New England. He reports that New Englanders object to Catholicism because the "laws and rules of the Catholic Church hain't got no joints in 'em; you can't bend 'em no shape or form." "The question for Americans," he continues "is not whether any particular form of religion be young or old, true or false, divine or human, but whether it suits the genius of the country." The American genius is one that knowingly moderates the rigors of the gospel in order that trade may go forth. "Had we not shaken ourselves free from the trammels of both pilgrim and priestly rules, could we have become in so short a period so intelligent, enterprising and powerful a nation?" Boyce could have mocked all of this. He could have undercut it as he would the ideas of Henshaw. There could have been the "horrible, senseless, mischievous laughter of an Irishman who comes," as Shaw put it, "at last to a country where men take a question seriously and give a serious answer to it . . . [and then] derides them for having no sense of humor." Later both Father John O'Brien's *Sacred Heart Review* and Father Cornelius Herlihy's *The Celt Above the Saxon* would do this. But Weeks is presented too generously for that. Certainly he was fond of money. Yet "he was just as ready to . . . lend it to a neighbor in a pinch, and think it no great obligation . . . He was by no means a mercenary man. Nor was he, like most lovers of money, envious of his neighbor's prosperity." Boyce found in Weeks a quality with which he could identify in that Weeks was a man responsive to experience. Throughout *Mary Lee* but especially in the character of Weeks, Boyce was faithful to his own insistence that a man's propensities are formed by his on-going experiences. In this light, Weeks is not to blame for his weaknesses since he was "born and bred in the midst of speculators." On the contrary, he is left essentially unchanged by his months in Ireland. Weeks departs "cursing Ireland and all the darned Irish in it . . . [swearing] you couldn't find such 'a tarnation set of varmints in all almighty creation.' "[63]

There would have been no place for Weeks, Kate, or Baxter Cantwell had it not been for Boyce's attitude toward religious knowledge. Boyce had learned in Ireland that religious knowledge results from experiencing the concrete historical situation where environment is yoked with whatever are the given powers of religious reflection. He had learned this well before Brownson nudged him in this direction. Given this thinking, Weeks had to be a Unitarian—pity him as you may—because spirituality is the outcome of a variety of religious experiences. The Yankee was born among "speculators" and would naturally respond to the call of commerce and come to discard Calvinism as "the old, stiff, evangelical rules" of his forefathers. Not that religious convictions could be predicted unerringly. For the totality of an individual's experience was boundless. Boyce in fact apologized to his readers in *Shandy McGuire* for generalizing from Ebenezer Goodsoul to all Bible readers. In the same way, he carefully distinguished the gentry's hold on Catholicity from that of the peasants. Shandy draws life and indeed sensuous enjoyment out of Catholicism. This is legitimate for the folk. But for patricians like Ellen O'Donnell and others who were carefully educated in Europe as befitted Ascendency times, Catholicism engaged the intellect. Because Alice in *The Spaewife* was also a Christian gentlewoman, she too was "not one of those who simply believe and practice religion . . . No, she studies it thoroughly." Father Domnick was expected to bring erudition to the religious instructions of Roderick O'Brien. "Stay with Roderick," Ellen begged of him, "to teach him the faith and practice of our holy religion,—to show him how grand, how royal it is in its mysteries and its worship! How like it is to the religion which a mind noble and generous like Roderick's would have selected for the worship of Infinite Majesty."[64]

As early as 1851, Boyce's lectures and writings had but one emphasis: Catholicity is a psychological phenomenon which uniquely recognizes the varieties of religious appetites and satisfies each. On January 24, 1851, he delivered a lecture which he would repeat often but which was first presented to the Catholic Institute in New York City. Its title was significantly "The Satisfying Influence of Catholicity on the Intellect and Senses." Boyce was as concerned with epistemology here as were John Henry Newman, Francis Weyland, Theodore Parker, or Orestes Brownson. As the title of the lecture suggests, he intended to combine epistemology and psychology. For this purpose he assumed implicitly the developmentist position of Newman regarding religious knowledge as well as a proto-Jamesian position on the importance of feeling.

The lecture begins with Boyce's assertion that he does not intend to take up a defense of Catholic dogma as Brownson had. Brownson left no space for mystery or for the enigma of the church attracting and repelling at the same time. But Boyce was less certain of how to make his own position coherent. He cited his topic as "the scope or genius of Catholicity" without really having found the right word. Somewhat later, he referred gropingly to the "spirit of Catholicity," a construction which he could only call "a communion of thoughts [among Catholics] inconceivable to the stranger, thoughts which we indeed are conscious of but cannot adequately describe." Even as the lecture ended, he was still in need of reassuring himself. "Yes," he wrote, "there is a poetry in the Catholic religion which we cannot describe, but which we can in part *feel* . . . It was the knowledge or *experience* of this mysterious power that has given to the Catholic Church the satisfying influence she has ever exerted on the intellect and the senses of man" [my italics]. He wanted to say that what religion reports are the facts of experience, facts not always coherent. But along the way he took fright, seeing as capitulation to relativity rather than insight the later assessment of James that "feeling *is* dumb and private and unable to give an account of itself. It allows that its results are mysterious and enigmas, declines to justify them rationally, and on occasion is willing that they even pass for paradoxical and absurd."[65]

The 1850's gave no ready ear to any argument on religious knowledge which allowed a place to the paradoxical or absurd. So Boyce yielded in his lecture to the need for logic to undermine the rationalists. He insisted that truth could not always be distinguished from error because these were not absolutes. "The very lowest and degraded forms of religion found in barbarous nations," he illustrated, "possess many relics of truth, whose lights tho' dim and obscured by the mists of error have not yet been totally eclipsed." Good and evil were also "only relative terms when applied to human acts and are ever varying in the circumstances in which they are found." Even if a herald were sent down to explain "what still remains obscure in the Christian dispensation" man would still be a plaything of doubt and error. "What then," he asked, "does man know?" And he answered, "Hardly anything but effects and results." This was the same kind of pedestrian proto-Jamesian epistemology which he had offered in *Shandy McGuire*. There, for example, he had verified the genuineness of a religious experience by noting "the change that takes place in the human countenance when the soul [is] engaged in prayer."[66]

Boyce maintained that the senses directed the intellect and, in that sense, limited it. He also stressed "the restrictive power" of Catholicity over the intellect, though this phrase was misleading. His meaning was that Catholicism faced the intellect with its own limitations. For he proposed that the Catholic religion was a "democratic doctrine" and that the apostles and their successors preached the truth "not to philosophers but to the multitude." He had wanted to humble Brownson and to demonstrate that religious belief was not an intellectual exercise but a complex experience. The point was well made. But in delivering it Boyce was forced into an extreme position himself. He was supporting an intellectual egalitarianism in maintaining that "the genius of Catholicity is to place all men on an equality on the road to Heaven" and that Catholicism "equalizes all classes in as much as one within its rule is obliged to believe revealed truth [not on reason but on simple faith]." But this same assertion undercut his own role in society.

What Boyce still required of a community was that it be a society of hierarchical grades and consequently different intellectual levels. Maynooth had taught him that the priest was a transcendent figure, servicing with different equipment the needs of a stratified society. He could straddle the levels of a deferential society but was socially and intellectually above the commoners. Boyce's main character in *Shandy McGuire* had successfully straddled the two Irelands. But this was because in 1848 Boyce was himself still optimistic about straddling whatever divisions of society America would present. After 1851, he was increasingly forced to accept the fact that America offered no social levels and that it lacked "those customs and habits [of other lands] that mark so nicely the distinction between the noble and the ignoble." In *Mary Lee,* he criticized Weeks as typical of the crassness and mindless mobility of American society. It was "a universal scramble in which everyone snatches at what came handiest . . . [where] the shoemaker struck his awl in the bench and ascended the pulpit." But he drew back from such implicit chaos in the same paragraph. "He [Weeks] was [after all] not an American gentleman by any means, either in habits *or education . . .* And those of his fellow-citizens *who could rightfully claim that distinction* would never have recognized him as one of their number" [my italics].[67]

It was equally important to Boyce that he be allowed to act as bridge between Protestants and Catholics, that the two groups "forgetting all sectarian animosity . . . [come to] fight [together] like children of the same father." To him, this kind of reconciliation had been the glory of Grattan's efforts and Young Ireland's aspirations. As a native of Ulster, it had been his continual experience. A society where such a reconciliation was at least viable was necessary to his career and to his self-image as "father." Yet Brownson was successfully closing the door on non-Catholics. And to try holding a candle to him as religious commentator was simply to illumine one's own smallness. Boyce did so out of desperation. He was incensed at Brownson's pretensions over the domain of Catholic theology. More personally and as the preface of *Mary Lee* made clear, Boyce's own abilities as theologian were being curtailed. Brownson drove him out of theology and in effect out of the ministry and into "scribbling."[68]

Shandy McGuire was written out of what troubled Boyce in 1848: the responsibility of the Irish priest in the nationalist peasant-led uprisings against England. But later writings arose out of his confrontation with a classless New England society, a lean society where Protestants and "gentlemen" were effectively cut away from him. He was forced to ask how Catholicity should be presented in the United States where it had to accommodate to egalitarianism. If a priest followed Brownson's course and made religion exclusively the quest of the intellect, then he could surely not be the transcendent father of many children.

Specifically, his work with the Irish immigrants—most of them illiterate—would certainly be to no purpose. But if he "forever moralized" and reduced religion to psychological "feelings," he then preached his way out of the society of learned men. He opened himself to the charge also that his interest in studies was only an empty pretension. As early as 1851, Boyce made an uneasy settlement with the latter alternative.

How uneasy this option was is clear in Boyce's continued efforts at writing and at making some kind of intellectual contribution. He was satisfied to write not as the theological scholar but as the *seanachy*, the Gaelic teller of tales. Using this form, he filled the only place that in his eyes Brownson had left for him. But the genre also best suited his self-imposed task of defrosting the spirit of Catholicity made frigid by Brownson. Bent upon this, Boyce had become progressively absorbed in reflecting on the experience of experiencing Catholicism. He saw the church conveying poetry by "speaking to man's soul through every avenue, through his sight, his hearing, his affections, his intellect, his imagination." But Boyce could also break out of this absorption and reflect on the experience of life. He admired the writer who chose to experience reality naked of religious clothing as firmly as Walt Whitman desired to experience it without material clothing. His protagonists in *Mary Lee*, Father John and Kate, defended Tom Moore and insisted that his poetry be judged on its merits. Henshaw thought differently. To him, Moore was "a very respectable songster in his way, but an immoral man, a bad Kaatholic." He had corrupted the minds of the young "because in losing his faith he lost his morality also." But Boyce persistently dismissed Henshaw's views on literature and concluded the discussion with Kate's exasperated retort, "My dear sir, we have nothing to do with the faith . . . Why, you drag faith into everything. Can't we admire a man's writings without inquiring into his faith?"[69] This was the kind of question which some Boston Catholic writers following Boyce continued to ask, thought it was progressively mistrusted as dangerously latitudinarian.

In the last half of the nineteenth century, Catholic literary culture was taking shape at two locations in the Boston area, Worcester and Boston.[70] In each locale there was a difference in the texture of thinking. In its own way, the essential difference was like that between Puritanism in Cambridge in 1620 and Puritanism in London at the same time; it was the difference between the functioning of Puritanism in the college town and in the nearby capital city. Similarly out in Worcester, Holy Cross College sat on one of the seven hillsides without disturbances. Even the battle for its charter in 1865 had been fought at a distance, in Boston. And when *The Worcester Spy* wanted someone to blame for the spread of Know-Nothingism throughout the state, it selected Roddan in Boston as *provocateur*. Worcester even went along with Boyce's unsuccessful educational experiment at St. John's on Temple Street, a scheme whereby the city would finance the school and pay a faculty selected by Boyce. The town, then, was once-removed from disputes like that over "the jail-lands" which, coming one after another, kept Boston tempers sharp. Holy Cross was small, staffed by Jesuits of the Maryland province and old-maidish in its discretion and gentility. Its spirit was typified in the 1850's by Charles Bullard Fairbanks, a talented young Bostonian who was assistant librarian at the Athenæum and, after a European trip, a convert from Episcopalianism to Catholicism. He was baptized at Holy Cross by Fitzpatrick in 1852, studied there for the priesthood until disqualified by poor health, and died in 1859 at the age of thirty-two while reporting events from Paris for both the Boston *Transcript* and *The Pilot*.[71]

Fairbanks wrote a number of essays which are significant for their interest in individual religious experience rather than an interest in how a religious group functions, what its politics should be and what defenses it has or should be prepared to marshall. Such concern for collective religious experience, as it were, came to preoccupy Boston Catholic writers, though not without exception. There it was not until the 1880's that an optimistic group of young Catholic writers gathered around

John Boyle O'Reilly and did begin to provide an atmosphere where Fairbanks' or Boyce's desire to scribble down individual feelings could be understood. Louise Imogen Guiney, Alice Brown, Jeff Roche, Henry Austin Adams, Eleanor Conway, Michael Earls, S.J., and Bliss Carman began to fill the pages of *The Pilot, Donahoe's Magazine, The Atlantic Monthly,* and an assortment of chapbooks with their verses. They encouraged "one another's muse" in voluminous, self-conscious correspondence. They set a new free style for Catholic writers in Boston because of their drive for sheer aesthetic production as well as their exchange as artists with "the Brahmins" and writers like Louise Moulton. John Boyce was one of the early Catholic writers of the Boston area whom they resurrected.[72]

One of the group, Michael Earls, S.J., sincerely admired Boyce. Unfortunately he also made a career from Boyce's writings, adorning himself with them and making discourse on them. From Boyce as from other Catholic writers, he took what he needed for his career both as teacher of literature and chronicler of American-Catholic culture. He set himself up as an expert on Irish-American literature and clumsily exaggerated Boyce's literary merits, obscuring his didacticism, pietisms, and general fumbling with plot. Still worse, he loosened Boyce from his own generation and from ways of thinking he shared with it. Earls missed the fact that Boyce was a man of the mid-nineteenth century and that like Darwin or Bushnell or Emerson he was fascinated with variety. Earls' generation, which was writing at the end of the nineteenth century, saw social groups as necessarily unharmonious. But Boyce had hoped that the varieties of social groups could be welded together and that a stronger type would emerge without annihilating any one group. "The Irishman coming to America," he had pointed out in a lecture, "asks for nothing but fair play. If, among the various social elements of the American social body which are being moulded into a new type of civilization, the Irish character be allowed development . . . he [sic] will be found to possess more than sinew." Earls missed this evolutionary thinking. He wanted Boyce to be a writer of the 1890's or, better, to be a prototype of how he saw himself: a classicist, a Thomist, a single-minded protagonist of Irish-American culture, a witty unruffled Irish-American priest. Boyce was none of these. Above all, he was a man concerned with the dynamics of religious knowledge.

The human mind undergoes revolutions as do kingdoms and nations, and will come out the stronger and purer from the struggle . . . *Experience* shall have taught men that the Church is the creation of Heaven, not the production of earth, and that her abuses are not to be remedied by her total suppression . . . but by an ardent and pious zeal on the part of her children to remove those unsightly blemishes.

But Earls found Boyce as a *seanachy*—just where Brownson had left him.[73]

Chapter II
1866 to 1880:
Polarization

The lives of the priests during this period were increasingly shaped by the impact of socio-economic conditions on the aspirations and choices of the Irish immigrants and their descendants. This formation was all the more direct because Archbishop Williams backed away as a real authority figure. The priests' lives might have been different if Williams had insisted on structuring Catholic life in Boston, moved quickly to order local conditions, kept at a minimum chaotic experimentation, and set policy. Boston was about to see the number of immigrants rise from 4,534 in 1866 to 70,164 in 1907. Most newcomers were Irish and Roman Catholic. They required Williams to confront new problems; the school issue was only one of these. In response, however, Williams and the priests who were his administrators generally operated on the unrealistic premise that somehow major adjustments should be allowed to have no substantially negative effect on the structure of "the pedestrian city." The two generations of priests working under Williams—those of the "generation of '45" who would rule the diocesan parishes in the 1870's and those younger men who would be reaching for power in the 1890's—appreciated that preponderance in numbers meant cultural, social and even political leverage on the city. Williams refused to enforce policies as much out of fear of Catholic visibility as out of his own inability to deal with the disorder brought by sudden Catholic growth. For a period, the general result was an orderless limbo. It was fruitful for the continued growth of several strains of Catholic thought. During these years, Boston Catholicism was neither a cultural nor a theological monolith. But this vagueness could not last. Gradually the dogmatisms of the local priests as well as the first intrusions of Rome moved into the vacuum where Williams had been unable to transmit "genteel," if provincial, Boston values.

THE IMMIGRANTS AND THE CITY

The city of Boston was able to provide a middle-class competence to a large number of its immigrants in the last third of the nineteenth century. Initially the massive influx of immigrants which had begun in the late 1840's meant location in cheap housing in what is now the North, South, and West Ends. Even as late as 1870, anything within a 2.5-mile radius of the State House was and would remain working-class settlements. But beyond that to a 3.5-mile radius was housing and transportation suitable to the aspirations of a central middle class. And before the depression of 1873 and again from 1885 to 1889, workers newly come to middle-class status were already clustering along streetcar tracks in areas like Roxbury, West Roxbury and Dorchester. By 1880 there was an extensive outward-moving middle class among the Irish population ringing the inner city but within a 3.5- to 6.0-mile radius of the State House. This was later appropriately designated "the zone of emergence."[1]

By 1900, one-half of Boston's families had come to share a middle-class, capitalistic environment in "the streetcar suburbs." Nevertheless back in 1891, there were still 71,467 Irish living in the city, 66.97% of whom still lived in rented tenements.[2] There were job opportunities, especially for the unskilled. Yet

it took about a generation for the Irish to have substantial numbers of their national group living in the zones of new suburban
construction.

Meanwhile the Boston Yankees among whom the immigrants
had come to live were moving toward the social and ethical
thinness which Howells caught in the 1880's. He saw the Bostonians "tied to a moribund provincialism, a quasi-tradition of
hypocritical benevolence, refinement, and respectability."[3] They
were encountered by the Irish, then, at a point of decline. Older
men like Dr. Oliver Wendell Holmes found defenses, judging
that "to be urban was an all but ignominious state of mind."
So the men of Holmes's generation kept touch with their country places, knowing all the while that prestige as well as the
balance of power was going to the city with its industry and
business. As for the younger generation, men like Henry Adams
had "lost the inherited ties that bound them to the rest of the
population; and, inasmuch as the population was urbanizing
. . . and was filled with strange new elements of every kind,
they did not even wish to know it." In fact, the rift between
themselves as writers and the public became "the corner-stone
of their self-respect."[4] They cultivated "the private life" in reac-
tion to a public life that was bound to get lost in "the mist and
mud of American democracy."[5] Surely their escapisms were
more subtle than those suggested in *Ballou's Pictorial,* a magazine which advertised Hyde Park as a residential area removed
from the Irish by a benevolent God. But ultimately they could
no more find isolation than Ballou. Edward Everett Hale also
failed to convince Irish workers that emigration out of the city
and into farming would restore the social conditions of the New
England town of two generations past where "a rented house
was an exception to the rule and general habit of the community."[6] Still there was hope. Such schemes as Hale's homestead-
ing plans might yet "take" insofar as the immigrant population
was not yet in a position to manipulate the Yankee community.
In fact, Irish Catholics were also well aware that they dare not
publicly question either the attempts of men like Hale to make
them suburbanites or the ethical values of the Yankees. Catholic

criticism was just gaining strength, just beginning to move in smaller and smaller concentric circles, from criticism of general issues to more intimate daring probings: from government, then to professional life, then to Yankee family standards. Only in the 1890's and then preferably through the words of a Protestant minister quoted in *The Sacred Heart Review* would the Irish come to criticize publicly the Yankee acceptance of birth control.

The Roman Catholic Church of Boston in 1866 was in no position to talk of strengths and weaknesses. It had found relief from the acrobatic theologizing of Brownson, Roddan, Boyce, and Nicholas O'Brien. *The Pilot,* under a new priest-editor, dropped theology in favor of discussing Fenianism and post-war reconstruction in the South. But at the opening of Williams' administration the church was desperate for institutions and personnel to service the growing Catholic population. There was no Catholic college in the city, and entrance to Harvard was effectively barred, except to the sons of the older Yankee-Catholic stock like the Blakes. There was no local seminary. The cathedral would not be completed until 1875 and then with funds raised for it by fairs and individual bequests. In 1872, the seventeen Boston Catholic churches gave a total of $6,015.27 in the annual cathedral collection. That put the average contribution at 1.8¢ if the number of those gainfully employed in 1872 was anywhere near the number for 1870.[7] By 1866, the St. Vincent de Paul Society had been organized but had not yet gained the right to incorporation.[8] Sunday school classes were held in church basements, a rectory or, as in Dorchester, a carpenter's shop. Public school teachers, if available, were generally the instructors in such schools. But an unintended pattern of teaching emerged from St. James parish. There, in 1866, Father William Byrne, the future vicar general, used the unemployed members of the St. Vincent de Paul Society to gather for instructions "the number of Catholic children not attending Sunday school and the number of those of our religion who are attending Protestant Sunday schools . . ."[9]

Meanwhile, the financing of church enterprises was a constant difficulty. The Lowell Bank trusted Williams with large loans, but there was no reason why an individual priest's credit should be particularly honored. He was, after all, receiving only $10.00 per week as a curate, he was liable for conscription during the Civil War, and he was individually responsible to meet payments on church construction. He might have as little collateral as Father P. J. Canny of Boston who, when he died in 1865, left $43.42, "one table, one what-not, two haircloth chairs, two seat-chairs, and two soapdishes."[10] Priests were not exempt from the wiles of business contractors.[11] They were equally vulnerable to high interest payments on loans.[12] To meet these needs, some dealt in "speculation and dealing in worldly affairs" as well as purchasing personal property in their own parishes.[13] Throughout this period and whether the immigrant was aware of it or not, even the liberals within Yankee society passed over both the greenhorn and the priest, preferring to work with assimilated Catholics like Thomas Ring— aged 37—or Yankee priests.[14]

In every way, then, Boston provided a discipline of prior conditions which preordained the structure of the immigrants' lives. The peninsular nature of the city, the growth of transportation which made for a grid pattern of settlement rather than clusters of communities, the natural fright, if not historic prejudice, of native Bostonians toward Irish Catholics—all of these were preexisting conditions with which the immigrant had to concern himself in making decisions. Added to this, he was generally unwanted by Boston Catholics of Yankee stock. Catholics like the poetess and essayist Mrs. John Blake had already unconsciously inserted themselves into Boston ways. When she wrote in 1883 of "our grandmothers . . . going from New York to Boston," whereas, in fact, her grandmother had never set foot outside Ireland, it was not to lie about ancestry but to betray an unquestioned, if unreal, sense of belonging.[15]

The immigrants upon whom these forces descended between 1866 and 1880 were of mean abilities. And they were well aware of this.[16] Economically unskilled and financially insecure, they came to see money and possessions as primarily important.[17] Thomas Ring, president of the Boston Council of the St. Vincent de Paul Society and a man of remarkably sound judgment, found them uncreative and unresponsive even to the needs of their own poor.[18] He found himself repeatedly opposed by Catholics who suspected any cooperation with the Associated Charities of the city although the nature of his work required this. "To stand aside in sulky silence," he argued in response, "would not be becoming our society . . . If without breaking down any of our honored traditions we can join hands with our fellow-citizens here, we will gladly do it."[19]

Dissatisfaction with their own cultural deficiencies led the immigrants to call again and again upon their "talented" leaders. John Boyle O'Reilly, a member of Thomas Bailey Aldrich's circle in the 1880's and a promising poet and speaker even in the early 1870's, was well aware that he was considered by the Irish as one of their "gifts" to Boston.[20] A local pastor too could be praised for his leadership, especially if he instigated parish affairs which neighboring Protestants might value, not to say, envy. One such pastor, Monsignor Patrick Strain, left a diary which contains a clipping from *The Boston Herald* of 1867. In it "a Subscriber" thanks the editor for his encouragement of the parish fair held in Chelsea. The letter, obviously from a parishioner, is noteworthy for its ingenuousness:

This result [a $3,000.00 net] is really encouraging and for this place it is thought extraordinary. Our friends have all labored hard, and strangers have given all the assistance they could . . . Several of the clergymen of the diocese have also been very kind and generous, and our city authorities, with a liberality not to be forgotten, allowed us the use of the City Hall, we may say, without any cost. In conclusion the old and the young Catholics and Protestants, all are not only satisfied, but are highly delighted . . .

Since Monsignor Strain as pastor had cooperated with Protestants and had heightened the parishioners' sense of belonging in the town, he too was copiously praised.[21]

The Irish Catholics, if they were ignorant and given to writing in jingles rather than poetry, were not naïve. Regardless of what late-nineteenth-century economists like Frederick Bushee saw on the surface or social workers like Vida Scudder good-heartedly stereotyped in novels like *A Listener in Babel,* there was not "complete religious conformity of thought."[22] Instead, the immigrants had a sardonic peasant ability to make individual devastating judgments in all directions. They were surprisingly selective about giving their *genuine* enthusiasm and money to the various Irish nationalist politicians who toured the East in the 1870's. John Boyle O'Reilly, a weathervane of Irish-American thinking, would not have assumed so effective a stance against nationalist plotters like O'Donovan-Rossa and Michael Davitt were it not popular.

The Irish were equally critical of priests. While consistently canonizing the Irish Dominican Father Thomas Burke, O.P., in the public press, private letters reveal that he was thought to be "ignorant and reckless" in his bouts with his English opponent Anthony Froude. "And the worst of it is," continued a letter from one troublesome Irish nationalist involved in "the spouting tour" (as they called the fund-raising lecture tour of the United States), "[that] our patriotic papers immediately cry out that Froude is knocked into a cocked hat."[23] The Irish Catholics were not averse to making a public show, if necessary, to recover funds from a dishonest priest or one with a bad business head.[24] In a show of another kind of independence, the men of the St. Vincent de Paul Conference in Gate of Heaven parish controverted and outvoted the pastor there, Father Patrick Higgins. This forced Higgins—himself a mail-fisted pastor —to make his peevish complaints known to Ring.[25] Higgins *was* in a helpless position. For at this time, Ring and his fellow-officers were in the position of *considering* the suggestions of Williams and Byrne regarding social work, making counter-suggestions that were acted upon, telling priests how to co-operate in working for the poor, and advising them on how best to handle the problems of unemployment.[26]

The power of the local clergy was, then, considerably limited. Not the wishes of the local clergymen but gain in terms of respectability determined who the local "day clubs" and "machine clubs" would put up for petty political offices.[27] Father Higgins did finally find a president for his parish's St. Vincent de Paul Conference who would "hand on . . . [his] . . . words with the devotion of an Apostle."[28] But for every such Mr. McMahon there was an equivalent Mr. McSweeney who resigned in 1879 as president of the conference in a Jamaica Plain parish after a dispute with the pastor, Father Thomas Magennis.[29] Less choleric but equally critical of the local clergy were men of realistic judgment like Thomas Ring. This man, in his private letters, betrayed a growing astonishment at the small-mindedness of the local clergymen. "Do you know," he reluctantly wrote to his cousin in 1877, "that even despite the warmest approval of His Grace, the most opposition to the Union [a cultural association set up by Williams] is among our priests, many of whom know very little about our hopes and work [and] seem to take a positive pleasure in saying sharp things against us, pooh-poohing the whole affair, etc."[30]

The most formidable demand the Irish population made upon itself was earning respectability, not learning subordination to the clergy. Real group consciousness came only after the mid-1880's. The drive for respectability in the 1860's and 1870's took the form of self-respect or of respect among friends within a close radius. There were exceptional men like John Boyle O'Reilly who managed to identify with "an Irish-Catholic community" sooner; such men sought respectability for themselves sometimes against this community and sometimes through it. But an article on "The Good Parish" in *The Pilot* of 1867 spoke for the majority, and it drew a perimeter which corresponded fairly accurately to the limits of its goals. "The good parish," it began, "is remarkable for its orderly, well-dressed people, who take a pride in appearing decent, and of being proper in their homes and conversation, and no brawls or tumults are ever heard within its walls." Particularly important, "the good parish never sends its children to school unclean." The people are industrious; they use the savings banks. "The good parish is social, intervisiting in delightful harmony, and keeping all the pleasant relations of neighborhood."[31] What the columnist realized here was that respectability had to be formulated as *individual* responsibility or responsibility to the parish at most. And the plea for self-respect would get maximum effect if framed in terms of financial security. For then it would dovetail with the widespread sense of achievement which the newness of the suburbs created, or with the good-hearted enthusiasm for hard work as in the case of Ring, or with the almost imponderable financial optimism of John Boyle O'Reilly.[32] Mythology aside, the Irish were not happy-go-lucky with money. Davitt was reduced to sounding like a leering wolf when forced to get money from those he called "the wealthy do-nothing Irish-Americans."[33] O'Reilly wrote letters to greenhorns which abound with admonitions to get a job and get ahead. He quite openly urged Home Rule for Ireland because "our hard-earned money is going there." The patterns noted within the peasant family economy in Ireland where the father assumed the burden of training and schooling all the boys for their careers did give evidence of continuing in Boston.[34] And to the extent that this obligation was fulfilled in the face of financial hardships, there was real generosity.[35] But this was within the family. Outside the family there was considerable apathy in contributing to the poor. Even regarding parochial school building projects, the majority of the Irish-Catholic population considered the public schools more than satisfactory for the general education of the children. Finally, the Irish, no less than other national groups, had to be urged to concern themselves about the religious education of their children.

Between 1866 and 1880, then, self-respect meant being able to exhibit at least the appearance of financial well-being, and Boston did much to satisfy this desire. For while one could not belong to Yankee society and could not even form a clear concept of city-wide society, one could locate in one of the clusterings at the crossroads of the streetcar metropolis and begin moving into middle-class competence. Whatever the good intentions, "the result was . . . a society shut up in a growing number of specialized social and political units, its citizens isolated from one another, its city-wide society needlessly uncontrolled because of the weakness of its agents."[36] The streetcar tracks and suburban traintracks did lead the way toward certain patterns of behavior among the Irish. Yet transportation companies like the Eastern Railway were not the only agencies to sharpen the abilities and desires of the immigrants.[37] By 1866, priests like the Redemptorists knew full well that their reputation and their magnificent Mission Church on a height dominating Roxbury could draw homeowners to the area, and it would be a "better class" of Irish at that.[38] They intended to influence and shape the lives of their parishioners, and they did. What was more subtle but just as real, however, was the shaping of their thinking and lives by the Catholics unto whom their massive church beckoned.

THE IMMIGRANTS AND ARCHBISHOP JOHN J. WILLIAMS

The immigrants had one kind of impact on Williams and his coterie of associates, and another on each of the two successive generations of clergymen. In the case of the latter, the immigrants were affecting the counterparts, first, of men like Henry Adams, a generation young during the Civil War. Secondly, they were affecting men like Henry Cabot Lodge who forged his career during the last decades of the nineteenth century and into the so-called progressive era. This was the generation to which William Henry Cardinal O'Connell belonged.

Williams' approach to his own role of leadership appears, on the surface, to be sheer drift, a kind of intellectual paralysis at the massiveness of the immigration and its accompanying problems. More than drift, it was refusal. He refused to think of himself as standard-bearer of what was now in fact the majority religion in the area. For accepting this new society and this new role would mean accepting the end of old patterns of existence for the city's native society.[39] Williams reacted against commercialism no less than Francis Parkman who "detested reformers . . . despised 'the morality of commerce' and . . . had made common cause with Godkin to save the Republic."[40] The archbishop was understandably nostalgic at the ceremonies marking the demolition of the old cathedral in 1860. But there was something more than circumstantial in his thinking when he referred to the archives of the old church as documents listing "the names of nearly all, if not all, of the merchants and gentlemen of Boston who were at that time prominent in the Society of the town."[41] The address on this occasion reflected a way of thinking which, even if it rose out of an early Boston provincialism, was decidedly genteel whether held by Protestant or Catholic.

Williams' dedication to Boston's earlier mode of life probably arose as much from his admiration for Fitzpatrick as from experience of "the pedestrian city." For he had left Boston in 1833 at the age of eleven to begin studying for the priesthood in Montreal and, excepting vacations, did not return to the city until after ordination at St. Sulpice near Paris in 1845. When he did return in that year it was to work at the cathedral in the center of a city not yet visited by the immigrants of '49. He knew Brownson intimately.[42] For recreation, he skated at Holy Cross, and sleighed with Father James Healy and the cathedral altarboys. He especially loved to walk in the New England countryside. His ordinary companion was Samuel Tuckerman, a convert to Catholicism from the illustrious New England family and a lifelong friend. Williams was handsome and marked by a prudence that was quickly taken to be holiness. Clearly being groomed to become administrator of the diocese, he was nevertheless unobtrusively kind to irascible figures like Father Hilary Tucker.[43] He never ceased to maintain the privacy which was typical of a Boston gentleman of his generation but remarkable for an archbishop of the last half of the nineteenth century. On March 12, 1864, when Williams was coadjutor-bishop of the diocese, *The Pilot* offered a sale of "card photographs" of the early Boston bishops and present outstanding local clergymen. And again on October 20, 1866, when he was bishop of Boston, *The Pilot* was again selling photographs, this time of six living American bishops. At neither sale was Williams' picture available.[44] The invisibility which Williams sought for himself in these instances was in its own way as admirable but as illogical as his maneuvring for Catholic invisibility in Boston society throughout his administration.

The overwhelming task of providing parishes and social services for the Irish between 1866 and 1880 gave Williams fair-weather allies among his clergy in the nonmilitant stance which was his by conviction and temperament. This position was supported not because it was a desideratum of Williams but because it was the only expedient posture, given the social and economic vulnerability of the Irish congregations.[45] So during this fifteen-year period, those Catholic priests *near* a situation cooperated with Yankee civic leaders and ministers, and some effectively so.[46] This cooperative stance was returned by Yankee officials and ministers, even if the response was in most cases a kind of testy tolerance of the Roman Catholic clergymen.[47] Ministers and Protestant officials found themselves dealing with priests and laymen whose endeavors seemed at times to threaten the integrity of the established order but which could not be controlled without being made much less useful. So to appropriate city funds for the support of Father George Haskins' school for delinquent and orphaned boys was equal to abetting Catholic growth. But not to aid him meant gross chaos on the streets and another kind of financial drain. Frequently state officials were simply indecisive. This is obvious in the on-again off-again grants of state aid to Haskins' orphanage.[48] Similarly, concessions were granted to priests anxious to catechize in the prisons or the House of Refuge and Reformation, but only reluctantly and over a limited period of years.[49] In all of these matters, the problem of state or municipal control over Catholic enterprises became steadily overshadowed in importance by the increasing difficulty of containing the priests and their parishioners within the structure of Boston Yankee society. Eventually, for example, even the combined efforts of Williams and Protestant liberals failed to prevent the establishment of parochial schools due to pressures from Rome and the power of certain local pastors. Yet, as they saw it, such severance from American Protestant institutions by Roman Catholics would destroy the whole social and religious fabric of the growing city.[50]

In fact, the overwhelming influx of the newer type of Irish moved Williams unconsciously away from the parish priests of Boston and from parish life where bitter realities were daily enacted. Samuel Tuckerman's daughter wrote that Williams "knew their [Irish] type, knew their density and . . . acted accordingly."[51] While this remains conjecture, it is certain that he did allow local pastors to move steadily away from him. At the same time, he placed more and more trust in a small group of priests and laymen. These were Yankee Catholics who were able to work on an administrative level above that of the parishes and who shared Williams' determination to maintain the small-city tempo and temperament of earlier years.[52] Two well-defined and antagonistic forces never emerged, except later on the school issue. And even in that case, the situation was acute only in the mid-1880's. After that and until 1907, the issue was becalmed.

Nevertheless, the split was real and it was based on fundamental issues. Both Williams and the parish priests recognized, for example, that the Irish-Catholic population desired to rise to middle-class status. Yet Williams' career and retrospective set of mind made him unable to comprehend the harsh realities of the immigrants' struggle for social upgrading. In reality, the city was experiencing vicious outbreaks of street violence and police brutality as the Irish cut into the old fabric of the city.[53] Still, Williams considered that their rise to economic well-being and respectability would be similar to that which Boston Catholic families had quietly attained in the 1830's and 1840's. In the face of social collisions which filled the daily papers, Williams urged nonviolence and submission even to the extent of tapering off the "anxiety to introduce priestly influence into prisons and workhouses."[54] But local clergymen like Father Thomas Scully were closer to the situation and were becoming increasingly dissatisfied with a pacifist posture. It was Scully who complained in 1876 that Catholics—obviously the many who were following Williams' style—had too long neglected the education of their children "lest perhaps [doing otherwise] we should disturb the *peace,* and lose the *good will* of our Yankee friends."[55]

Basically Williams and local clergymen like Scully were divided on whether or not it was credible that the Boston community would ever be receptive to Catholics. Williams noted the antipathy of the Bostonians to the Irish in an 1879 report to Rome, but he hastened to add that it was daily diminishing.[56] The local priests were not so sanguine.

Again, both Williams and the local clergymen knew that the immigrants, especially the children, needed religious instruction.[57] Williams maintained throughout that the mother's instruction supplemented by Sunday schools and private academies, especially for boys, would suffice.[58] The parish priests increasingly knew otherwise and rightly so. For financial demands, either self-imposed or otherwise, were driving down the benefits of family life. There was little interest in the children's religious instruction in many instances.[59] Williams was satisfied that somehow the faith would secure itself through a diocese-wide pattern of religious instruction. But the pastors were distrustful of vagueness and wanted "salvation by acre." Thus while the bishop hoped to make increased use of the Vincent de Paul men as teachers, the pastors were individually dislodging these men, successfully replacing them with men and women of the religious teaching orders.[60] Similarly, Williams and the parish priests disagreed on the less formal techniques of providing religious instruction. Williams espoused those earlier Catholic liturgies whose quiet and decorum had drawn praises from men like Nathaniel Bowditch. The pastors supported their parishioners' enthusiasm for public processionals, highly embroidered oratory, and revivalistic meetings.[61] Thus in the very act of erecting massive church buildings, the local pastors were making a radical and assertive gesture against the "Catholic establishment" and, at the same time, contributing to the general backlash against the Yankees.

Another point on which Williams differed from the local clergy was the matter of intellectual leadership of the Catholics in Boston. Both Williams and the local clergymen were well aware of the intellectual inferiority that characterized the priests. Sherwood Healy made it quite clear to Williams—if the bishop did not already have other sources of information—that the clergy were not a highly intelligent group nor even necessarily well trained. Healy was a professor at the seminary at Troy, New York, and in a position to suggest, as he did in 1868, that the young priests be examined in theology every year for five years after ordination and given faculties only annually. "It is astonishing," he wrote in proposing this, "how young men forget what they learned in the seminary. They study not and become stupid. I could give many examples . . . I cannot think . . . that you know how ignorant are some of our clergymen: you might not sleep easy if you did."[62] Regardless of whether the problem of leadership affected Williams' nocturnal hours, it did drive him toward a solution, though again it was not one which pleased the local clergymen. Williams wanted an intellectual elite, formed quietly and willing to work with Catholic laymen as spokesmen to the Yankees. To this end, he initiated the Catholic Union, literally instituting it to challenge the clergy into intellectual firmness of some kind.[63] Chancery circulars also encouraged parishioners to assume creative and responsible roles in the parishes. There was no intention that feudal holdings grow up in the archdiocese. The pastor "together with one or more of . . . [his] parishioners" was invited to meetings for relief projects.[64] Similarly, Williams encouraged local Catholic writers and gave O'Reilly complete autonomy in handling *The Pilot*.[65] However, the local clergy, always with the exception of Yankee priests like Joshua Bodfish and Theodore Metcalf, did not "think better of the Union by and by," as men like Ring had hoped. Nor did they think better of the Jesuits whom Williams brought in to staff the boys' "college," nor of Father Isaac Hecker who was given such honors as speaking at cathedral dedications, nor of converts like Henry L. Richards or James Kent Stone, men whom the Union held up for emulation.[66] Yet the pastors, for all their peevishness, made no counterproposals during this time since the situation was still too fluid.

Part of the truth was that even if the immigrants had not widened it, a gap would have existed in any event between the thinking of Williams and that of the next generations of clergymen. It was a spread between two sets of values. Yet these were seldom articulated explicitly on either side. Williams' values were small, hesitant roots of that Americanism which came above ground with Archbishop John Ireland of Minneapolis in the 1890's. They were real and to some extent shared, but Boston, as it turned out, gave them no hearty life. Moreover as early as 1885 a myth was growing up among the Boston Catholic population. It held that all Boston Catholics had one set of values, that they all thought like Irish Catholics and that this had always been so. The different patterns of thinking of Cheverus, Boyce, and Haskins were already disbelieved, forgotten, or twisted into whimsy by Catholics. Those of Williams, Mrs. Blake, and Thomas Ring, individuals who were *still alive* in 1885, were equally passed over. *The Republic,* an Irish-Catholic paper begun in 1882, had to cut through this myth in 1907 when it presented an obituary of Williams. It consciously set about to startle its readers with the fact that a Catholic of Boston could think in categories other than Irish Catholic. Its initial reference was to Williams' "sympathy even for those whose opinions differed radically from the creed in which he put all his faith." Then, as though exposing something startling, the author intelligently picked out the components of Williams' character and thinking. He pointed out that these were basic to Williams' view of life and yet, at the same time, incomprehensible to the famine immigrants. "The young Williams . . . brought to his task the . . . sweetness of Cheverus and the sturdy American spirit of his predecessors. He was liberal in his viewpoint, always going more than halfway [*sic*] in meeting those around him . . . He was a link between these [present] electric and tingling days and that period when the saintly Cheverus helped to build the Boston Athenæum,[67] and to hold lengthy converse with John Adams in the glamour of those days of stateliness." To assess him as a churchman, *The Republic* typed him as a "liberal." In doing this, it applied a term which carried notorious implications as of the 1890's and which *The Republic* knew "bore the odor of heretical teaching," to use its own words. Nevertheless, it contended that Williams always insisted upon "a rational 'American' point of view . . . He was a friend of what may be called the 'liberal' tendency in the Catholic Church in America."[68]

Finally the author, who remained unnamed but claimed he knew the archbishop personally, fixed upon Williams' central conviction and deftly illustrated it with suitable examples. Williams, he wrote, "saw that the strength of the American Republic lay chiefly in character. It was not by brilliancy, by intellect or even by genius that Washington and Jay and Adams impressed themselves on their fellow-citizens . . . [he believed that] it was by character that they conquered, by their moral individuality."[69] The author had isolated Williams' essential values, though he did not draw out any implications. For it would seem that Williams did judge an individual on his character, on his "moral individuality." But again this was old fashioned. The priests of the next two generations, because of the heavy Irish dominance, thought of character in terms of nationality. Quite like Henry Adams or Henry Cabot Lodge, both Father John O'Brien and William Henry O'Connell deified national history as the source of all explanations.[70]

Williams also differed with younger local clergymen on the matter of engaging with the Yankees in warfare, as it were, on behalf of a particular religion. It was not within Williams' memory that Catholicism had been used by any Boston bishop against the Yankee. But for the Irish, religion was in fact at the very heart of hostilities ranging from bitter polemics to military engagements. What was worth bloodshed in Ireland would be worth verbal warfare in Boston when the opportunity would come. For the Irish, religion had always had to be a linen cloth bound around a serrated sword. Even when unwound, religion and matters related to it would have an angularity not present in Williams' thinking.[71]

Finally, Williams' definition of success was different from that of the local clergy. He put a low value on material possessions. Yet he had a possession more important, namely, the respect of the non-Catholic community. In the last decade of his life, a Universalist publication did a "sketch" of the archbishop. It found him "a man of good general culture and wide reading . . . No one could pass him by in the thoroughfare without recognizing an impression of force."[72] But the immigrants' children, those who were beginning to establish their own families in the 1870's, did not have the respect of the community. Material solvency, if not gain, was already uppermost in their minds. In fact, the first public act in which Williams and thirty-one priests combined forces was an open and successful declaration shoring up confidence in Boston savings banks during the depression in 1878.[73] In the same way, the priests of the two generations after Williams' were obsessed about financial security. It was they who worked most closely with the first-generation Irish-Americans, who petitioned the state for a charter for the Union Institution for Savings on their behalf, who loaned them money, or who were themselves the sons of such families. They, too, were plagued during depressions and were victims of phoney insurance companies. Yet they were expected to raise churches quickly and without diocesan funds.[74] In fact it was with this last expectation in mind that canon law defined the person of the parish rector. This role was not that defined much later by Vatican Council II, to form "a genuinely Christian community." The priest was defined as an administrator of property. Not surprisingly, success in *this* role brought as a reward the title of "monsignor."[75]

Although Williams' public leadership during the depression of 1878 showed that he recognized new needs and new values, still he continued to honor privately values which the immigrants and their descendants could not possibly share. For him, the result was an increasing separation and a progressive sliding into passivity and ineffectiveness. He continued to act like a "typical Yankee" toward the Irish immigrants, operating from a sense of *noblesse oblige*. At the same time, he continued to tolerate in Boston a social structure which in turn tolerated only such opposition as was within the framework determined by constituted authorities. He assumed that what was right and true was also moderate and pacifist. The *acceptable* truth about conditions in Boston and other cities of his archdiocese was sufficient. He dared not, as Father John O'Brien was forced to do on education, address himself to the questions of defining truth and power. Often he avoided any analysis of the social and political costs of peace, although these costs might well be very dear. He concerned himself with the structure of power only insofar as he might help it exist *as it was*. So, in a real way, he contributed next to nothing to the kind of restructuring of society that the immigration demanded. It is important that he allowed freedom to Louise Imogen Guiney and the writers at the turn of the century. But, in the long run, his policy allowed freedom to powers of institutionalization and bigotry within the church, forces which proved to have stronger roots and choked out more fragile growths. With blind loyalty to Boston's provincial culture, he sought to insert the Catholic population into a kind of social and religious milieu that was already decaying. In the 1880's, when the literary center of the United States was beginning to shift from Boston to New York, he sought to eke some cultural tone out of a Catholic population that was still largely subliterate. Yet this, after all, was the type of contribution Boston expected. And while he looked out for these endeavors directly, personally attending the weekly evening meetings of the Catholic Union, he disposed of Irish affairs by passing them into others' hands. He adopted a liberal policy toward Irish nationalism in the early 1880's, officially supporting the Land League of Parnell and Davitt.[76] While to Bishop McQuaid this appeared totally inconsistent with Williams' hopes for quiet assimilation, it was actually in perfect accord with Williams' policy: any extreme of permissiveness that would insure peace.

WILLIAMS' ASSOCIATES AND IRISH CATHOLICISM

The coterie of clergymen who were closest to Williams during this period were by no means "Irish" though the Irish immigration affected their careers directly and decisively. Who were these men? By the time of his consecration in 1866, Williams' closest associates as a young priest had died or were out of the diocese. Of the remaining eighteen secular clergymen who were living in 1866 *and were of some prominence,* six priests were a generation older than Williams. Twelve men were of his own generation.[77] Among the older men, Williams especially relied on Fathers George Foxgrove Haskins and James Fitton. Fitton was a friend from boyhood, a man who before setting out on his missionary career had pastured his father's cows on the Boston Common.[78] Within his own generation, Williams turned to the Healy brothers, to Joshua Bodfish who was born in Falmouth, Massachusetts, and had served as an Episcopal minister until his conversion in 1863, and to William Byrne, a man who was a schoolmaster in Baltimore before ordination and continued to teach Greek and mathematics for a short time at the Emmitsburg, Maryland, seminary. Bodfish was chancellor from 1881 to 1886. Byrne was vicar general from 1879 to 1907. As the years passed, choice of associates became narrower. For by 1878 six of the eighteen men had died, including Haskins and Sherwood Healy. During the same time, James Healy and Patrick T. O'Reilly left Boston for episcopal appointments elsewhere. When Williams had to make appointments from the young men of the next generation, he chose for roles of leadership in the archdiocese three young men who were native clergy; like Bodfish, one of them selected for immediate advancement was a convert from a Yankee family.[79] When he was free to fill such offices as promised prominence, Williams adopted the policy of chosing either nonimmigrant priests or, as in the case of Byrne, men who were both scholars and Irish, and who consistently spoke like moderates on Protestant-Catholic issues.

Before the mid-1870's, then, Haskins, the Healy brothers, Bodfish, and Byrne were Williams' immediate associates. They served with him in the inner city of Boston at the cathedral. They were the brightest men available and could in no way be connected with the Irish immigration.[80] They cooperated with Ring in the work of the St. Vincent de Paul Society and they cooperated with Williams in fighting desperately against the growing characterization of Catholics as "uncultured." As they died or were promoted out of the archdiocese, their endeavors were proportionately crippled.

The immediate effect of immigration on priests like Haskins and James Healy was that it gave them increasingly mobile careers. The growth of the Irish-Catholic population in inner Massachusetts and Maine called for bishops. And James Healy, a young priest who was half Negro and brought into the diocese by Fitzpatrick, was ambitious for such an office. He got the bishopric of Portland, Maine, in 1875. His more gentle brother, Father Alexander Sherwood Healy, was needed for the seminary at Troy, New York, when Catholic population growth made it mandatory to have an American seminary on the East coast. Convert-priests like Haskins, Bodfish, and Theodore Metcalf (a generation younger) were pitched into liaison roles. Each man was aware of a hesitant acceptance from both Protestants and Catholics. With some sensitivity, Williams tried to protect them from needless exposure to either hostile camp.[81] They were among the intellectual leaders of Catholic Boston. Not only were they at home with the members of the Catholic Union, but at least one Boston Irish journalist also attributed the Union's development directly to Bodfish.[82] In 1873, Metcalf was the Union's first president, chairing sessions where Yankee Catholic priests—never Irish Catholic priests—were frequently speakers along with Dr. John G. Blake, Mayor Patrick Collins, Father Robert Fulton, S.J., John Boyle O'Reilly, and Samuel Tuckerman.[83] In addition, Metcalf was co-chairman with Phillips Brooks of a hospital fund-raising affair in 1873; in 1874 and only five years after ordination he took over as chancellor of the diocese until Bodfish replaced him in 1881.

More than Metcalf or Bodfish, Haskins found himself pitched into liaison jobs and public appointments which could not have been predicted when he accepted ordination in 1844 and which would not have been entrusted by Yankee liberals to any other Catholic priest. Haskins had always been interested in delinquent boys. Now under the pressure of the immigrants' ignorance of legal matters, he doubled his appearances in the courts, saving numerous wayward or destitute boys from imprisonment. Only Haskins could have filled this role in the 1860's. He had done it as a young Episcopal minister and had gained the respect of the Boston community. He was older than Williams by sixteen years, had attended Boston Latin School and was graduated from Harvard in 1826 in the class of Richard Hildreth, Charles Russell Lowell, and Robert Rantoul. He was ordained as an Anglican minister in 1830, and thereafter centered his life on delinquent boys, following a career which prefigured the later social gospel movement. This interest continued after his ordination as a Catholic priest and afforded him both an independence from the immigrants—for he was saving individual boys, not Irish boys—and, at the same time, a certain reverential regard from them which he used to advantage. Creative and dedicated, Haskins was accepted as a knowledgeable critic of the State Reform School as early as the late 1840's.[84] By 1865, he was a member of the school committee and was operating the House of the Angel Guardian for delinquent and orphaned boys. The latter remained essentially an individual endeavor. Its reputation rested on his reputation and its financial solvency on his contributions and good business sense.[85] Haskins' approach was to appear in the courts, act as voluntary legal aid for individual boys, and get them from the courts "on probation." In describing these incidents, he never allowed Catholicism to isolate him from the larger community.[86]

In fact Haskins reveals himself as one who, although a Catholic and a clergyman, refused to see himself as anything but an individual Bostonian.[87] Much as his job brought him into proximity with the Irish immigrants, he resisted identification with them. He was a confirmed "humanitarian" and never used the word pejoratively, as later Catholic writers would in order to grace "Catholic charities." He made two necessary trips to Ireland in the 1850's and 1870's, later writing of the country and its people. But in these works his prose is paralyzed and unconvincing.[88] On the other hand, his *Reports* of the boys' home, which should have been dull financial accounts, are graceful, humane, and intense. After several pages of figures, he personalizes the account and offers "Remarks on the Financial Report." Of these remarks, his first citation is one of gratitude to the state: "to our relief, the State [*sic*] came to give us a lift. May God bless the State."[89] It was in these writings that Haskins set forth the theories that occupied his mind and career, concerns that were never overlaid with dogma. He was not interested in Catholic growth in New England, although in this he was quite different from later priests who could not get that concern out of their bones. Much like Metcalf's safe association with the Catholic Union, Haskins' work allowed him to put one toe in the water but not get thoroughly wet. His closest and lifelong friendship was outside Boston altogether and with another convert, Bishop James Roosevelt Bayley.

Publicly Williams set a high value on Haskins and his *modus operandi*. He demanded that the respect which Haskins had earned in 1866 when he was selected to preach the eulogy at Bishop Fitzpatrick's funeral be shown him at such important events as the second diocesan synod in 1868.[90] Not only was Haskins a diocesan consultor at this time but the sessions were held in the chapel of the boys' home. Yet when he died in 1872 few of his ideals or sensitivities had been transmitted to younger clergymen. Certainly he had little effect on James Healy who worked closely with him at St. Stephen's parish but whose thinking was already formed along other lines. The Boston School Committee ordered the public schools in Haskins' parish closed on the day of his funeral.[91] In the future this would be looked upon as having been entirely gratuitous. It was not such a gesture. Rather it represented a liberality of mind which existed among a diminishing number of Protestants and Catholics. It was also a symbol of a mental flexibility that could still transcend the fractured city but that could scarcely be understood later. Nor could it be exercised later, as Bodfish, for example, was to discover when he requested permission from Archbishop O'Connell in 1908 to address a Universalist Church group in Charlestown. O'Connell "forbade him absolutely," wrote the archbishop's chancellor to a friend, "[and] I see by the papers that Father Bodfish did not appear at the meeting."[92]

Haskins' answer to the Irish immigration was a careful dramatization of his projects as humanitarian rather than sectarian. In the same way James Healy self-consciously and wherever possible avoided identification with the Boston Irish. In fact what is remarkable about Healy is the total abnormality of his presence in Boston. Here, in a city where the Yankees and Irish were going to divide the power was a Negro priest selected to be rector of the cathedral at the age of thirty-two, chosen by both Fitzpatrick and Williams as secretary, and eventually selected for the bishopric of Portland, Maine. His priest-brother was Williams' personal theologian, his *peritus* at the first Vatican Council.

A clerical career was all-important to James Healy, and the overpopulation of the East coast with Irish provided the rails over which his ambitions could ride. Healy was the son of a mulatto slave girl and a Missouri planter; he was the oldest of ten children, all of whom were eventually placed under the guardianship of Bishop Fitzpatrick.[93] In a diary written in 1849 at the age of nineteen, "Jeems" showed himself to be a finicky rather than an analytic student, already hypercritical of his priest-professors and fellow-students at Holy Cross College, Worcester.[94] There Healy moved through an identical college curriculum with the same few boys, just as he would have at Andover or any other college. He was pitted against these same boys for medals in theology and philosophy. He knew what it was to earn these prizes one term only to lose them the next, and always on the basis of disputation.[95] This system encouraged in Healy competitive mental habits that never changed. It strengthened an already developed tendency to quick and inflexible value judgments.[96] It fostered the reading of Paine, Augustine, and Byron but only for the purpose of successful argumentation. The same insensitivity that made Healy a distracted reader made him, like countless other American boys of the time, ready prey to the pieties of small-town educators. Self-congratulatory rather than introspective, he idolized externals, especially the external effects which he himself could create. All his life, he watched first his own performance and then his critics.[97] There was a home-grown conservatism and coldness in Healy long before the Puritan city could influence him. It was natural not imitative.

Healy's decision to enter the seminary in Montreal in 1849 was not a decision to serve the immigrants of Boston as a parish priest, though Fitzpatrick was like a father to him, housing one of the Healy girls in his own sisters' home in Boston. Even in the Grande Seminaire at Issy, he was thinking of a career teaching theology either in France or America. He developed little if any genuine social conscience by his contact with Haskins who, with Healy and Fitzpatrick as companions, was searching the Paris slums in 1854 for ways of rehabilitating the criminal poor. Yet Haskins was Healy's "first hospitable host among the [Boston] clergy," and with him the young priest began to work at St. Stephen's and the boys' home. Within one year of ordination and at the age of twenty-five, Healy was diocesan chancellor; seven years later he was rector of the cathedral. With such support and from the 1850's until his death in 1900, he was able to make it up to himself for his grievously burdensome racial origins. Very quickly he became adept at "taming" Irish congregations.[98] He became excessively sensitive if overlooked. On one occasion, he was outraged at Roman church officials who had received him with honor in 1864 not, as he put it, because he was a priest or the secretary of a bishop but because he was the confessor of Mrs. Ward who had married into European nobility. By 1865, he had developed the urbanity and pomposity of the *nouveau instruit,* criticizing the student body at his alma mater as "a little uncouth in manners."[99] He made himself the "favorite" of the wealthy Catholics at Nahant, possibly conducting himself with the same obsequiousness which he assumed among wealthy Catholics in California in 1891.[100] His writings reveal him as a person who never quite pulled himself up beyond the level of personal opportunism.

From 1866 to 1880, Healy preached the same sermons that he thought out during the 1850's. There was no significant change in either style or content.[101] His basic finicalness as well as the sentimental Sulpician spirituality would serve to explain both the impeccableness with which the sermons were written out (and some discarded as "imperfect") and their almost feminine "dulcet . . . maxims." Training at Holy Cross would be sufficient to explain an argumentative style which used scripture rather than interpreted it. But what best explains the arid timelessness and essential theological neutrality of the sermons is the *quid pro quo* attitude of mutual unconcern which dully passed between Healy and his various congregations week after week.[102] The Irish were to him an undifferentiated class whose prejudices and fears could be played upon and who could readily be made to feel shame at their lack of faith and pursuit of money. This is clearly seen in the sermons.[103] More important, while the sermons were catechetical efforts and therefore abstract, they were more really almost hygienic efforts to keep aloof from the human condition. They contained no similes or concretizations; ethical violations were hastily typed as though to be thereby less contaminative. The results are fleshless, not because of the Irish species of Jansenism but one would suppose because of Healy's need for distance from his own human misfortune. Neither the preacher nor the listeners are anywhere in the sermons, which leaves them harsh but jejune.

Healy's sermons were symbolic of a transition. They registered a change from a period when Catholic priests wrote or lectured in order to persuade to a time when they were really talking only to themselves. The timeliness of Roddan's or Boyce's writings gave way to the tepid timelessness of Healy's sermons and to their pitifully indifferent presumption that theological error in 1865 will be the same in 1895.[104] Furthermore, Healy's sermons effected what they symbolized. For they both reflected and strengthened the intellectual paralysis of the Irish congregations. Healy, for example, strongly criticized the kind of open debate with Protestants that Roddan, O'Brien, Brownson, and Haskins had so eagerly taken up on the lecture platform. In a sermon of 1858 delivered at the cathedral, he cited such open debate as disloyal: "one [Protestant] accuses the church of superstition, [and] we acknowledge the charge; another of fostering poverty, [and] we have tried to excuse her;

another accuses her of slowness, of want of progress . . . of want of appreciation of the great movements of the age . . . and we have stood by."[105] Healy felt that this must change, not by debating such charges but by the docile performance of simple pieties.

So much for the Irish-Catholic populace, those who were to exercise the timid virtues and contemplate Healy's favorite passage, "the just man lives by faith." The real advancement of the church in Boston as Healy saw it, rested on the cultivation of a monied elite. A manuscript of a speech to the Boston Union in the 1870's reveals markedly Healy's sorting out of the worthies among the Boston Catholics and his tortuous efforts to manipulate their thinking. His structuring of the speech is deceptive, starting out, as it does, with a long tirade on the diabolical effects of prosperity. But his main message eventually emerges as quite otherwise. The prosperous men of Boston are to understand that they are "naturally" (a word crossed out for delivery of the address) leaders of the church in the city. And the church, as Healy sells it, is not opposed to prosperity but is in fact the very font of it, despite evidence to the contrary. The church has gifted the world with "the gentler arts," and these in turn "make life beautiful and"—inserted after the final draft —"prosperous." Still, he began nagging, how were the wealthy Catholics behaving? Were not those of "better financial, political, social and public condition" absenting themselves presently from active participation in parish activities? Were they not, by implication, absenting themselves from submission to the clergy, men already "overburdened and little appreciated?"[106] In all of this, Healy differed radically from his patron Williams. For although rib, as it were, from Williams' side, Healy lacked the bishop's esteem for a Catholic laity independent of the Church. From Healy's perspective, such independent activities undercut structural organization and left no room for institutional controls. Healy, like O'Connell after him, had a mind for organization. What was insanity to Williams was imperative to him.

Healy's elevation to the bishopric of Portland in 1875 had consequences for Boston. For him, the move was a step upward but also a further step backward into unimaginativeness and authoritarianism. For in terms of calendric time, Maine in 1875 was eastern Massachusetts of not later than 1830. And individual priests of the Portland diocese were involved in the problems of drink, drugs, and violations of celibacy found in missionary times.[107] These problems plus open insubordination called out the fussy, intolerant, and exasperating qualities which Healy had always manifested.[108] And with these same qualities, together with a still more constricted view of ecclesiastical affairs, he came back to Boston, delighted to dedicate a church or graduate a seminary class. No less than before, he still saw the Irish as a necessary evil and still practised his predatory craft upon them. Nothing had changed; his use of phrases like "our Protestant brethren" and "our Catholic laity" rang with the emptiness of the bureaucrat who had laid claim to these groups but only for his own purposes.[109] Unable to respect his Irish congregations and unwilling to respect the Yankee, he was, by the age of sixty-five, a man kept intact by belittling others— Jews, Indians, Easterners on Raymond tours, and bishops who had lesser "palaces" than he.[110]

William Byrne, who served Williams as vicar general from 1879 to 1907 was a more graceful gentleman, something of a pedant but with aspirations for the intellectual life that were genuine.[111] He was far less willing than Healy to manipulate people or situations and retained his esteem for Thomas Ring and the St. Vincent de Paul Society into the 1880's.[112] Similarly, while Healy dropped the first person singular and referred to himself as "the bishop" after 1875, Byrne continued to sign "Wm. Byrne" to his letters to Ring. He encouraged the autonomous work of laymen. On one occasion he hoped that even at a Retreat "most of the speaking [be] done by the laymen." "Yours," he reminded Ring, "is a lay society."[113]

By the late 1870's Byrne was often the voice of Williams on public issues. His comments were generally *ex post facto*, never strident, and typically introduced by a phrase or two such as this: "This important question had been discussed with much heat and too much haste during the past week in and around

Boston." In exactly this manner, he spoke for Williams on the public school issue in the autumn of 1879. Presenting a very cautious opinion on the issue, he brought his audience (as well as readers of *The Pilot* where the address was later printed) to the question, "Are our public schools here in Boston so dangerous that a prudent Catholic is duty bound to keep his children away from them, where no Catholic school exists?" Having begged the question and weighted it as Williams would like, he followed through with only indirect reference to the bishop. "This doubt has never been settled by any formal decision of a competent authority. The tolerated usage of the public schools that obtains here is the nearest approach to the solution that we have." He conceded that the public school system "as reduced to practice, varies enormously as to its danger in different places, and even in the same place for different persons." But he maintained that whatever dangers are present arise from defects within the system not from the system itself, and that "most of these incidental evils are absent from the public schools of Boston." He continued, "The children are not required to read the Protestant version of the Scriptures, or to recite un-Catholic prayers. The books in use now are pretty thoroughly purged of all sectarian or anti-Catholic leaven; the mouth of the reviler is closed and at least no open or direct attempts at proselytism allowed."

Byrne was aware that diocesan priests like Father Scully were fighting in every way to establish a comprehensive Catholic school system and had to be answered. He carefully rejected the argument that "our use of the Public Schools, or our cooperation in carrying them on can *fairly* be construed as an approval of them." Rather he admitted that he was not "quite content" with them. Yet, as he pointed out, "in most of our parishes, the burden of church debt carried, the pressing calls for the support of our hospitals, orphanages, asylums and homes for the poor, are so urgent and imperative, that little can be done toward establishing Catholic schools." He saw a case for the education of all children in schools common to all. He would not concede that to admit that spiritual training is rightly preeminent is necessarily to endorse a separate school system. Rather he concluded that the rapidly growing fairness of public opinion may, " 'ere long, discover a way of making a system of common school education acceptable to Catholic minds, and safe for Catholic consciences."[114]

Byrne reflected the conciliatory policy of Williams in presenting the public school issue as "not absolutely insoluble." But it was an increasingly difficult stance to maintain.

A DIFFERENT RESPONSE: PRIESTS OF THE "GENERATION OF '45"

Throughout the first fourteen years of Williams' administration, the prominent clergymen of his own generation probably numbered nineteen. These were men like Bodfish and Byrne whose names appear frequently as chairmen of clerical celebrations, speakers at public functions, diocesan consultors, or simply men appointed to care for such matters as the priests' retirement fund. By 1880, nine of the nineteen prominent clergymen had died, were out of the diocese, or were absorbed in nonparish offices for Williams.[115] The English-speaking parishes of the archdiocese, multiplying at an enormous rate, were progressively in the hands of a generation of clergymen born a full generation after Williams, between 1842 and 1862. By 1894, ninety-seven were pastors of English-speaking parishes.[116] Of these men, forty-five were born in Massachusetts, thirty-nine were born in Ireland, and seven were natives of Canada or of the United States outside Massachusetts.[117] Of those born in Massachusetts (forty-seven percent of the total), twenty-three were natives of the city of Boston, four from Salem, four from Lawrence, and sixteen from such towns as Abington, Amesbury, Dedham, Milton, Waltham, and Weymouth. Taking the twenty-three men born in Boston, nineteen were educated in the public schools there, and seven of these attended either Boston Latin or Boston English high schools.[118] Taking the same twenty-three young men, eight went to Holy Cross, four to St. Charles, Maryland, three to Canada, two to Boston College, and two to colleges like St. Bonaventure, New York.[119] There was similar dispersal for seminary training: six to St. Joseph's Seminary at Troy, New York, nine to Montreal, six to St. Mary's in Baltimore, one to Paris and one to Rome. Of the group, Father Christopher T. McGrath was ordained the earliest, in 1865. The last ordination was in 1881, although most of the men were ordained in the mid-1870's at the average age of twenty-four. Excepting two men, all were pastors within an average of 11.5 years or at the average age of thirty-five. Five were made pastors in the 1870's, ten in the 1880's, and eight in the 1890's. The only man of this group to get a bishopric was Father Matthew Harkins. The priests held an average of 2.0 curacies, several becoming pastors within three or four years of ordination. In this respect, the case of Father John W. McMahon, however, is the most noteworthy as he was created pastor of the venerable St. Mary's in Charlestown within eight years of ordination.

Of the twenty-two young men born in Massachusetts but outside Boston, fourteen were graduates of the public schools; each of three in Salem took advantage of the parish and public schools, and for five data is incomplete. Like their Boston counterparts, they dispersed themselves to the available Catholic colleges: three to Holy Cross, four to Boston College, five to St. Charles, Maryland, four to New York, and two to Villanova.[120] They were trained at seven different seminaries: eight at Troy, New York, five at Montreal, four at St. Mary's in Baltimore, one at Niagara University in New York, one at Trois Rivieres, Lower Canada, one in New Brunswick, and one at Villanova in Pennsylvania.[121] The latest ordination was in 1883, but most ordinations fell in the mid-1870's when the average age of the group was 24.5.[122] None were pastors in less than nine years. Six had parishes in the 1880's and the remaining men became pastors in the 1890's. They had an average of 1.9 curacies as did the men born in Boston. John J. Nilan, born in Newburyport in 1855, was elected bishop of Hartford, Connecticut in 1910.

Of the thirty-nine priests born in Ireland (forty percent of the total), only seven were ordained there.[123] Seventeen had been brought to the United States as children and received public school education here. Twelve more were in the United States by the time of college studies. Of the total of twenty-nine receiving their education in the United States, eight attended Holy Cross, seven went to St. Charles, Maryland, four to Canada, one to Boston College and four to colleges along the East coast of the United States.[124] Most of the men were ordained in the early 1870's at the average age of twenty-five: fourteen at Troy, New York, four in Montreal and two elsewhere in Canada, five at St. Mary's in Baltimore, one in Philadelphia, two in Paris, and one in Rome. All became pastors. None were singled out for work in the diocese and only one became a bishop. Compared to the American-born men, they were pastors sooner (averaging 8.2 years as curates), usually founding parishes in outlying districts.[125] Nine were pastors within four years or less of ordination.

It is evident from such statistics that this generation of priests was an unjelled group from the outset. With only eighteen percent ordained in Ireland, they certainly cannot be seen as the kindly nineteenth-century Irish clergymen whom pious imagination has created as dispensing ministrations on the "coffin ships" or later immigrant ships.[126] But neither are they young men solidly rooted in American culture. Most of them were too young to have participated in the Civil War, and both college and seminary training necessarily took them out of their birthplaces or frequently out of the country. The geographic discontinuity already evident in the life of Father John T. Buckley even before ordination is typical. He was born in Boston in 1854, educated at the Boylston School and Boston Latin School, started college in Maryland in 1869, and was ordained in Montreal in 1878.[127] Unlike Longfellow and Holmes and Williams, he and the others had no "growing days of the young republic" to remember; nor were they their own sufficient center. Local attachments were not deep. And coming from widely different backgrounds, graduating from various colleges and seminaries, they had little in common among themselves save Salesian spirituality taught in all nineteenth-century seminaries. They did not step into any definable clerical structure in the Boston diocese after ordination. They were still seminarians during the 1868 and 1872 diocesan synods, and during the same time possibly influential men like Haskins and Fitton had died. If there was any well-defined episcopal policy emanating from Williams' desk, any structure with which they were to identify, it was invisible.

However, certain lines were starting to come clear. Training in Rome meant (as it had for Roddan and would for O'Connell) a more responsible position in the diocese or a better parish. In fact, the evidence indicates that being born in the United States (as opposed to Ireland) increased one's chance for a prestigious future in the diocese. Each of the three young men of this generation who had moved above the level of pastor to positions of greater responsibility in the diocese was born in Massachusetts. Richard Neagle had been born in Bradford, Massachusetts, educated in public schools there, graduated from Holy Cross College, and ordained in 1877 in New York. He was appointed chancellor of the diocese in 1886 and served until 1896. John F. Ford was born in Weymouth, Massachusetts, educated in public schools there, graduated from Boston College and ordained in Rome. After serving as curate in one parish he was selected by Williams to be director of the diocesan Working-boys' Home. The career of Theodore Metcalf is most remarkable and must have seemed so at the time. A convert from a Dedham family whose ancestors settled the original plantation in 1635, he was ordained in Rome in 1870 and within four years appointed chancellor of the diocese. He served in that capacity from 1874 to 1881. Meanwhile other young priests of his generation were erecting new parishes in places like Beverly or taking over old ones, like St. James in Boston. These parishes were already feeling the disturbances of "inner city" population movements in the 1880's. Each young man was thrown into a pastorate involving serious and individual responsibilities.[128] These tasks were so centrifugal that efforts requiring the sustained organization of the pastors—like *The Sacred Heart Review*—were still a decade away.[129]

This was the group which additionally experienced polarities with Williams and rejection from the Yankee and Yankee-Catholic elements of the city. The real effect of the tragedy of rejection is to be traced in the intangible area of self-esteem and from it, the area of theology. From the time immediately after his seminary days, the priest of this group was considered "stupid" by Williams' trusted theologian, Father Sherwood Healy, and he was expected, for example, to cheat on the diocesan examinations.[130] All of this put the parish rector in an unexpectedly threatened position. He was dissociated from the bishop as a person who might see realities about him in the same way. At the same time, he was also only second choice when either the Yankees or the bishop wanted a public representative.[131] If he tried to be involved on a level of action wider than his parish, he found himself immediately subordinate—resentfully so—to such Catholic laymen as Thomas Ring, Charles F. Donnelley, Patrick Donahoe, Patrick Collins, and John Boyle O'Reilly on the supraparish level.[132] But with increasing success the same hiatus between the bishop and the pastor allowed the latter to tyrannize on his own estate, the parish. Williams' agenda for the Third Diocesan Synod of 1872 was prepared to deal directly with the abuses that had arisen as a result of such autonomy. It proposed for discussion such matters as "bringing private affairs or politics before the people in church," the tendency of pastors to engage in "speculation with parish funds for personal gain," and the act of a pastor "refusing absolution to or denouncing members of secret societies without authorization." Other problems were "frequent talking of money," and "absence a week without permission." Williams had sought Sherwood Healy's advice on the remarks he should make as presiding officer. Healy, in reply, had suggested putting the following questions to the clergymen: "Are the sick visited often enough? Is not a priest obliged to visit all, whether they pay well or not, have friends or not? . . . What about pastors obliging assistants [curates] to sing [High] Mass and interchange intentions [stipends] with them, the pastor retaining the larger fee?"[133]

Parishioners, however, needed the priest and accommodated. The sacraments aside, he had built the church and it provided

God and all good things. James Healy concentrated on this sort of absolute dependence at ceremonies dedicating the Mission Church in 1876. Heavy with images of an uprooted people and their leader, Healy's sermon was both a balm and a focus. "At the end of their pilgrimage," he intoned, "the Israelites had arrived at the Promised Land, [and] *their leader . . . assembled the people, [and he] renewed their covenant with the Lord*" [my italics]. He then swept ahead historically to the ages of persecution, overlaying the image of the migrating people with similarly meaningful similes of triumph over persecution when "the raising of the church [was] equated with the end of persecution." In itself, the enormous church edifice, Healy subtly pointed out, was the end of secretiveness. It allowed the Irish to demonstrate that they were not a subversive group. In fact, even the ceremonial was most prized because it was "a figure of adaptation." Finally, in a city rich in historic monuments which the Irish immigrants could envy but not claim, the Catholic church building should "stand as a sign and monument for our covenant with God."[134] As Healy so satisfyingly testified, the church was the sole location of one's commerce with God. And in this spot, characterized by an immobility so out-of-joint with late-nineteenth-century America, the priest both increasingly fixed himself and was fixed by the people. One popular metaphor portrayed the church as a health-giving and convenient well in the midst of the city, and the priest as its full-time keeper.[135] Moreover, the need for the priest became absolute as specifically external Catholicity won respect. Religious protection rackets, as it were, could and did take hold in these situations where the presence of an "irremovable rector" combined with the injunction of canon law forbidding parishioners to join congregations outside their own parish boundaries. One example of this involved Father P. V. Moyce and a young couple in his Northampton parish in 1868. When the case finally reached the bishop's desk, it appeared that Moyce, on his own reluctant evidence, had charged the gentleman the usual fee of $25.00 for performing the marriage ceremony and complaints followed. In responding to Williams' questions, Moyce admitted to "having received more than this sum, more than four or five times since my entry into these parts. Of course, it was on all occasions voluntary, excepting this one." The letter ends fearsomely, "Tell this queer-minded soul [Mr. Killeen] to see Father Moyce or to write to him, and that he will be sure of ample satisfaction; and so he will."[136]

With this generation of priests, uniformity of thinking was obviously more circumstantial than the result of dictated epis-copal policy. This was so, as has been cited, even on the public school issue. It was only by chance that Father John O'Brien of Cambridge found himself the storm center of that issue in 1880, and simultaneously found himself in a moderate position coinciding with Williams' and opposite to the belligerent atti-tude of Scully.[137] In fact, Reverend J. P. Bland, the Unitarian minister who first assailed O'Brien from the pulpit and then in *The Boston Herald*, actually *was wrong* in insisting that priests could have no opinions of their own. That time might come. But presently to charge that "they were simply officers in a for-eign army" and "not allowed to have any [opinions]" was false and, moreover, unfortunate insofar as it radically transformed O'Brien's thinking. By the 1890's he was reactionary on the pub-lic school issue whereas in the 1880's he was as moderate as Williams.[138]

There was simply no single way of thinking in the 1870's. The clergy were not convinced that the city would inordinately choke out religious fervor. But this was not because Williams loved old Boston and imposed this attitude. It was true that for him and Haskins Boston was the gateway to past ways of thought.[139] Charles Bullard Fairbanks and Louise Imogen Guiney also regarded "city" not as an economic category but as a cultural framework providing thoroughfares which could be paced off to recapture the past.[140] The city was accepted for countless reasons. Father Joseph V. O'Connor, who wrote for *Donahoe's Magazine* and who identified with the Irish immi-grant, insisted in 1879 that the Irish would not plough the fields of Goshen if there were not "neighbors . . . someone to *see* their work and share their abundance . . . The city is civilization."[141]

Pastors like Peter Ronan and the rector of the Mission Church considered the city safe insofar as the parish could be raised within it as a citadel of protection.[142] Only in the 1880's when the same pastors wanted to build parochial schools would the "city" be suggested as dangerous to faith and morals.[143]

As on the matter of the city, consensus was never assured on other issues like the role of women or the procedures of the diocesan synod. There were almost as many reasons why "the Church" opposed women suffrage in the 1870's as there were priests. Similarly, the diocesan synod of 1868 was not a rubber-stamp affair; as a group, Williams and the priests did not even know precisely how to conduct one.[144]

For all its liabilities then, being cut off from Williams also provided a priest with scope for creativity. Despite the impression that *The Pilot* ineptly created and which reactionary ministers like Bland made popular, the priest had a good deal of autonomy.[145] Many used it to good purpose. Father Thomas J. Conaty's intellectual development is an interesting comment on what a talented man could make of his career in an open atmosphere. Immediately after ordination in 1872, Conaty interested himself in the field of temperance and the Irish Land League, becoming prominent along with Terence V. Powderly and Boston's Mayor Patrick Collins.[146] At the same time, he served on the Worcester School Board and the Worcester Free Public Library earning praise from G. Stanley Hall and Senator Hoar for civic services given for fourteen years. In the 1880's, Conaty decided to turn his attention solely to education, organizing the Catholic Summer School at Lake Champlain, editing *The Catholic School and Home Magazine* for his parish in the 1890's, and appearing with G. Stanley Hall who was then president of Clark University at the insignificant but pioneering Child Study Congress in 1898. In 1897, Conaty was appointed rector of the Catholic University in Washington; he was one of the founders of the National Catholic Education Conference and served as its president from 1899 to 1903.

The times were such that, like Conaty, men of the generation after Williams would be esteemed not on the relative amount of their knowledge, but on their ability to enter new fields of research and inquiry and to occupy advanced positions there. But for the most part, it was only the generation of Boston priests *after* Conaty's that actually capitalized on the functional use of knowledge. Conaty was an exception among his own peers. He was flanked on the one side by a priest-contemporary, James Kent Stone, a Bostonian who was the grandson of the jurist, a convert from Anglicanism, and a Passionist priest. This man saw nothing purposive in knowledge and viewed Christianity as "the hoarded wisdom of sixty generations." He spoke of "looking forward to the future without any very definite aims or plans, but with a vague anticipation of something glorious, waiting for the realization of a bright but hazy dream of limitless progress": limitless Puritan conversions to Catholicism.[147] On the other side were the majority of local clergymen for whom entering new fields of knowledge could only mean learning how to enlarge a parish plant. They were not especially open to the ideas of laymen. Opponents were frequently labelled as "malcontents." In the matter of city-wide projects that might have engaged Protestants and Catholics, they were uncooperatively biding their time.[148] So while Ring was appointed in October of 1878 as an Overseer of the Poor and his horizons proportionately widened, he was working with more than one parish priest who was "jealous of an organization [the St. Vincent de Paul conference] existing in his parish and not completely under his control."[149]

Converts to Catholicism added little to new ways of religious thinking. Men like Henry L. Richards, Isaac Hecker, and James Kent Stone were never accepted by the local clergy.[150] And if they had been, their writings would simply have added to the growing conviction that Catholicism had nothing whatsoever to learn from Protestantism.[151] At the very time when the intellectual virtues might have been encouraged among the clergy, men like Stone were, for the sake of their own security, denigrating the intellectual qualities of religion and reassessing Protestantism as "an illogical effort of the human mind to put itself in possession of revelation without the aid of authority."[152] In addition, they were feeding the myth of Catholicism as somehow achieving a unique spiritual "heroism" and a Manichean sort of transcendence. Stone wrote rhapsodically in 1870, "to Catholics, the unseen world is a reality, and they live for it *alone.*" Preaching something like the "social gospel" would have been enacting the Trojan Horse over again.[153]

What resulted was a generation of priests that fumbled opportunities for initiative, or so they were judged by contemporaries like Ring and the next generation of clergymen. In fact, Louis S. Walsh, a perceptive and earnest young man, *expected* them to fumble, to botch affairs even within the parish.[154] Later, in his capacity as priest-professor at the diocesan seminary, he summed up Healy's thinking and style as obsolete.[155] O'Connell looked back on Byrne as an intellectual snob.[156] James Gillis, whose career as a Paulist took him out of the diocese, looked back almost psychotically to this generation as men whose drinking habits were not to be imitated.[157] Many of these assessments were unfounded exaggerations and failed to take account of the adverse conditions for priests in the last quarter of the nineteenth century. In this respect Conaty's situation was somewhat unique in that he had the advantage of being able to distance himself from the religious factions of Boston by withdrawing to the college town of Worcester. But someone like O'Brien lived within the increasingly disintegrating relationship of Yankee and Irish in Boston—worse, in Cambridge. Like Conaty, O'Brien too had interested himself in exploring "adult education" in the 1870's, and had set up the Charlestown Catholic Lyceum. It was by serving on the Cambridge School Committee and taking a stand as a moderate that he got into difficulties with Reverend Bland. In the late 1880's, he started *The Sacred Heart Review* literally on an intellectual shoestring, namely, with editors who were the children in school. Yet by this time he had become a rebel against Williams on the parochial school issue and a reactionary toward the Yankees. Neither of these forces moved against him, however. Ironically, what destroyed him was precisely his identification of the priesthood with the common people, especially as it was symbolized in the simplicity —often the discourteous simple-mindedness—of his *Sacred*

Heart Review. For O'Connell *did* suppress the paper five years after his administration began: to him the *Sacred Heart Review* was a well-intentioned but unpredictable mongrel making noises on a track where only greyhounds could run.

THE THIRD GENERATION OF PRIESTS
AND IRISH CATHOLICISM

The generation of priests who would come to maturity in the 1890's and who would look backward to O'Brien, Conaty, Scully, and Healy were beginning their careers in 1880. O'Connell, Walsh, Gillis, Hugh Blunt, and Michael Earls had grown up in Lowell, Salem, Boston, and South Bridgewater. Each knew the thinking of the priests a generation older, and each admitted in diaries or later writings to feeling confined in a society of "badges and names . . . large societies and dead institutions."[158] As young people, they were unusually serious about life. Gillis, O'Connell, and Walsh were irritable "scolds" in their own homes even as young men, and knew it.[159] They were unsure of the clear demarcation between childhood and adulthood because of poverty. They were obsessively fascinated by material possessions. All came from very close family situations, although with the exception of Walsh and Blunt, the fathers had died by the boys' teens. With each, the events of childhood and schooldays were to remain fixed, and these heavily reinforced adult decisions and attitudes out of all proportion. There was a relentless drive to excel intellectually. Each was dogged by a sense of repeatedly adjusting, of fitting in where one was not wanted, though circumstances in their careers did provide escapes unavailable to an earlier generation of priests. Each eagerly took advantage of these. With the exception of Walsh whose father taught him to love Boston, each sought special dissociation from Boston's Irish-Catholic culture with more than average alacrity.

Unlike Charles Fairbanks, Healy, or Haskins, these young people naturally found nothing mysterious in Catholicism. There was neither Stone's expectation of some mysterious merging of Puritanism and Catholicism nor Fitton's memory of times when "after the discourse or lecture [of the missionary priest], one or other of the mixed audience, generally a Protestant, would invite him to luncheon, which consisted of pie and cheese and a mug of home-pressed cider."[160] Catholicism had sprawled out and was now commonplace and static. They were quite conscious of the enduring and irreconcilable cleavage in the society they had inherited. As a Holy Cross student in the 1870's, Walsh could size up and condemn the Jesuits as emotionlessly as he had gauged the pettiness of the priests of his parish in Salem. For this generation, the mysterious factor in life was the Yankee, a figure whom they both admired and despised on different levels simultaneously. Throughout his life, Gillis was fascinated by Yankee society; Walsh was captivated by London and Westminster Abbey; with O'Connell, the fascination reached obsessive dimensions. Every value was somewhat consciously held up against Yankee culture.

Gillis, O'Connell, Walsh, and Earls were constantly taking measurement of themselves. But this was not in terms of virtue or character—almost as though to concede inwardly that the Yankee had the corner on character anyway. Rather, they were asking, Where do I fit in? Did I extract every possible drop of value out of that experience? How much have I yet to learn? Enamoured of bigness, they admired the city—whether London, Rome or Boston—for its technological promise and its receptivity to organization. To them, the congeniality of a city was unimportant. Like the most brilliant of their contemporaries, they gave away wisdom in favor of facts and data. "Education" was both a status symbol and an avenue to "arrival." Both Walsh and O'Connell made an equation between one's education and the possibilities of one's spirituality. All of this would be significant, later.

SIGNS AND PORTENTS: 1866 TO 1880

During this fifteen-year period then, there was still social and economic fluidity; if there were solidifying attitudes of mutual rejection, their outcomes were yet unpredictable. Priests like

Father E. Holker Welsh, S.J., were still being invited to speak at Unitarian churches.[161] On the Brahmins' part, the meaning of existence was increasingly elusive, and this in turn was aggravated by a vague distrust created throughout the community by the presence of the immigrants' children. So they stepped back into a mean retrenchment. Williams' and Haskins' values were forwarded too timidly and were by nature too unstructured to prevail. Moderates like O'Brien and O'Connor were being forced out of neutral positions but by confrontations that were still comparatively rare.[162] The parish priests were just getting underway. The result was an uncrystallized situation best articulated by Stone. He counted on this suspension to have a hospitableness for Protestants. He could still manage to see New England Puritanism open to such new religious forms as Catholicism. In his estimate, Puritanism had left behind it "a sediment of refined naturalism, sickly spiritualism, and rude indifference," and now "a new departure" was at hand. It would be one in which the present younger generation would see Protestantism first "played out" and then searching—as he had—for some new "strong foundation." It would be Catholicism, of course. But this required a continuation of the present mercifully unjelled state of Catholicism. The church would spread but unpretentiously and harmlessly. Without much credit to the clergy or to the Irish, he preached that its conquest would come about "not by any plan of human forethought, not by any concert of human energy, not by any conspicuous and heroic sanctity of her children, not by any care of splendor or outward rituals, but . . . by the expansive power of an innate and irresistible vitality . . ."[163]

But there were definite signs of change. The day when Stone could appeal to an unaggressive Catholicism was fast disappearing; and so was the day when a Protestant convert could assume to speak authoritatively on Catholic matters.[164]

Time was running out too on the haphazardness with which Williams was deliberately letting the archdiocese grow. First, after 1875, Boston became an archdiocese, and there was the expected increase of correspondence between the bishop and

Roman officials. But in addition to this, the centralizing policies of Leo XIII would soon begin to move the Boston archdiocese into a closer rapport with Rome. Yet for the present, Williams and the clergy were decidedly not a part of that separate and separatist world directed by Rome, and they assiduously avoided the fate of being its enforcing agents.[165] Thus Williams' uninformative diary during Vatican I may be taken as a mark of his typically prudent silence. However, it may also be seen as reflecting his deliberate disentanglement from Rome. Similarly his diocesan reports to Rome, looked at in comparison to those of bishops like McQuaid of Rochester, were guarded and sparse, not to say careless.[166] In 1875, Rome opened the tug-of-war with Williams over the public schools.[167] Two years later, when the Office of the Propaganda was still dissatisfied with the progress of Catholic schools in Boston, it received back on its own letter to Williams, a noncommittal note from him stating he would try to better the situation.[168] Yet all that Rome learned of the public school situation in Boston from Williams' diocesan report of 1879 was that "the schools are public, that even in the smallest town they are set up according to law, and that this is defended as doing nothing contrary to the children's religion."[169] Even McQuaid, who was Williams' best friend among the bishops, wanted Rome kept uninformed on American church affairs. He fought repeatedly against the prospect of an apostolic delegate residing *in* the United States. "We shall then be," McQuaid wrote to Cardinal Gibbons, "victims of spies, eavesdroppers, meddlers and every contemptible species of humanity" who might appeal over our heads to Rome. His opinion that it would be "too late to howl when the screws are on" and when Rome was legislating all things was shared by Williams as well as Bishop James Healy of Portland.[170]

But Rome was not the only factor spelling the end of autonomy and the undefined place of the Catholic Church in Boston life. The new generation of pastors never knew Boston except as a mélange of hostile ethnic units. Naturally, they burned no sacred fire to the citizens' city. Nor were they familiar with the Yankee in the way that Williams was. Yet they were increasingly the "leaders" of Boston Catholicism, displacing men like Ring, Bodfish, and, in reality, Williams. The lever of power was the parish. It was made clear to Ring that the St. Vincent de Paul Society, to use Ring's paraphrase of one priest's words, "depends so very much on the pulpit for the maintenance of its charities . . . nearly three quarters of the receipts are [gathered] directly or indirectly through the medium of the pastor . . ."[171] In addition, religious Sisters, who were a new-fangled phenomenon and would be subject to the pastor, were increasingly making their appearance, much to the consternation and antipathy of the parishioners.[172] There was a shifting definition of words like "prosperity." For Williams' generation, it had the biblical meaning; O'Brien's generation took its lead from the people, and it came to mean, quite narrowly, financial improvement.[173]

In 1879, Williams was pessimistic regarding the future of the Church in Boston. There was the oblique but real suggestion in his report to Rome that the Irish served to impede conversions.[174] In the same year, Stone capitulated with reluctance saying, "I do not think that the glowing anticipations concerning the future of the Catholic Church in this country . . . will be speedily realized." Nevertheless he was still convinced that Catholicism could become admirable by becoming truly American. No one yet knew the outcomes of what Stone called "the great experiment of throwing the Catholic Church upon the hearts of the people alone."[175] He remained somewhat optimistic because he saw Williams and other clergymen in brown hats and ordinary shirt collars; he observed no churchly bureaucratic trappings.[176] What Stone could not know was that Williams' successor would fasten Boston Catholicism not upon "the heart of the people alone" but onto Rome. "The great experiment" would go through some exhilarating paces in literature and theology in the 1890's. But portentously here in the 1870's, John Boyle O'Reilly, in order to make himself and the Irish more acceptable to the Yankee community, was already unfairly stereotyping the Catholic populace and clergy as naturally conservative and submissive to ecclesiastical authority.[177]

Chapter III
1880 to 1890: Drift, and Some Mastery

Throughout the last third of the nineteenth century, members of the Roman Catholic clergy were the dynamic religious force in Boston, holding a crucial position in the socio-economic development of the city. There were no giant figures among them. But in the 1880's and 1890's the code of values espoused by Archbishop Williams lost whatever momentum it had, and that proposed by the generation of '45 was further refined and its application steadily widened. These values determined the policy of the church toward the Yankees, French-Canadians, and Italians. Yet the swelling wave of Irish-Catholic group consciousness did not give the clergy the expected sense of decisiveness and self-assurance. Rather the clergy were experiencing a chaotic decade. In their overreacting to these anarchic circumstances, they sought a kind of control that in turn softened the ground for acceptance of the rigid bureaucracy created by Cardinal O'Connell after 1907. At the same time the next generation of priests were absorbing a classic humanism at the Jesuits' Boston College. This was becoming their intellectual framework. But even this new emphasis in piety was not articulated until the 1890's, and therefore it did nothing to dispel the clergy's sense of drift in the 1880's. The generation of '45, while it was toilsomely and sometimes with understandable belligerence working its way off the harsh probation that Boston society put it on, remained "the lost generation."

AN UNSETTLED DECADE

Even if it endangered the city's cultural purity, Irish assimilation into the life of Boston was a necessity if there was to be reasonable comfort for all. But there would never be the satisfying sense of honor as before. The community was disfigured by segregation. One Bostonian, Eleanor Abbott, reminisced in *Being Little in Cambridge* that "nobody except day-laborers ever patronized the Mt. Auburn Street [streetcar] line at either morning or night, if he could help it."[1] In the 1880's a group consciousness on the part of the Irish and a greater sense of disintegration on the Yankees' side had forced a preoccupation with social preservation. This meant, more often than not, concern for one's own preservation, whether as Catholic pastor or Yankee businessman. At any rate, the parish priests assumed the responsibility for adjusting the Irish. One of their number, Father John McMahon, regarded this inculcation of manners as a misguided endeavor. He saw an unsavory "desire for self-advancement" in the fact that young men "even encouraged sometimes by the clergy" were joining "literary, social and temperance societies." Yet the clergy persisted, actually only piping a way that the immigrants and their children were determined to go anyway. Starting in the 1870's, strong and conspicuously prosperous parishes were established in "the zone of emergence." The dynamics of religion began to function on this level in Boston. It remained the location of power (though certainly not of intellectual leadership) until the organizing days of O'Connell when power moved above the parish to the diocesan level.[2]

By the end of the 1880's, Dorchester had become a middle-class area; men like Mayor Patrick Collins and Thomas Ring had moved there during this decade. In the same ten years, the Irish gave over the North and West Ends to Italians and Jews. In fact, Robert A. Woods, the noted Boston settlement house worker and self-styled sociologist of the late 1890's, insisted that the immigrants' children were now being confronted with lower-middle-class problems and that the "new type" of immigrant from Ireland was less destitute.

Another factor in parish-building was the accepted (and unexplored) assumption that ethnic and racial groups would want to band together exclusively. So in 1884 Father William Byrne felt obliged to set up a "Colored Conference" of the St. Vincent de Paul men, although in this and in the general setting up of parish boundaries, there was not the hostility toward threatening, non-Irish groups which would mark the 1890's. In most parishes then, the average priest was addressing himself to a congregation of poor and lower-middle-class Irish or a mixture of lower-middle-class and middle-middle-class Irish. The retreat of the Yankees before this swelling power of the newcomers became precipitous between 1880 and 1890. The Irish then constituted a majority of the city's population. They enjoyed permanent control of at least one Congressional seat and had experienced the pleasure of electing their first Irish mayor. However, they by no means as yet governed the city on their own terms. Still less had they mastered the psycho-sociological factors. For both Yankee and Catholic, the result was a decade of rejections, discouragements, and self-delusions, all made more acute because the final outcome was unpredictable.[3]

The Irish continued to resent their poverty in the self-pitying, often mean and primitive way presented in George Bernard Shaw's *John Bull's Other Island*. The fact that they defined "bigot" as any Yankee who looked down on a *lower class* indicated that they resented scorn of their poverty at least as much as scorn of their religion. O'Connell remembered later that when he was a curate at St. Joseph's Church, every Sunday sermon held up both the ideal of poverty and—an ambivalence he seemed not to note then or afterwards—the ideal of getting out of it. As such, these homilies both satisfied and disappointed the listeners. O'Connell later recalled that "the same old round of instructions and sermons [were given by us at St. Joseph's], done more or less in a hurry, and no wonder we get [*sic*] weary and tired, and less wonder still that the congregation gets more so." The Irish were being exploited and their entrance into the professions unjustly barred. Still the only safe way for the priest to attack the situation was by pointing out the lack of virtue in the exploiters, not by attacking the system head-on. To do so was absurd. At best, it meant putting into question the clergy's Americanism. In some situations, it would result in getting the parishioners into trouble "at the factory." In Sacred Heart parish in Cambridge where most of the parishioners worked at J. P. Squires, Women's Hose, Inc., and Millers' of Wakefield, the workers would have been extremely distressed had Father John O'Brien, their pastor, not cooperated with the companies for the workers' good. As it was, he did cooperate and directly, if only in arranging a day off annually to attend the parish picnic.[4] Further, to preach against the capitalistic system would require a condemnation of those Catholics who were managing factories and employing tactics exactly like those of the Yankees—and who were renting the front pews of the churches in considerable numbers in the 1880's. In a town like Lawrence, it would mean destroying the parishioners' belief that they belonged to the whole community in some genuine organic way. Besides, apart from the fact that the clergy themselves needed people like Mr. Squires and could make good use of their "generous proofs of interest in the [parish] works," they were getting no complete picture of affairs from the archbishop. Generally they observed municipal or statewide economic problems from the limited perspective of the parish only. As a result, they treated the socio-economic inequalities on the level of psychology, reducing the causes to the seven capital sins. Yet the Irish, though they seemed satisfied with this reduction, simultaneously resented a do-nothing Church. Even Father John O'Brien in his weekly Cambridge newspaper, *The Sacred Heart Review*, felt compelled in the late 1880's to stress what the Church had done traditionally "to better the lot of its people." Still the people found themselves captive to their own miserable ways of pulling up out of poverty, and so did the clergy. Both groups knew they were as determined as the Yankees to be money-makers. Like the Yankees, they worried over it and questioned their own self-respect.

Not that this was admitted publicly or even to themselves. Rather, they sank into the comfortable myth unconsciously exposed in O'Connell's autobiography: *we* would not allow *our* lives to be darkened by such *efforts* for money; only if money comes *naturally* is it acceptable. In the same volume, O'Connell used the word "capitalist" for the Yankee, while the Catholic who was engaged in similar business ventures was "a quiet man . . . of enormous wealth." With progressively dangerous myth-making, the Irish came to define Yankee wealth as ill-gotten. Everything it bought, like seats at the symphony or opera, was similarly tainted. In the mid-1880's, the mentality was such that George Appley *could not* have worked his way up: only the Irish did that.[5]

Irish Catholics also continued to resent their inability to make a cultural contribution to Boston. They imitated the Yankees widely but unsuccessfully. To compensate, they stressed in their writings the great families and baroque architecture of Catholic Europe for which achievement, it could be argued, they could claim some undefinable but real credit. In this decade, parishioners delighted in gigantic Gothic churches which were erected as a defensive gesture of effrontery. The subject of such buildings arose at one of the faculty meetings at St. John's Seminary (Boston) in 1886. "Here [in Boston] this [construction of churches] is a common object of the zeal of the priests. Considerable sums have been spent here ending in results so unhappy from various points of view that it is not only the bishop who has deplored them." After 1900 and when security had been achieved, parishioners reversed themselves and praised the pastor for "quietly" having built up the parish. In the 1880's isolation within the parish persisted, and parishioners had the example of the priests in this manner of behavior. Edward Everett Hale reluctantly noted in 1881: "Thousands of Protestant clergymen have spent and been spent in the physical relief of poor persons belonging to the Roman communion. But who can name ten instances in America where the Roman Catholic priest in any neighborhood has lifted a finger for a Protestant beggar." Starting in the 1890's, the generation of priests born after 1845 would be more able to meet these same Yankees on cultural grounds. But then they would be ostentatious in their newly defined Catholic culture, betraying a deep and persistent resentment at their cultural impoverishment when young.[6]

The sense of humiliation and inferiority as part of a poorer class accompanied these Irish families as they reached middle-class status during the 1880's. They did begin to strike back not only in their architecture but in their literature. The *Sacred Heart Review, Donahoe's Magazine,* and *The Pilot* carried countless stories in which priests or immigrants scrutinized their situation and found defenses. Few stories were set in Boston; most writers used a protective covering. Their plots were played out by classes within European society of bygone days. Peasants, the stories told, were really the noble people; noblemen (read Yankees) were actually only *parvenues.* ("Once there was a young peasant girl who was the handsomest maiden in all the country round, but she was wretchedly poor in everything except good blood.") Ancestry was spotlighted but not for the same reasons as, nor in the scholarly way of, the 1907 Gaelic revival. This literature handed ambitious middle-class persons the opportunity to identify with guileless, if motley, peasant ancestors. But it could scarcely have been entirely satisfactory. Nor was it in any way a cause of abjuring the comforts which middle-class living afforded. Father Flatley still went to Florida; Fathers John E. Delehunty and Daniel O'Callaghan still went to Europe; and Father Peter Crudden, pastor of St. Peter's in Lawrence, left an estate of $500,000 when he died in 1886.[7]

The mentality of the clergy during the 1880's was formed more by incoherent, particular circumstances than by heightened group consciousness. Above all, the local clergymen were experiencing patternless instances of suffering, greed, family breakdown and general cultural malaise. The diary of Richard Keefe, a caseworker for the St. Vincent de Paul Society in 1888–1889, is filled with notations on individual cases referred to him by priests of Boston. Father Denis Lee, a curate at Saints Peter and Paul Church in South Boston, called him in on twenty-three occasions for almost as many "cases" in four and one-half months. Father Lawrence P. McCarthy of Most Holy Redeemer Church in East Boston asked that Keefe remove a drunken woman from her home to the House of Good Shepherd. Father John Nilan petitioned aid for Mary Gallagher, an unwed mother. Father H. H. Sullivan at the cathedral encouraged Keefe to "use every legal means" to arrange for the daughter of a woman repeatedly arrested on "disorderly conduct." Many clergymen were directly involved in and often overburdened by numerous cases of desperation in their parishes. Yet their accounts suggest that they saw no pattern in these cases; they could not reduce them to any order. Each case remained singular and inexplicable. Moreover, the parish priests lacked sufficient information on the interlocking city charities to see the cases referred to these agencies as part of a whole. Rather than watching the integrated frames of a motion picture, they were looking at lantern slides, seeing only singular tragedies that "legal means" or one of the unknown agencies in the Charities Building would settle.[8] Even the vicar-general of the diocese did not know how the Associated Charities operated until 1880, and then only sketchily from Thomas Ring. In fact the St. Vincent de Paul Society itself was continually altering course during the 1880's, necessarily relying on the reports of individual "visitors" to the poor of a parish. From these and from the fluctuations in the hesitant pulse of the city-wide, nondenominational Board of Overseers, the Society learned when it should switch emphasis from aid to the poor to "giving more attention to catechism in public institutions." Sudden circumstances propelled the Society from coal distribution to casket-making to flood-control. The decade was bombarded with episodic needs that even those closest to the organizational forces of the city could not gather into coherence.[9]

The Catholic literature also demonstrates the individuality in suffering—poverty, unexpected disease, and unemployment. The most ominous of all the notions with which the fiction deals is individual failure of nerve; the only remedy is the proper use of one's individual courage and endurance. Death is a lonely, solitary event. In fact, aloneness and unpredictability are emphatic. And the ultimate horror is not to die but to die without honor, to die having acted against one's personal convictions. In other tales, individuals make the most awesome decisions utterly unassisted, some bereft of parents or prevailing against their wishes.[10]

In circumstances which touched their lives most closely, the priests also sensed anarchy rather than the sure progress of a confident Catholic ascendancy. This was true in trivialities like the fact that "many estimable Catholics" refused any contact with church societies; even some Vincent de Paul members did not wish to attend Mass in a body for the General Meeting.[11] But apart from trivialities, it was also common to encounter among the clergy and laity completely individual interpretations on such vital issues as education, pietism, and the family. The local clergymen managed to bring some order to the matter of education by the end of the decade. It was the orderliness of organized defiance (against Williams) and it crippled any possible moderate position in the future. But it afforded an answer and therefore quiescence, at least on that subject. The priests were not as successful in filling with new wine the old and increasingly discarded wineskins of traditional Irish-Catholic pietism. Only in the 1890's would the younger clergymen of O'Connell's generation offer an appealing approach to religious behavior, that taught by the Jesuits at Boston College where most of them were educated. Finally, the clergy were too successful on the matter of the family. Even before the end of the century, their desperate, if psychologically faulty, formulations had made a swollen monstrosity of the omnicompetent family and destroyed the balance between it and other social institutions.

More important ultimately, the need to find direction in the face of the utter particularity of incoming experiences soon shaded into an impulse to control. When someone like O'Connell finally appeared, his policies were found to be—if testily in some cases—acceptable.

In the mid-1880's, the question of religious education in Boston became visible and was publicly aired. More significant than the details or broadsides, however, was the surprising diversity of attitudes among Catholics. When the dust cleared, forces had lined up in peculiar ways. Williams, despite clear evidence that pressure was on him from Rome to build parish schools, resisted, just as the American bishops had resisted the calling of the Baltimore Council knowing they would tie their own hands in the matter. Many Boston priests supported Williams in this position, some writing the chancery to discredit Catholic schools and urge public education. Byrne, of course, continued to speak peace and propose conciliation. Only after "the orphan, the sick, and the hungry [are] provided for" should the education of Catholic children in Catholic schools go forward "unless in the meantime, the public mind, now growing rapidly more fair as it becomes better informed on this subject, shall haply [sic] discover some way to amend the situation."[12]

Throughout the 1880's, the Catholic people were satisfied with the public school system. Rochester's Bishop McQuaid wrote of education in Massachusetts that "Catholics have held back from establishing Catholic schools in the hope that their neighbors, the majority, would listen to reason and agree upon a plan by which all classes of citizens may be secured in their rights." Patrick Donahoe was indecisive in 1883. Calling upon "American fair play," he suggested that the state "aggregate our Catholic schools to the public school system and open a teacher's career to our convent girls." Yankee Catholics like Mrs. Blake made nothing of the issue. They were quite satisfied to concern themselves with the needs of the public schools from which they had been graduated. Boston Catholic women, Donahoe generalized in 1888, were "opposed" to the parochial schools and were clearly "doubting the sincerity of their priests."[13] Others wanted a general education for their children. A public school education was considered to be a supremely good one, a training which would in fact answer the need for leadership in the church. Thomas Ring was continually conscious of this need and looked desperately for young leaders for the St. Vincent de Paul conferences. At the same time, he was not satisfied that the Sisters of Notre Dame de Namur should be teaching the older boys at Sunday School sessions. He felt that St. Vincent de Paul men should teach them catechism; for the rest, a public school education was satisfactory. The trickle of criticism of Sisters in the 1870's mounted in this decade. Father Abram J. Ryan spoke out with unexpected pique against expensive convent-schools patronized only by rich Catholics and non-Catholics. "Now," he followed up, "because a Sister or a nun wears a veil, it by no means follows that she is competent to teach. What is in the head, not what is on the head settles that." Another clergyman admitted the validity of current criticism—with a bit of self-exposure here—that "children in the parish school don't learn nothin'." In 1889, the *Review* was forced to defend religious teachers, insisting, by way of praise, that many were formerly public school teachers. Many parents continued to want a utilitarian education for their children. Still others argued that "harmony and mutual respect between citizens of different denominations [is] more effectually promoted by having all children in 'our common schools.'" Mythology to the contrary, Irish Catholics resented supporting two school systems. Nor did O'Connell's generation of priests universally thank their predecessors for the parochial system. One of them, Father James Gillis, later specifically spoke out on political issues, so he said, because that was what fully educated men did. To be recognized as learned in the profane sciences was his consuming desire; it was also his covert way of repudiating a Catholic education. The same is true of O'Connell who urged Catholic education for the masses but himself garishly displayed his "wide learning."[14]

Nevertheless some of the priests, arguing from increasingly shifting positions and aware that the children were not being schooled at home in "the religious dispositions," kept up a barrage of small fire, each parish priest handling the issue as he wished. Father Thomas Scully, who never got over being a Civil War chaplain, now spoke throughout the diocese and was delighted that the school question was "being happily agitated." As early as 1875, he was in correspondence with Bishop McQuaid on the education issue. McQuaid was a vigorous promoter of parish schools in his own diocese and had encouraged Scully's efforts. In return, Scully had assured McQuaid that he would persevere, despite the lack of leadership from Williams. "I will fight it out," he wrote. "The struggle is coming. The army is ready if we had the leaders. You are I may say almost alone." In 1876 Scully wrote McQuaid to express his gratification that the bishop was coming to Boston to speak on education. He assured McQuaid that he would find a home in his Cambridgeport rectory or, as he put it, in "our camp." He referred to his parish as "the fighting ground in the school question" and to his school-children as "our little army of 460 boys." The battle for Catholic schools, he maintained, was one he was fighting alone. "All the Catholic politicians," he wrote, "have denounced me." The same tone of persecution pervaded his letter to McQuaid shortly after the lecture. He called for a declaration of war on bigoted Yankees and at the same time implied that Williams was the traitor. "We," he wrote, "have too long neglected [setting up Catholic schools] lest perhaps we should disturb the *peace,* and lose the *good will* of our Yankee friends." Boston has lagged behind noticeably. "I need not," he concluded, "tell you why *we* are so backward."[15]

At Malden in 1882 Scully attacked his fellow-priests publicly. "Some of the Boston clergy . . . are proud of being graduates of the State schools and are amongst their most loyal patrons." He openly questioned the efficacy of seminary training on "priests . . . out of Godless schools," and he pointed out that Williams' diocese was not "in perfect accord with Rome." Possibly in desperation he had opened his own "college" in Cambridgeport. His skirmishing was even watched outside the diocese, although his insistence on attendance at parochial schools "under pain of sin" was still a novelty in places like St. Louis, Missouri.[16]

Other priests were beginning to accept Scully's position, but gradually. In 1889 O'Brien was forcing the school issue in the *Review.* Still, until the 1890's even he continued to represent both sides as offered by readers' letters. Volatile as the issue was, the rebels sustained their position against the archbishop, the Yankees and their own people. They were radical in their fears and plans. Yet they could count only two-fifths of the Catholic children in parish schools in 1907 after twenty-five years of effort.[17]

The school issue of the 1880's had serious results nonetheless. A whole new rhetoric developed, a stiffness of mind, a set of logical and illogical arguments on a plethora of side-issues, and finally the visibility of the old split between the archbishop and many of the parish priests. The school issue also split many parishes internally. Father McInerney at the Mission Church had difficulty in 1887 convincing the parishioners to accept the parish school. First he brought in the Jesuits to give Lenten talks on the subject of the Baltimore decrees and the obligation of sending children to the school "under pain of mortal sin." Soon only parochial school children were in the processions and other favorite church functions. Parents with children still in public schools were second-class parishioners, judged—in an odd inversion—in terms of their children. Outside a specific parish situation, Catholics who approved public schooling were called "rankest" Protestants. For perhaps the first time, a whole group of Catholics were assailed by fellow-Catholics as disloyal to the Church.[18]

Yankees like Edwin Mead who had always favored one school system were now forced to take a definite stand, cornered into a given position by the Catholic clergymen and then berated for it. Williams and Thomas Dwight, who was Ring's successor as president of the St. Vincent de Paul Society, tried to smother part of the conflict by stating that Catholics were happy to support two school systems. This was untrue and the *Review* reported it as such. Still more fundamental, once given the parochial school system, it had to be defended. Tactically this involved some priests in maneuvers ranging from private intellectual contortions to new alliances with local politicians. In this way the schools that were established especially to teach the nonsecular further secularized their builders. For the first time priests publicly insisted that the church had certain rights over "citizens."

Finally the issue showed the priests that acquiescent pacifism

115

need not always be the answer and that Williams' ideas need not always be mildly accepted. Clearly, having carried this "rebellion" off rather successfully, a policy of more aggressive tactics was reasonable. In addition, Williams had used a local parish pastor, Father Magennis, as spokesman in public cases involving the school question. It was indeed a turning point in the balance of power between Yankee Catholics and the groupings of local pastors.[19]

Divisiveness on the issue of education was only a visible symbol of a deeper cultural formlessness felt by the clergy and others in the 1880's. This world of anarchy and fragmentation which, for example, William Dean Howells had to strive so consciously to recreate in his novels, came alive quite unconsciously in the pitifully bad stories written for Catholic readers. Characters like Rodolfo in "An Event on the River" by Louise Imogen Guiney as well as those presented in the parables of the *Review* were morally crippled and could only act chaotically because they had lost touch with their past, they had lost continuity with their traditions. And this was to have lost touch with one's conscience. Put another way, the ancient Irish pietism, itself an indivisible triptych of race, creed, and nationality, had lost its meaning as a mode of religious response called forth by the experience of the sacred. The dismay at this was one cause of the insistent Irish-American nationalism of the 1880's. The sanely qualified nationalism of a man like Roddan in the 1850's was replaced by rigid protestations of the purity of the ancient piety and unflinching devotion to the various causes of the nationalists. The cautious Irish nationalism of John Boyle O'Reilly during the 1880's stood in contrast to such shrill protestations but the radical spokesmen nevertheless made use of his every word.[20]

The shattering of each of the three components of Irish pietism was quite complete, despite strident assurances to the contrary. Social Darwinism was especially damaging to the Celtic race. Even Roddan had acknowledged in 1850 that "the Celtic type of civilization . . . is less fitted to make a nation great in our times than it was two thousand years ago." He insisted that "the world *now* has no place for the Celtic type of civilization, and the nation which clings to it will be left by the others whole centuries behind." Readers of the 1880's were familiar with his warning that "the type of civilization . . . best calculated to meet those wants [of the 1850's] is the one represented by England and America." Reverend Joseph V. O'Connor, a frequent contributor to *Donahoe's Magazine* in the 1880's, sturdily reminded his Irish readers that according to Max Müller's hypothesis "the Irish race should have been stamped out long ago."[21]

More devastating to the stability of Irish pietism was the attack upon "nation" and the haunted house in which its course was enshrined, Irish history. For the concepts of "the nation" and "the faith" were inseparably joined, resulting in the unfortunate bilateral agreement that an attack upon one would be considered an attack upon both. This identity, when expressed theologically, resulted in the faulty assertion that faith was inherited, was passed down through the national history from father to son. Preaching Irish piety on this contorted limb of an argument, such contenders then sawed it off by making the same inheritance factor the sole source of the present "enduring faith." It is, as one priest wrote, "generally the traditional gift of the martyrs—a belief of the ancient Church which explains theologically the enduring faith of the Irish people." Given this rigid identity, piety was emptied of meaning when nationalism was. Yet this was precisely the state of affairs. In 1880 one priest cited "the new generation since the Civil War" as grown "weary of the foolish and incessant 'blathering' about Ireland." And at the end of the decade, Martin J. Roche, a columnist for the *Review,* had to admit that the same "rising generation of Irish Americans" saw the history of Ireland as "a wild, dreary chronicle of internecine slaughter." In the same decade, Father Joseph O'Connor defended the younger generation's general resentment at "the older generation's . . . constant whine about the wrongs of Ireland." Such articles, while seemingly innocuous, in fact were a signal that dispositions necessary to keep alive an older mode of religious expression could no longer be fired up.[22]

Irish pietism was a tenacious mode of religious ritual and behavior, although its base was actually unorthodox Catholicism. Like a lichen, it rooted in the daily peasant routine, governing a system of controls, duties and sentiments which made up family life. It fixed the position of parent as one of extreme superordination, while the retention of the name "boy" marked for the child a life-long subordination that was never relaxed. More widely, "saintliness" was a matter of fulfilling one's role, but specifically one's role for the village. In accord with both pietism and an organic concept of society, the "leading classes" were expected to bring decency and order to the village or parish. As late as 1889 in Boston, Father Bernard O'Reilly was writing with these village roles in mind, warning that "servants will follow their masters in way of life, amusements, and recreations." And "only the good example of the men of the leading classes" could "provide a standard for the poorest of working classes."[23]

The implied doctrines of this way of life were part of Jansenism, the all-pervading reaffirmations of the rigorist doctrines of Augustine. Original sin was not mere imputation; rather, it expressed itself in the depravation of nature, in appetite, and concupiscence. In this respect, Irish Jansenism was contrary to official Catholic teaching, severing the natural order from the supernatural order. "Poor mortals," wrote a priest in 1881 betraying this substantial horror of the natural world, "[they are] charmed by that which they cannot approach familiarly, that which they cannot understand or fathom, that which is forbidden." Sin was not an intellectual matter; it manifested itself best and continually in sex which was, perforce, joyless. So, the priest-writer continued, mysteries (false religions, secret societies) govern men; one of these mysteries is women and "mysteries lead [inevitably] to sin." Yet the depraved state of man demanded a still more fearsome psychological assumption: "What is done today in fear and trembling is committed tomorrow with boldness and impunity."[24] This anthropology, which housed man's nature in the squalor of sin, came to be the pre-existing groundwork for the socio-psychic conditions that both embodied and nourished Irish pietism.

The discourse of theology only deepened the gloominess of the scene. It focused attention upon the nature of man, not God; like the Calvinism experienced by Harriet Beecher Stowe, it was effectively without a warming Christology. By its own psychology, such pietism rejected the autonomy of the individual. It insisted in every instance that religion was an attitude and choice—indeed an inheritance!—*before* experience. Out of this insistence came the proposition that "correct dispositions have to be nurtured" and then the experience of the divine will inevitably follow. Yet in fact, and as the 1880's were proving, such conditioning did nothing to close the gap between the God young people were being told about and the God they were—or were not—experiencing. Such a piety was merely calling forth a massive list of induced words that failed to transmit any meaningful concept of God. At the same time it was exhausting itself in anecdotality, a sure sign of decay.[25] There was no effort at making the presence of God (or the Incarnate Word) meaningfully commensurate with the dimensions of the circumstances of present society. Anecdotes like that of Boston's Mary Catherine Crowley on Louis xvii of France ironically held up a model of Christian pietism while at the same time never suggesting any meaning for God. In such episodes, explanations of how Blanche of Castile or little Carmelita or a model Irish newsboy acted and were rewarded took the place of explaining how God acted. Yet such anecdotes were the theological discourse of the day. But while Miss Crowley wrote of little Louis xvii "seeking consolation in prayer" and while the clergy eagerly published such easily digestible ascetic tracts, the young people "of the poorest working classes" were disinterested. One priest wrote with picturesque dismay that they were "swarming to [cheap theatres and dances] from the crowded districts like flies in midsummer to a putrid carcass." At the same time, serious Catholic youth in Boston were frankly planning to imitate the ymca, hoping to establish a kind of meeting place free of "some pious old cronies who want to have

prayers as soon as they find a number of Catholics gathered together."[26]

Rejection of this pietism came wholesale to Boston in the
1880's. A wedge was being driven disastrously between "faith"
and "nation." Indications of this ranged from commonplace admissions that "lectures in behalf of the Irish Home Movement"
were fiascoes, to more subtle signs. In James Riley's charming
"Songs of Two Peoples," the loved home was in rural New England not Ireland. And one commentator arguing for better
Catholic newspapers moaned in *exasperation,* "The unsophisti-
cated reader . . . might suppose that Home Rule in Ireland was
a religious question."[27] But perhaps the point at which the
wedge completed a clean break was at the mass meeting in
1883 regarding Irish emigration. The meeting was held in the
Boston Music Hall and presided over by Mayor Albert Palmer,
John Boyle O'Reilly, and Patrick A. Collins as well as Judge
Fallon and Joshua Bodfish. With their thoughts on "material
prospects," they resolved:

That while the resources of this country are unbounded, and its reception of "the oppressed of all nations" generous and hospitable, the
wholesale introduction of indigent people . . . would at this time add
nothing to the material prospects of the American people, and would
cause untold evils to the emigrants themselves.

This unmasking of a shift in loyalties away from Ireland and
its incessant problems was, if flagrant here, not exceptional.
O'Connor was one priest who recognized that American experience was accentuating the autonomy of the individual, forcing
him to regard the Catholic faith and Ireland from a new perspective. To O'Connor this experience was a blessing. It rescued
the immigrant from a hierarchical village structure. But O'Connor was an exceptionally realistic priest, having worked among
both the Mollie Maguires and the Quakers. *Donahoe's Magazine*
was similarly open and, in the 1890's especially, served as forum
for a number of priests. How many Boston priests matched
O'Connor's kind of thinking we do not know. What we do know
is that even he referred to "the liberal view of the Church" as

"semi-pelagian" and that his attitude toward marriage and sex was tainted with Jansenism. *Donahoe's Magazine* also made a talented, consistent attempt to make Americans of its readers and to respond positively to their changing habits of thinking. But it was the conservative *Review* that speedily built up circulation among the local clergy from the time of its first appearance in 1888.[28]

The priest-editors of the *Review* twisted and turned desperately in a vain effort to keep alive the old pietism. Father Bernard O'Reilly whose column appeared regularly seemed unable to realize that Boston was not "old Ireland." Similarly, in 1889 the *Review* was still counselling that "if you cannot set apart a room 'for God,' then at least have a corner of some room for Him. Let it be your oratory . . ." Elsewhere the editors alternately falsified the old pietism or preached frightening exhortations to the fallen-away. They insisted that the church believed in broad reforms and was "humanitarian." The church, they continued, "traditionally stood for democracy." But having made these concessions to modernity, the editors swerved in another direction. They preached jeremiads and called for penance under the terms of the old Jansenistic piety. Like the data coming at them from every side, their exhortations were helter-skelter and not "methodized." The faithful must not drink or attend the theater; they must stop swearing; they must not wish to be "independent of the control of the church simply because someone else . . . is independent"; they must not be "ashamed of their religion"; they must accept God's displeasure for the times were "days of lukewarmness in religious matters." They must be made aware that their children "have no Catholic instinct . . . [that] there is [in their ways] a coldness, a suspicion, a blighting spirit of criticism in their position toward the Church." These troubled utterances reflected clearly that God had another controversy with New England. Yet they seldom betrayed the total alarm of the clergy on this matter or on the place of their own status as the rush from Irish pietism seemed to take on stampede proportions. Their alarm was a double one, and both concerns were enunciated in 1889. "The problem which presents itself to the Catholic priesthood especially in our large cities is a very serious one . . . [For] a considerable number of Catholic children are being detached [from Catholicism] without entering into any new religious relations." And: "they [the children] . . . have lost all regard for the church and priest . . ."29

During the 1880's the clergy took these statements seriously. An old order was passing and no "new religious relations" were even predictable. Still worse, if the truth were admitted, not only children but grown men were throwing off the old pietism. One could read that the menfolk were sick of "a chapter and a half of a continued story of Irish peasant life, a ten-column sermon on original sin, [and] editorials on the Tenants' League." As for the status of the priest, this too was questioned as much by men as by the adolescents. One clergyman generalized that fathers did little to encourage priestly vocations specifically because they wanted their sons to have that occupational mobility honored in America but "denied the priest." In this way the priest's role was being increasingly seen as a structural variant of the ordinary occupational patterns in America. In addition he was being dissociated from "the men" and correspondingly feminized. One layman, in analysing Catholic newspapers, pointed out that they were not attractive "to the men." Immediately, however, he imputed a difference between these discriminating stalwarts and the manipulable, effeminate clergymen. "They [newspapers] tickle the clergy with compliments . . . and they charm the women with stories, recipes, etc." Further accentuating the contrast, the writer's next sentence returned to dealing with "the men."30

In the end the rejection of the older pietism by the rising younger generation and "the men" did leave behind the impression of a stronger likeness between the clergy and women. Instead of being able to break away from this identification, they found themselves calling to their aid "the wife and mother [who] feeds the sacred fire and the lamp of piety."31

But religious leadership by the 1880's was not left solely to a baffled local clergy. They were not even the men who were influencing the intellectual training of the younger priests or seminarians. They feared that this influence was being exercised by the Sulpicians at St. John's Seminary which opened in Boston in 1884. Yet it was the Jesuits at Boston College who filled this need because they were able to provide a kind of learned pietism which, with its particular symbolism and ideals, was both personally meaningful and honorable.

THE ROLE OF THE JESUITS AT BOSTON COLLEGE

By the 1890's Jesuit ideas and practices were a decided factor in the mentality of the younger Boston clergy. In January of 1893 an article on Boston College appeared in *Donahoe's Magazine*. The author was a loyal graduate, chauvinistic and interested in sharing his statistical study of the college. He described a current enrollment of 376 students with a faculty of nineteen, five of whom were laymen and graduates of the college. Going back to 1878, he counted 243 graduates, with this vocational breakdown: eighty-nine secular clergymen; six regular priests; twenty-five doctors; thirteen lawyers; thirteen teachers and nine journalists. Forty-one graduates were still pursuing ecclesiastical studies; fifteen were studying law and medicine. This enumeration was followed by a proud exposition of the college's philosophy of education and the quite accurate claim that "nearly the entire body of the younger clergymen of the archdiocese is made up of Boston College men."[32] The more illustrious graduates were especially cited: Reverend Garrett J. Barry '80, "considered one of the most eloquent preachers among the younger Catholic clergy"; Reverend John F. Ford '81, director of the Workingboys' Home; and Reverend William H. O'Connell '81, "recognized as a preacher of great ability." Just as Cambridge University was the training ground for the Puritan divines, so Boston College prepared the clergy of O'Connell's generation. Even the subsequent experiences of many of these same young men in Sulpician seminaries did not dispel the influence of seven years spent with the Jesuits. John Wright, who was archbishop of Pittsburgh in the 1960's and a graduate of Boston

College (1931) and then St. John's Seminary, attributed his cultural formation exclusively to Boston College in the days when it was frankly "a small Catholic College." In 1963 he reminisced about the graduates in an interview. "They were typical of a whole generation. It is not a question of whether they were *better* than others; the point is they were *different* and their differences contributed mightily to America."[33]

The kind of delirious enthusiasm which the unknown writer showed for his *alma mater* in 1893 was building momentum in the 1880's. By 1886 applications for entrance had to be submitted very early. Local clergymen, however, were not enthusiastic about Boston College, either in the 1880's or in the earlier years. In spring of the institution's first academic year, 1865, Father John Bapst wrote his provincial in desperation. "There is hardly a secular priest," he informed his superior, "who will say a good word on our behalf, but a great many will be disposed to say a bad word against us; and yet the parents are generally influenced by their pastors as to what college they should send their boys." By design or otherwise, the announcement in *The Pilot* of a fair for the school gave no indication that it was a Jesuit institution, and there was no "S.J." after Bapst's name. Nevertheless the college soon had the financial support (a matching loan) of Andrew Carney. It also had the kind of encouragement from Williams and Yankee Catholics which is found in the writings of one of the latter. He cited Boston College as "the most important single agency in elevating the mind and manners of that [the Boston Catholic] community." More directly, Father Robert Fulton, an extraordinarily assertive man who served several terms as president, noted in his diary as early as the mid-1870's that by his count, "40 of my boys have [either] entered the Novitiate preparatory to entrance into the Jesuit order, become [secular] priests or gone to theological seminaries." In the '77 graduating class of nine boys, one young man died, two became physicians "and all the rest became priests of the Archdiocese of Boston."[34]

The content of the education which the future Boston clergymen were getting at Boston College in the 1880's indicates the error of Archbishop Wright's contention that the graduates were "different," that is, dissimilar to graduates of equivalently small but non-Catholic colleges. It would appear that on the contrary a Jesuit education at Boston College made a student "different" from other Irish-American Catholics. It set them apart from immigrants of the previous generation (and a previous generation of priests), from uneducated Irish-American contemporaries, and from Yankee Catholics who were still sending their children to Harvard. But it made a student *like* other graduates of small American colleges. For the Jesuits found nothing equivocal in accepting an American version of Catholicism. "Yes, faith, hope and charity leave Europe," wrote Father Bapst, in the 1860's, "and take refuge in America." Protestantism, he was certain, was dying. Unlike the priests who would later write for the *Review*, he did not see "the American character" as dead or, worse, hopelessly depraved by original sin. It was "too noble, too religious, has aspirations too lofty to content itself with sterile infidelity." There had even been progress "since the [Civil] war." "Prejudices that once existed against the Church have gradually disappeared and now an educated Catholic whose conduct is upright, is esteemed, *to say the least,* as much as a Protestant of like character" [my italics].[35]

The premise behind this thinking was the opposite of what the *Review* was preaching, whimpering that the norm of Americanism was "blood and lineage" not "fitness." And the deductions from this premise carried the Jesuits and their students away from the inevitable, sullen defeatism of Irish pietism and into battle. Boston College men developed the conviction that a cultured, educated Catholic could equal any Protestant in "American character." Under Fulton's direction, they eagerly became members of a college club with an intriguingly familiar title, the YMCA. Members hoped to assimilate into Boston society, bringing to the task a suitable degree of polish and cultured refinement. Therefore its meetings were largely educational. The society's primary function was to shape the benevolent man. In this endeavor it was supported by other college groups. The YMCA, the sodality groups, and a strong alumni association were the means whereby the Jesuits mobilized the men for good works. And benevolence not only provided a merciful release for the activism of these young Americans, but it also guaranteed the hope of dazzling success at convert-making. What has been said of Charles Grandison Finney in the 1830's might well apply here, namely, that "it took the gifts of . . . [the Jesuits] in a country devoted to business, to gain attention for the interests of eternity."[36]

This emphasis on the benevolent man seemed to announce a harmless enough goal. It even coincided with the Jesuits' traditional humanist emphasis on making man himself central. Nevertheless the ideas which they introduced into Catholic piety eventually displaced the pietism itself. The mutation shows up best by returning to parallels with the small sectarian New England college. Both operated to graduate "the whole man," that is, men mildly conversant in all fields of learning. In both instances, the piety that emerged was, as a result, oblique. In "the whole man" the college produced a priest (or minister) or layman whose acquaintance with Cicero or Shakespeare gave him just the coin to provide him with cultural affluence. It provided him also with additional ornaments like a highly embellished rhetorical style and a kind of mannered verbal obscurity that could pose as ultimate clarity.[37]

Boston College used the metaphor of "the whole man" as a rival ideal to "usefulness" and to a narrow professionalism. But basically it served as an affirmation of the value of culture, of the power of "the faculties of man . . . moral and intellectual," and of "the power of free will to normalize appetition." The origins of this salutary emphasis upon reason may be found in Ignatian spirituality but need not be located there exclusively. An examination of the life of Fulton reveals experiences which were wholly American and which called into play both intelligence and determination. Fulton was a Virginian whose father was a Presbyterian, whose mother was a devout Catholic, and whose ancestry included Governor Wise of Virginia and President William Henry Harrison. He frequently reminisced to his students about his days as a page in the United States Senate where he heard Webster, Clay, and Calhoun debating. His family owned slaves and it was he who gave them their freedom when he entered the Jesuit novitiate at Frederick, Maryland. This man's mentality becomes profoundly fascinating when it is remembered that, like the small New England college, Boston College deliberately planned its curriculum to build men like the president. The students were to imitate his classicism ("Such men as Emerson and Browning he did not admire or read."), his traditionalism, and his tendency to convey his point of view with affectation and archness. Unfortunately, Fulton's theological position was openly anti-intellectual and complacent. What passed for balance was too often stagnation, and his humanism was that of the party of Memory. Yet he combined a multiplicity of functions as president and as such was greatly admired. He was what one Yankee convert uselessly hoped all Boston Catholics might be: "a genius, an infatuated lover of the classics, a witty and brilliant conversationalist, and yet an energetic and powerful administrator." Clearly in a graduate like O'Connell the stamp left a successful impression.[38]

With the idea of benevolence attached to the larger concept of "the whole man," it was a small step to the enthronement of *character* as the ultimate ideal. Whereas the college took seriously its aim in 1864–65 "to educate the pupils in the principles and practice of the Catholic Faith," by 1870 Fulton was lecturing on "Christian Character." Even by then, Christianity had become but a part of the harmonious total, "the whole man." The college graduate was to be the Christian gentleman. This is far different from the early product, the Christian, and would appear to be hazardous when the graduates are potential priests. "Setting up altars to gentlemanliness" was, as it turned out, a seductive kind of worldliness for the Protestant clergy educated in small northeastern colleges. The results were no different at Boston College. O'Connell's Baccalaureate Sermon of 1894 is an excellent instance of this redirection. He wanted the young men to be concerned about "reputation." They were to consider the need to enhance the reputation of the college and the reputation of "a Boston College man." He argued for the acceptance of the self-help model of behavior and for a reverent respect for the proprieties of the social world. Allowing himself no time for transcendental digressions, he described civilization as the "product of work"; it displayed its character as "the pleasure and grace of refined life." A diploma was the answer to social ambitions, he agreed, but even a good education was insufficient. "Your education," he warned, "may give you the *entree* into all that is best in social life, but without good manners you will never get further than the entry . . . [If] you determine to live among the educated and refined, you must conform to the best usages of such people. Say what you may, there is generally good philosophy behind etiquette."[39]

The remarkable quality of this sermon by an ordained priest is its lack of any doctrinal or dogmatic affirmation, and its scaling down of the meaning of such words as "reverence" and "philosophy." It could more suitably have been delivered by any prominent businessman. The young men, if they followed O'Connell's paradigm, were not to become men of fiery faith; rather they were to be "whole gentlemen." O'Connell, for his part, lived out the model, displaying much of its balanced superficiality in his writings on social issues in the 1890's. In an 1895 article in *Donahoe's Magazine,* he remarked that it was never his intention "to champion either side of the question [of the problem of widely separated economic classes in the cities], though it does seem that in the face of all the outcry against wealth, it might be well to consider just how much of the accusation is true."[40]

Eventually, O'Connell's consistent position on social and economic matters was to support the rich as benevolent and paternalistic while arguing for patience on the part of workers. This position was less a mannered acquiescence to the Yankees' social principles and endeavors than a logical deduction from "the whole man" metaphor. In this way—and more so than might be suspected—the metaphor was remarkably influential. It pointed a man towards the assumption of an essentially conservative social philosophy as well as towards certain modes of personal conduct. Enunciations of this sort were not to be articulated by Jesuit-trained clergymen before the 1890's. But given the metaphor one could predict their form even in the 1880's. The parts of society should fit together in cultured harmony just as the faculties of "the whole man" were perfect when harmonized. There should be no essential conflict between the individual and the community or between groups within the community. The wealth that would make one Catholic more powerful than another should not be despised by—or despoiled by—his Catholic subordinates. For the wealthy Catholic's duty was to acquire wealth; those who fell short, namely, the poor could exist in blissful organic union with these wealthier co-religionists and bask in their good will.

Andrew D. White, who commented on late nineteenth-century American colleges, probably would have dismissed Boston College as "stagnant as a Spanish convent and as self-satisfied as a Bourbon duchy." Yet in large measure he would have been wrong. For while the college was not in the mainstream of American reform, first, it never claimed to be so and, secondly, its social and intellectual impact was in fact significant. The Jesuits there always remained within the limits of their particular theology. Nevertheless, they did make some response to Darwinism, and they were directing the young men's minds toward the acceptance of natural phenomena as scientific data about God. They retained an outmoded Newtonian notion of the universe and left unquestioned the "laws of the mind" which governed the individual's reception of that universe. In these assumptions the faculty was decidedly early- and mid-nineteenth century. But there was always a salutary veneration for the intellect and reason. And this was a promising first step toward bringing theology into harmony with culture.[41]

Unfortunately men like William James and Charles Eliot were just then redefining the process of learning and promoting the *method of experience* as generative of basic principles. This made antiques of the new cultural gifts the Jesuits were bringing younger clergymen like Louis S. Walsh and William H. O'Connell. Yet having tediously proved the reasonableness of faith by "the laws of the mind" and having established the primacy of the intellect *against the powers of pietism,* these educators were not about to abandon speculation or the deductive method. Like Josiah Royce and the Scottish realist philosophers, they refused to capitulate to the scientific method in logic and philosophy. Yet in this refusal they denied to their students any methodology which would question formalism whether in literature, social theory, or theology. This tenacious grip on unalterable truths also significantly affected the on-going intellectual development of Boston Catholicism. It meant that though they were the official cultural leaders of Boston Catholicism, the Jesuits nonetheless withheld any real support from imaginative writers like Mary E. Blake, James Riley, Louise Imogen Guiney, and Jeff Roche. Typifying this, Fulton wrote to Louise Guiney that "hardly any of the present poetry gives me pleasure . . . I really think that the present taste [for romantic, subjective poetry] will blow over."[42]

As much out of misplaced self-satisfaction as principle, Jesuit scholars and the priests they trained in their image left it to free-lance writers like James Riley to produce poetry honoring the Boston Public Library and to Jeff Roche to join Yankee writers' circles or spoof them in "The V-A-S-E." In utter humorlessness the clerics sat at the literary critic's desk enunciating the traditional principles of the trade. In philosophy, their adherence to the traditional was especially strengthened by the frightening spectacle offered by Fiske and other Protestant theologians who were accepting Herbert Spencer's theories. This prompted them in the 1890's to reverse their earlier tendency to see themselves as part of the American culture. For whereas earlier the Jesuits had been foremost in supporting acculturation to American standards and values, they now refused to march any further forward. They came to the determination that Catholic culture could now stand on its own merits without an "American" component. This determination was held the more tenaciously because the university movement became a directly threatening and nasty reality in the 1890's. Harvard Law School refused to accredit Boston College graduates at the beginning of the decade. President Charles Eliot of Harvard and Father Timothy Brosnahan, president of Boston College, debated the merits of the elective system in the public press from 1894 to 1898, and often very acrimoniously.[43] As universities and colleges gradually accepted both the elective system and Spencerianism, young Jesuits like Michael Earls of Southbridge, Massachusetts, were learning that they could cultivate their own cultural garden. There—but never outside the hedges, as it were—they could attain professional preeminence and self-esteem. Earls, who was in his later years exclusively "bent on expounding a vision of humanistic Christianity," was not so narrowly motivated before his years with the Jesuits. In something of a cockeyed mutation from butterfly to cocoon, he changed from an amateur writer of notable feeling and freedom to one whose every writing, as one of his pupils at Holy Cross College in Worcester put it, "imparted a sense of Catholic belonging . . . of corporate Catholic self-respect." Ironically, scholarship served to isolate the younger clergymen still further from the larger community. Jesuits like Earls lived their professional lives in a limited world of collected (Catholic) editions and classics. Yet they readily won the admiration of their Catholic contemporaries, especially of secular clergymen like O'Connell.[44]

In the 1890's, Boston faced the depression, "new immigration," war, and constant psychological tensions. The younger clergymen became commentators on these issues. But the 1880's was a period of drift. Even the most observant local pastor could not predict that Boston College would have extensive influence or how that influence would function. In the 1880's, Boston College was still largely a small school directed by Jesuits—most of them southerners—and ignored as irrelevant by *The Boston Daily Advertiser* and *The Boston Evening Transcript.*

The massive disorder among their congregations in the 1880's did not move the clergy to call for help from any of the numerous social agencies in the Boston community. They had not learned that in the United States the official church was just one competing vehicle of social amelioration and social change. Instead and on principle they kept aloof. Because of their disapproving attitudes, Thomas Ring wrote to his cousin that he "had to work . . . quietly" for the incorporation of Catholic almshouses under the Board of Overseers. They rejected the public schools and even Catholics who supported them; similarly they rejected the Jesuits. They also sought to undermine the influence of the Sulpicians at the seminary. So, for example, at a faculty meeting of 1896, the French priests there saw as a cause of bad student-teacher relations the fact that the young seminarians were "too intimidated and put on guard by the prejudices fairly poured into [them] by the [local] clergy, and of which they are not ignorant, on the spirit of the Sulpicians." However, the managerial rights of which the local priests felt themselves cheated in the areas of social work, education, collegiate life, and seminary training were seized upon in the area of the family. Yet because they did not, for example, make themselves knowledgeable on the efforts of other agencies to better conditions for parental control, they could not profit adequately from surveys and investigations done under municipal auspices. They took no notice of causes for family breakdown offered by the Municipal Board of Survey in 1894, namely, that "many evils [attend] the want of a comprehensive system of streets." Consequently, their assessment of family breakdown in the modern industrial city was faulty. In fact it added to the dilemma.[45]

By 1889 the *Review* was assuming, and correctly, that the family was together only at night, if then. In fact, the priest-editors had at their fingertips all the external data on the apparent deterioration of family life: the father's absence from the home; the excessive timidity of the young children; the mother's overburdened day; quarrels and drabness and religious indifference and drinking. What they did not have was a knowledge of the internal conflicts and their intensity. Sometimes this was true because a parent could not make clear his or her anguish. At other times, the data was too raw or the problem too new. The clergy often refused to see the problem; or in other instances they could make a very canny judgment but found themselves forced to capitulate to the only manageable solution.[46]

The real picture was not in the evidence of families fragmented except at night but in the *unspoken* dilemmas faced by "scores of unhappy households." The father sought the home as a place of rehabilitation from work and the business ethic only to find himself or his wife forced to prepare the children for these same demands. He also found his wife, like himself, bound by a code of morality which refused them free sexual enjoyment. Whatever they did privately about birth control, outwardly they were not expected even to know of contraception. The clergy presumed the parents' agreement that "preventatives" were "mysterious" and "Anglo-Saxon." The men knew their homes were prudish—"parents," they were admonished, "should see that no newspapers with vicious pictures come into the home." But they were caught in an inescapable tension. They were made to feel all the psychological pressure connected with the generally held belief that the moral virtues —or tendencies to disregard them—were hereditary. In addition, there was the demand for the impossible sort of sexual restraint implied in one priest's comparison of married women to vestal virgins.[47]

The priests who wrote for the *Review* did not really know what the father's role should be. O'Reilly's articles on paternal responsibilities repeatedly switch unconsciously to those of the mother. The father, it was clear, generally found the children a burden rather than a source of recreation. Often grandparents lived with the family. A man's wife was not expected to be his friend; his kind words to her were a gift, not a right. In all this the father found himself irritable. He was not to bring home his cronies, yet neither his wife nor the priests wanted him out at clubs or the theater. Real issues regarding marriage were not to be raised. To admit real issues was only to point out the irreconcilables with which one had to live anyway, given the Church's stand on divorce. The clergy "helped" the situation by stressing "dispositions," calling for a calming of emotions to solve all problems. "The quiet life" became part of the clerical rhetoric, and it was a term with two different meanings. The wife was to hear it as "doing household chores"; for the husband it meant study. Both were therapeutic, the latter not to be construed as promoting intellectual excellence. Yet the father remained "irritable," as the *Review* acknowledged. And the mother continued to be—to recall the current understatement —"predisposed to nervousness and hysteria." In general and as the *Review* also acknowledged, "Home is associated with repression of the natural virtues."[48]

Both husband and wife were aware that, for all their middle-class comfort, their lives were nonetheless drab and ugly. Some of them looked to the church-hall for social involvement. What they found, in many instances, were clergymen leading the same drab lives as their own. Even the *Review* acknowledged a general criticism in 1889 that the priests were "too dull, too fond of routine, too uninventive." The *Review* recognized this drabness but chose to cope with it, again, on the level of externals. Or to offset the truth, stories in the *Review* and elsewhere perennially portrayed the clergymen as "cheerful . . . [and] kindly." The local clergy did join Williams in striving to elevate cultural standards but solely in terms of family and home. Ambivalently, they encouraged imitation of the Yankees but simultaneously issued warnings against these practices. They placed the burden of deciding these matters increasingly on the mother, cheering her with the reminder that marriage was a greater comfort for her than her husband. She was expected to manage the home and to save the faith. Everything in the literature and sermons points to these days as religiously lukewarm: there was no reason why the faith should not have died out. The priests knew that it was unnatural for the women to have sole responsibility for the religious education of the children, especially the boys. But "in our present condition, the father takes no leisure." So, like the Biblical valiant woman, the mother was "charged with the care of the servants, the children, and the poor of Christ."[49]

At the same time, priest-writers betrayed the fear that they were worsening a developing problem, namely, society's growing signs of effeminacy. Yet with no real familial role for the father and a recognition of their own ineffectualness, there remained no alternative but to rely on the mother. There was no other educative source qualified as both trustworthy and available. Consequently they urged her to form the devotional life of the child. In this she was reminded by the *Review* that there was always a "kind of timidity about our young men, a kind of modest humility, or rather humbleness." The boys *were* timid— it would appear that the word which the *Review* was searching for was "repressed"—and the priests more than suspected that it was because of her. So they struck out at the mother for allowing the girls to read about "the 'ologies" while boys were let sleep late and generally pampered by her "depraved indulgence." This state of affairs, they warned, could only result in the same spoiled boys becoming tyrants later in their own homes. Actually their worry was not about male tyrants but that the girls, by reading and becoming more intelligent than the boys, would be in a position to perpetuate the matriarchal homes which the clergymen themselves knew as children and now unconsciously resented. The same matriarchs would make increasing demands on them as pastors and would fill the seminaries with young men prepared to bow supinely before the French Sulpicians.[50]

If their approach to the father's role in the family was one of helpless bewilderment, the clergy's set of directives to the women was also scored with a fundamental contradiction. It was contradictory to support as they did the Victorian image of the noble, sheltered woman *and* to demand that the same Dresden figurine "get out and vote" in the school board elections of 1884. One would have to be an artist in balancing contradictions to condemn, as they did, the authoritarian family because of its "very silent children" and in the same scenario make remarks about "the inconceivable cruelty of childhood which would prove that the ferocious instinct of cruelty should be repressed in children whenever it asserts itself." In fact ambivalence marked the priests' whole approach to the acculturation of children. They strove to encourage the formation of the emancipated individual. "Let our young men," the *Review* liked to recite, "not be content to stand shabbily in the background in free America, where pluck, talent, and energy must ever win richest rewards." Let their parents stop preferring for them the "gentlemanly professions" rather than "the more lucrative callings of a less genteel profession." In the same way, fathers too were encouraged to immerse themselves in the competitive, if impersonal, economic order. Yet at the same time as the priests encouraged this kind of mobility, they refused to accept the consequences of their own preaching: emotional breakdown within the family. So when the father's central social concerns came to be outside the domestic area because of a multitude of business demands, the clergy countermanded their own orders, insisting that "the sanctification of a home (not business) is the first duty of a Christian man, after his own salvation." In this way, they added to an already precarious balance between the home and the market place as foci of opposite sets of values, the one stultifyingly static and the other recklessly dynamic. The *Review* summarized its advice as "advance-with-safety, progress-with-restraint, exploit-with-control."[51]

If they had leveled a real critique of the values of the market society, the priests would perhaps have ended in the position of the later social gospel ministers, constructively criticizing themselves and the Church. As it was, they went on to defend the system and, in their own bailiwicks, to "dot the land with magnificent churches." Out of it all, they took into receivership a mildly willing Catholic population. They directed all their effort to these clients, either individuals or families. Thus there was a continued avoidance of search for the sins of the community, even of the parish as a whole. The search was exclusively for the sins about which menservants gossiped or the sins against "the family sense." Yet they might have congratulated themselves as having been eminently successful. Archbishop Wright, who was a Boston priest in his early career, did so later in asserting that "probably nowhere in the world [except in the American Church] has there been so great an emphasis on the rights of the working-man *precisely as the head of the family"* [my italics].[52]

The role of controller did not assure self-esteem. Every reader of the *Review*'s short stories in the 1880's knew that his was a country rife with revolutionary ideas and exhilarating proposals for regeneration in fields like workers' rights and political practices. The stories themselves simplified it, dividing people into the supporters of change (liberals) and those who stood in opposition (Catholics). Readers would have recognized that to the liberals, Catholics were part of "the ancient, worn out social edifice raised by barbarism, ignorance, superstition, and despotism." Even the heroes of their own romances could sort out the two groups. The liberals were "the men of the so-called cultured classes," and the Catholics were "those . . . met with in a narrower sphere." Interestingly, stories like "Honor Before Honors" (1889) did not draw out inordinately either the disparagement of the liberals or the defense of the Catholics. The clergy also knew that they were the latter and that their own narrowness of operation was undeniable. Yet horizontal mobility in the form of moving from parish to parish was suspect even when it was possible. The career of a man like Father J. Antonio Molinari lurked behind such transiency from parish to parish, diocese to diocese. The ordinary clergymen would not have been surprised that in Williams' files was a letter of 1874 from Bishop Richard Gilmour of Cleveland identifying Molinari as requesting "a place in the diocese of Cleveland." Yet, as Gilmour continued, "I said I must have satisfactory reasons why he should leave Boston and [why] his Bishop would be willing to let him go. He mentioned that you had chid him for drinking and he also mentioned that he had been many places in the diocese—grave matters." Yet priests, as the parishioners drew to their attention, quickly became "too dull, too fond of routine, too uninventive" when they remained in stable jobs within the parishes. Local clergymen had no prestige as scholars; there was no Hilary Tucker making weekly jaunts to the Athenæum as in the 1860's. The pious literature consistently gave the *learned* clergymen either a Jesuit or Benedictine vocation. Pastors like Thomas Magennis, Arthur J. Teeling, and Peter Ronan were growing in prestige and power in the 1880's but this was still undiscernible.[53]

While the job of controller was handled assiduously and with talent in some parishes, in others the pastor operated with executive aloofness. A year after the decade ended, a manual of behavior for the members of the parish was made available. In fact Lelia Harding Bugg's *The Correct Thing for Catholics* was in its twelfth edition by 1891. It was written and published because of the distress of "clergymen" at "the ignorance and thoughtlessness, the blunders, ludicrous and annoying when not serious, encountered in their parochial work." This book of manners advised Catholics on how to *behave* after receiving the Eucharist and revealed a different emphasis in spirituality from a time like the 1840's when Father James Fitton's *Familiar Instructions* tried to explain the *nature* of the Eucharist. Yet the handbook was more than evidence of a change in pedagogy. It was an admission that a sense of meaning had gone out of such earnest, optimistic, evangelical efforts as Fitton's. The book also testified to the clergymen's desire to be vaccinated against their own people. Parishioners were warned not to pre-empt the priest's time, not to borrow money from him, and not to ask him to "go security." They were not "to harry the clergymen for letters to officials, political or otherwise, to obtain employment"; they were not to "reveal their ignorance . . . by criticizing the use of ecclesiastical titles." There was, it seemed, the unspoken assumption that in setting forth the minimal bylaws of religious conduct, the officials would be thereafter relatively undisturbed and the faithful would have the respectability they wished.[54]

The mentality of the generation of '45 becomes still more comprehensible when one surveys the devotional literature which priests were reading, especially works exclusively on the priesthood and written by "an insider." By 1890, they had before them *Daily Thoughts for Priests* by Abbé John Hogan, a Sulpician and rector of the Boston diocesan seminary. In substance it was a

Jansenistic plea to cultivate the ascetic virtues. It was also an illuminating admission that even the seminary rector could not answer the unarticulated but persistent question of what a priest was. In the Preface, Hogan set up "men of business" as the priests' exemplars. The book was to act as "a substitute for morning meditation" in the lives of men hopefully as busy as "merchants, the lawyer and the politicians." But the ideal of the priesthood, as it emerged in the manual, also required a set of qualities which were antipathetic to the businessman: the priest was "the great comforter of his fellow-men"; he was a man of pity; he was "the servant"; he was devoted to children; he was a man for whom "self-restraint is natural." While the priest was expected to fulfill each of these roles, he was also of "a higher nature." People would be as uplifted by the sight of him as was Winklemann at the sight of Apollo Belvedere. Hogan's priest was "a mysterious preternatural being" who would find ease in "the positive dislike" of the persons and things dearest to him.[55]

Hogan was writing because these light-bearers were falling like lightning from the sky into the corrupt world and its ways. Hogan's world was an excessively dark one, a world still darker than that of the local clergyman who already had his own cellarful of pessimism about himself and the world. Actually Hogan's world was nineteenth-century France. An exposition of tne gospels by American priests to a wide Catholic population had really only got underway in America by 1890. Yet Hogan and other writers superimposed the French situation on the American scene and were already talking of "the age" as "an *afterglow* of the Gospel where its direct radiance has been lost" [my italics]. Hogan was unable to forget the republicans whom he watched demolish St. Sulpice in the 1848 revolution. To him the fact that faith had "disappeared" was not a limited historical reality but a universal one. Comfortably, others than the clergy were responsible for this. They had as little need for self-scrutiny on such matters as they had for reasoning out their own vocations. "Every priest, in his ordination," he laid down, "has at all times a special assistance from God to see where his duty lies and to do it. He has special impulses . . . an intuitive sense of the proprieties of the priesthood." If, as Hogan felt compelled to warn, the priest did "grow self-indulgent and shift most of the burden onto others," the remedy was not reason but emotion. He was to read works like *Daily Thoughts;* he was to bestir himself to repent for his "love of comfort, and lack of prayer; . . . [for his] regard for outward proprieties, but scarce anything of the inner spirit."[56]

The decade of the 1880's baffled those who lived through it, but it does yield some secrets to latter-day students. Local Catholic clergymen struggled away from the sense in the early 1880's of being on probation in Boston society. By 1890, they had picked up an issue, "the school question," which seemed to release their hidden animosities and tell them where they stood. In this dispute, local non-Catholic political leaders of the Republican and Prohibition parties as well as the newspapers that supported them were ironically the priests' allies. For these forces bluntly told the priests that they had no place in Boston society and that they were consistently wrong and narrow-minded on public issues. Insofar as this justified the clergy's own hatreds and restricted "theology of election" ("it is no part of the Lord's teaching that *de facto* all men would be members of his church"), this was exactly what they wished to hear.[57]

The priests were clearly conscious, then, that by 1890 strident "ultra-Protestant" groups rejected them. Strangely they welcomed the openness of this. They also welcomed the increased interest of Rome in the affairs of the archdiocese. The Vatican politician, Cardinal Simioni, was determined to carry out orders and promote a flourishing parochial school system in the United States. He had conspicuously let it be known to Bishop Louis deGoesbriand of Burlington, Vermont, that deGoesbriand's friend Williams was in disfavor at court on the matter. Remarking on this Byzantine politicking, deGoesbriand wrote Williams in 1879 relaying Simioni's "exact words." "They write to me," offered Simioni, "that they have no Catholic schools in Boston and that there are priests there who are opposed to Catholic schools." Simioni repeated these words, deGoesbriand continued, a night later. The Vermont bishop added that they "may have been said with a desire that I would relate them to you." Williams did not grow in grace and wisdom before Rome, however, and by 1890 there was already sufficient evidence to convict him, if they wished, of "Americanism." Meanwhile he did nothing (if indeed he tried) to intercept the honor of *monsignor* that Rome could now confer on local priests. Such a title came first to Patrick Strain of Lynn. All that his brief diary tells us is that he had learned how to be cunning about finances and indifferent to his inability as pastor to retain both curates and housekeepers.[58]

This was the generation of clergymen—most of them five years away from silver jubilees as priests in 1890—that was in many ways responsible for the growing ineffectualness of the St. Vincent de Paul Society in the parishes. In effect, the society was lifeless by the end of the century. But the conference men were not the only victims of the clergy's psychological needs nor were they the most afflicted. Those most painfully affected were young curates. This group of priests was identified by William L. Sullivan, a Unitarian, in 1911 in *The Priest*. This novel is a failure partly because the struggle to understand Catholicism is vital in the author's mind but fails to animate his characters. The tension arises from the conflict of his admiration for and yet despair of the Roman Catholic Church. Sullivan sets all of this conflict into the painful relationship between a young American-born curate, Ambrose Hanlon and his "old Irish pastor," Father O'Murtagh. Abbé Hogan in *Daily Thoughts* had avoided the pastor-curate question or laid the blame for such "absence of harmony" on the "faults of boyhood" which a curate retained. Sullivan blamed "the consecrated mental inflexibility" of the older priest. Neither pointed to "a generation gap." Nevertheless Sullivan made it emphatic that there was a very real difference in the two mentalities. The young curate's longing for "honest intellectual inquiry" ran directly against the pastor's blustering ignorance and the chancery official's "patronizing air and . . . assumption of infallibility." Sullivan assumed that young curates had intellectually inquiring minds at the turn of the century. This in itself is remarkable. For to all appearances and into the 1920's and 1930's, all clergymen seemed to follow set patterns of thought, reduplicating the narrow dogmatism of the O'Murtaghs. There is no evidence of publicly bothersome gadflies within the system after Williams' death in 1907. Yet Sullivan's novel suggests something about this inexplicable disappearance of young nonconformist priests. In his creation of Bishop Shyrne (archbishop of Boston), Sullivan introduces a churchman who represented for him not only everything that ranged from gross discourtesy to interference in politics but also authority's answer to intellectual curiosity. Shyrne in *The Priest* was clearly O'Connell, the man who became archbishop three years before Sullivan wrote the book. He could not have written the novel before 1907 when Williams was still administrator. Nor could the clergymen born a generation before O'Connell have realized as they headed into the 1890's that they as well as younger men were going to feel the full weight of imperial authority shortly after the turn of the century.[59]

Chapter IV
1890 to 1910: New Sources
and Functions of Authority

PROLOGUE TO THE 1890's

In May of 1895 Archbishop Williams addressed the civic and religious dignitaries gathered to celebrate the golden jubilee of his priesthood. It was his last significant public address. The speech rounded out a commemorative week and was painstakingly preserved because of the occasion and because the bishop spoke so infrequently. He seemed aware of being the last spokesman of a past generation of Catholic clergymen and presided over the meeting with unaccustomed vigor. His address ranged from memories to assertions, and from past recollections to expectations of what the lives of Boston's priests and laymen should be. Yet his words were not merely serviceable generalizations for another polite banquet. They were intended to be taken seriously. For they presented a lifetime of experiences and from these a proposal of well-being for the Boston community. More than anything else, they reflected the vast changes in the Catholic clergy of Boston, changes that had set Williams apart from the younger priests and laymen he was addressing. Williams was well aware of the progression of circumstances that had brought this about. Midway through his speech he acknowledged of his own clergy that "the greatest trouble was not to urge them on, but at times to prevent them from going too fast." In the same way but at an earlier celebration during the week, he had given conscious recognition to a way of life which he had brought into existence for Catholics, and then lost control of. In that address, he appeared conscious of the unsure, catapulting Catholic milieu which had been created and in which he and his audience of schoolteachers and children had all been involved. "I take such pleasure in your goodness," he said, "not for myself alone, although I am mixed up in it all, but for the Church whose history we are making." He concluded the speech by implying that he was the sole representative of an earlier, cultivated Catholic tradition now subterranean in Boston and he would speak for its founders. He would, as he put it, "stand the brunt of all their effort, and what they stood for."[1]

But at the banquet Williams discussed wider issues. He insisted that "the good old Commonwealth of Massachusetts" had preserved religious liberty for all. He set out to warn his younger priestly confreres that the security of Boston Catholicism lay not in hustling along the growth of Holy Mother Church but in each priest and layman fulfilling his role as a child of the Commonwealth. In the presence of men who regarded Massachusetts laws as policies directed against them, he dared to praise the old Puritan Commonwealth and speak peace. "The Commonwealth, with its own peculiarities [is] somewhat cold and stern," he acknowledged, "but to her children who know her well, [she] is warm of heart. Whatever qualities she may lack, she has inherited a precious one from old times, and that is respect for religion." And to this he tied what must have seemed a preposterous conclusion. For to pastors who desperately drew strength even from so defensively narrow-minded a newspaper as *The Sacred Heart Review*, he proposed that "the old constitution of Massachusetts" would not let the ill-humors of the time "grow up and prosper."

Williams continued to outline his filial devotion to Boston and propose it for general imitation. "I love the old city of Boston," he recounted with feeling. "I was born there when it was only the town of Boston. When I first remember it, it was a city of lanes, alleys, courts and crooked streets . . . I have always lived in it, except while in college studying." He continued by discarding the fact of many *ad limina* journeys to Rome as well as travels throughout the United States in his tasks as bishop. "From the time I was born, up to the present, I have never left it for long; and I love it above all cities. I am accustomed to its ways; I know many of its people though I am not acquainted in the last few years with those who govern the city. I remember when I was a boy, I knew all the Catholics of the city—they all went to one church." Williams cited Boston as the meaningful context of his life. Yet before him sat Catholic pastors who were a generation younger than himself and who tied their lives to the remarkable growth of the church in New England. Realistically, they were not "of Boston stock." They were "paddies" to their Yankee neighbors as Cheverus, Fitzpatrick, and Williams never were. Their heroes were not Josiah Quincy or the converted transcendentalist, Orestes Brownson. Their idols were Charles S. Parnell or Pope Leo xiii. There was no Theodore Parker to battle. Instead there was a cruel and vulgar Protestantism which called for matching sums of cruelty and vulgarity, coin easily raised. With them was a still younger priestly generation for whom Catholic institutions like Boston College, Holy Cross College, and the North American College in Rome were starting points in life. These institutions offered a different cultural world which was, if sectarian, nonetheless altogether satisfying.

Williams' obsolescence continued to spin itself out throughout the week. To the members of the Catholic Union he reiterated that he wanted no aggressive Catholics. He wished for "Catholics who shall stand on their rights as American citizens, no more." Yet this was a major oversimplification. It combed out all the knots of immigration restriction, parochial school disputes, and Italian (not to say Irish) ignorance of what citizenship rights were. Where there had been the presence of controversy for decades, he called for "no controversies." Where there was largely distrust of whatever sort of government the other side might promote, he exhorted Boston Catholics to "pass on to their progeny the same faith, the same kindness, the same trust in their government." All of this was sincere but retrospective. He had not intended that the Irish should take over the city. He did not suppose that conditions in Boston after 1849 would call for redefinitions of concepts like "character" or would demand new approaches to education, municipal social services, and property-buying. He miscalculated badly because he was so certain that Boston and Massachusetts would remain the familiar world of Yankee supremacy. He was convinced that the well-being of Catholics would be served by conciliation. He counted on irenicism, a certain amount of childish hiding out, like building St. Cecilia Church in so unprepossessing a style that people to this day cannot readily locate it. He placed a heavy reliance on educated converts in high offices to bridge interdenominational differences and, finally, he hoped to avoid Rome's accumulating demands for greater Catholic visibility. The clergy could pass on the message of "the strong liking for fair-play in Massachusetts" as he was willing to do. "We do not ask for special legislation to further our interests," he summed up. "[Rather] let every man have his share, his liberty to serve God as he likes, so long as he keeps the laws of the state." Let every Catholic realize that Massachusetts is his home. "I do not say make it a Catholic state; we don't care for that, but make all true, faithful citizens, make them lovers of justice, and the Catholics will take care of themselves."

Eleven years after this celebration, another banquet took place. Williams had honored a young and dear friend, Louis S. Walsh, by personally consecrating him as bishop of Portland, Maine. The toasts offered at the subsequent dinner suggest a transformation vitally important to the course of America's social and intellectual development.

First toast: Our Holy Father, Pope Pius x
                Response by William O'Connell,
                Coadjutor Bishop of Boston

Second Toast: The New England Hierarchy
                Response by John J. Williams,
                Archbishop of Boston[2]

"AMERICANISM"

The elevation of Leo XIII to the papal throne in 1878 was a turning point for the Boston Catholic clergy. The lives of the priests of Williams' generation and that of the generation of '45 had been formed by proximate circumstances. The careers of their successors were formed largely by the far-reaching institutions of Rome. The papacy functioned with an increasing centripetal force that had substantial social and theological outcomes for the Boston diocese. To Williams the power that emanated from Rome was restrictive. But other clergymen who gained access to that power discovered in its encroachments security and opportunities for advancement. For clerics like William Henry O'Connell—in his thirties in the 1890's—Rome and its empire became magnetic. Ironically, identification with the Chair of the Fisherman afforded a certain air of privilege, a cultivated style, and an exuberant politeness with which one could compete with cultural Boston and win. For Rome of the 1890's was bedecked with wealthy Americans, a colony of "charming, elite society." These people shared with numerous European worthies the high-stepping, "hydrangea-tinted" pleasures of the Edwardian age. Like O'Connell, who became one of this number, one could have "the distinct impression" in Rome of being "not at a periphery of a circle here," as he put it, "but at the very center of things."[3] As for the lowly Boston clergy at home, they had no choice but to arrange themselves under the dominance of this new influence. Williams' sluggish Bostonian attitudes had long since alienated them or left them nonplussed. And actually O'Connell left no room for choice. He was consciously an agent between Rome and the local rectories. Fully aware of this role, he became the most successful of an emerging colonial officialdom with first loyalties to Rome. He meant to work perfectly for the new Pax Romana, and he did.

At the same time, the shaky leadership of cultural provincials like Williams, the Blakes, John Boyle O'Reilly's literary "circle," Thomas Ring, and convert-priests like Bodfish and Metcalf was further undermined. The zestful theological bouts regarding

"Americanism" as well as the merriment of writers like Louise
Guiney, Jeff Roche, Mary E. Blake, James Riley, and Father
Julien Johnstone lay a smokescreen over altering conditions of
thought. New and stronger forces than the Catholic Union or
the writers' genteel exchanges were at work. In fact, when the
papacy decided in the 1960's to shift from patterns laid down by
Leo in the last quarter of the nineteenth century and loosen
control, it failed to realize that its earlier imposition of rule had
brought lasting functional and intellectual changes. One key to
the thoroughness of these ideological changes was the degree to
which they adversely affected both the genteel intellectual leadership and the presently ruling pastors. The ways of thinking
held by the first group were *still operative* into the 1910's, but
not beyond. These men and women fitted into the *fin de siècle*
literary scene of Boston and the East coast. Their exuberance,
superlative courtesy, and *joie de vivre* were more characteristically Bostonian than Catholic. It is not surprising that it was
they who voiced "Americanism." As for the pastors, after 1907
they succumbed to proposals originating in Rome and enforced
from O'Connell's new episcopal palace on Granby Street.

"Americanism" was an ideological separatism from Rome
promoted by a number of the American bishops (including Williams) and touching upon one of the most fundamental theo-
retical problems which still challenges the Church: the problem
of integrating Christian belief with the everyday experience of
contemporary man. Evidence of this creeping separatism can be
accumulated from as early as the 1860's. By 1894 even a Baptist minister in Rochester, New York, was able to put the actors
as well as the issues correctly, if cryptically, in order. "One [of
the parties among the American hierarchy] is led by Archbishop
Ireland and it stands for Americanism and a larger independence. It is sympathetic with modern thought. It believes the
Roman Catholic Church should take its place in all the great
moral reforms. It is small but progressive, vigorous, and brave."
Reverend Anderson considered the other party out of touch with
modern ideas. "It is the old medieval European Church, trans-

planted into the nineteenth century and this country of freedom, interesting as an antiquity and curiosity, but fast losing its power and consequently growing in bitterness."[4]

In the same year, one "Americanist" felt justified in generalizing his own thinking. "The tendency in this country," wrote Father John Conway, editor of Bishop Ireland's newspaper, "is not to rattle the dry bones of heresy. Theology will continue to grow . . . for this is nothing more than saying doctrinal development will continue and in the region of morals new conditions of society will present new cases for solution." He insisted that "the Apostles' Creed . . . doesn't . . . contain the full body of Christian teaching." Rather, "definitions are the work of time." "Whether or not we shall reach the point of having Mass celebrated in the vernacular . . . as suggested to Rome by Bishop Carroll, is more than I can say, but we do insist more on . . . essentials than phylacteries."[5]

"Americanism," however, was a term coined not by American prelates but European. It was given further substance and definition abroad in Leo's encyclical of 1898, *Testem Benevolentiae.* Despite much evidence of "Americanism's" very obvious reality, the conflict was later hurriedly dismissed as a "phantom heresy." James Gillis explained it away in 1950 as a "disturbance [that] should never have arisen . . . Its sound and fury signified nothing."[6] American church historians have persistently argued that the American church has never voiced a real heresy, thereby simply begging the question.[7] Without raising all of the details, it is a fact that Abbé Felix Klein's French translation of Father Walter Elliott's biography of Father Isaac Hecker opened a transatlantic controversy in 1898. As late as 1948 the issues were still unresolved; vague distrusts and questions lingered. In that year, Klein was declaring the controversy a fantasy out of one side of his mouth and out of the other still justifying Isaac Hecker's fear that the Vatican Council had bound the church to the failing fortunes of the Latin races. And he was still making a seer of Hecker, still supporting Hecker's dismay at the passivity of Catholics, still repeating Hecker's disapproval of Catholics' "submissions to small tyrants and mere pasteboard absolutisms, their neglect of the press, their absorption in provincial interests, their clinging to antiquated machinery, and their lack of personal initiative." Archbishop John Ireland had entered the controversy by writing the introduction to the American edition of Elliott's biography. To the European clergy, Ireland was championing in it illuminism, activism, and cultural relativism. And in the same remarks he was calling the traditional Church "repressive." He was angering the Jesuits and secular clergy by charging that "the work of evangelizing America demands new methods" and by calling for "newly equipt men, i.e. more disciplined than usually are the parochial clergy, and more subtle in the character of their institutions than the existing religious orders." He accused the European Church of corruption, and he saw America's immigrant priests "from the Shannon, the Loire, or the Rhine" as men who did little "to make the Church in America throb with American life."[8]

It is necessary and still more illuminating to see "Americanism" not as the projection of European clergymen's temper tantrums but rather as a disturbed imperial relationship. The Vatican now faced the same problem of insubordination in America as did the English monarchy vis-à-vis Massachusetts after the Restoration in 1660. Similarly, it was not the people or local clergy that had got out of hand, but the magistrates there —in this case, the bishops.[9] In any parlance of power, this was treasonable. Some American Catholics were seeing the Catholic Church in the United States as unique, and they intended that it remain so. And some American bishops recognized that the Church had come ("intruded") into a worthwhile (though Protestant) heritage, and that for the legitimacy of this pluralistic culture a stand must now be made against Rome. That confrontation with Rome would result in a possible defeat was anticipated. In a letter of May, 1890, to Archbishop Corrigan of New York, Archbishop Ryan of Philadelphia described Leo xiii's reign as "a sort of inauguration of a new regime."[10] Under the explosive leadership of Ireland, the controversy was a repeat of the pamphleteering of Increase Mather in 1684—and it was another defeat. For the conflict ended in the removal by Rome of the rector of the only university set up by the American bishops; in the public censuring of the Paulist Fathers, the most American of religious orders of priests in the country; and in the calling to Whitehall, as it were, of the fiery archbishop from Minnesota. During the same initial spasms of centralization—and altogether reminiscent of Andros' mission to coerce the Commonwealth of Massachusetts into obedience—an apostolic delegate was sent for the first time to the United States. In 1894 he took up permanent residence in Washington, D.C.[11] Finally, "legitimate authority" was further restored by Rome's tighter control over the appointment of bishops. The raising up of such useful agents as O'Connell of Boston was part of this strategy. If there is any meaningful ratio between cause and effect, the conflict cannot have been just a problem of language. It was one of belief and action. As Leo aptly put it in *Testem Benevolentiae*, some unknown number of Americans desired "a church in America different from that which is in the rest of the world."[12] This angry indictment from the throne of Peter could not have been more correct.

Testem Benevolentiae was first and foremost, then, the clarification of an imperial relationship. This explains why the document was addressed to the throne's highest-ranking colonial official in the United States, James Cardinal Gibbons of Baltimore, and why it immediately and pointedly located Gibbons *"in gente vestra."* It testifies too to the perfect consistency in Leo's climactic exhortation: "One in the unity of doctrine *as in the unity of government,* such is the Catholic Church, and, since God has established its center and foundation in the chair of Peter, one which is rightly called Roman, for where Peter is, there is the Church" [my italics].[13] Leo's understanding of what could eventuate in a Wilderness Zion was marked not by senility but remarkable insight. Typically he was meeting a danger head-on, this time the separatist policies of the American church.[14] Apprehensions heightened on both sides of the Atlantic. O'Connell was in Rome at the time making his way into a prominent career in the church. He recognized this imperial context but, already learning the skills of politics, avoided the issue. Rather than be drawn in as lobbyist for the American church—a role which, as rector of the North American College in Rome, he might have been expected to assume—O'Connell played the royalist, a role that in the eyes of some of the American hierarchy must have seemed the sorcerer's apprentice.[15]

Williams, on the contrary, was guilty of "Americanism," though certainly not guilt-ridden about it. Operationally, neither he nor the other American archbishops went to Rome for explanations or dogma. The annual meetings of the archbishops in the 1890's were intentionally subversive wherever possible. In the 1894 meetings in Philadelphia, the bishops agreed to pay for the house of the apostolic delegate. But in return they warned the Vatican that one of its important collections would suffer unless *their* terms regarding American contributions were met. At the same meeting, the archbishops decided that they would not promulgate Rome's decree prohibiting secret societies unless forced to do so. A year later, minor suggestions from Vatican officials regarding the procedures of the archbishops' meetings were casually dismissed.[16] Even after *Testem Benevolentiae* the "sentiment of the bishops," as Williams noted in April of 1899, "is that they object to legislate [*sic*] for the whole country—many things should be left to each province." So, as the bishops well knew, Leo was directly on the mark in his encyclical when he isolated the principles upon which they were operating. "The principles on which the new opinions . . . are based," it read, "may be reduced to this, that in order the more easily to bring over to Catholic doctrine those who dissent from it, the Church ought to adapt herself somewhat to our advanced civilization, and, relaxing her ancient rigor, show some indulgence to modern popular theories and methods."[17]

Williams was guilty by association and was equally censurable as an individual. For he had, if the truth were known, "designedly" omitted "certain principles of Catholic doctrine" or "buried them" in oblivion. In 1888 and in what appeared to be the exercise of a loyal subordinate, Williams delivered a Thanksgiving sermon. Later he allowed it to be reproduced in *Donahoe's*

Magazine and at that time cited its basis as Leo's recent encyclical, *On Human Liberty*. What actually appeared, however, was an expurgated and freely interpreted gloss of Leo's treatise. Williams placed the natural virtues ahead of the supernatural virtues (as later condemned in *Testem Benevolentiae*), and argued for individual liberty from the nature of man's intelligence. Then in a mixture of innovation and orthodoxy, he built two cases simultaneously. Aiming the first at the Boston Irish who were still chafing under the school disputes of the late 1880's, he made an apparently easy, iron-clad deduction on their behalf, namely, that intelligence and liberty would result in truth, that principles of right would survive "as long as common sense . . . fills our community." At this point, he leaped ahead of logic, Leo and, most important, European ways of thinking. He insisted that men in the United States recognized these principles and he rejoiced "because of the fair-play extended in this country."[18]

Williams then turned to the functions of liberty in social and political life, ostensibly still following Leo's thinking. He praised the American liberties found in freedom of speech, opinion, conscience, and worship. Williams was equally pointed in supporting freedom of the press although ten years later Leo would denounce "the habit of thinking and of expressing everything in print." He argued that restraint would lead to tyranny. Always, he concluded "we prefer license to restraint." ("License," wrote the pope in 1899, "is confounded with liberty.") If Williams was adding to the confusion on this issue, he was somewhat more the traitor on the issue of freedom of worship. Still doing his twisted gloss of Leo's *On Human Liberty*, he wrote, "We must . . . worship God; it is the universal cry *of the nation* that we must do it, and *intelligence* tells us we must answer to God for it" [my italics]. But he was subtly substituting natural "intelligence" for grace or the magisterium of the Church. This was followed by circumlocutions about "the law of God" and hints that man's obligation before God for "following out the principles which God gave him" required religious pluralism.[19]

Unaware of Williams' "designedly" omitting "certain principles of Catholic doctrine," *Donahoe's Magazine* carried the full

text of Leo's encyclical two months later. Then it could be seen
how purposive Williams' omissions were. He had omitted in its
entirety Leo's long and searing denunciation of those who "style
themselves liberals." Among these Leo denounced "rationalists
. . . who follow an independent morality." Williams was clearly
unwilling to support these categorizations and had omitted
them. He also failed to pass on Leo's pontifical warnings against
"Socialists" and other "sedicious societies whose one object is
revolution." Needless to say, it seemed equally appropriate to
delete the pope's denunciation of "that fatal theory of the separation of Church and State." Again, whereas Williams sounded
like Vatican Council ii on freedom of worship, Leo called for an
examination of "that liberty in individuals which is so opposed
to the virtue of religion, namely, the *liberty of worship* which
rests on this principle, that every man is free to profess, as he
chooses, any religion or none . . ." "Justice," we continue to
learn from Leo but not the bishop, "therefore forbids, and reason forbids, the state . . . to adopt a line of action which would
end in godlessness, namely, to treat the various religions, as
they call them, alike, and to bestow upon them promiscuously
equal rights and privileges." It also becomes clear that only
after Leo's insistence that "the profession of one religion is necessary in the state," had Williams returned to the encyclical's
outline. But soon again Williams omitted touching upon the
fifth of the areas of liberty Leo discussed: teaching. Plainly,
neither Williams nor in his estimate the Boston populace would
accept the pope's judgment that "true science [should not] feel
aggrieved in having to learn that just and necessary restraint by
which, in the judgment of the Church and of reason itself,
man's teaching has to be controlled."[20]

Much of Leo's encyclical was plainly a phillippic against liberalism. Leo may have been judicious in his confrontations with
the real problems of church and state in Europe; however, he
was dangerously creating them in America. Or so he would have
done had there been hierarchical approval of such statements
as his final remarks on liberty. "Although in the extraordinary
conditions of these times," he concluded, "the church usually

acquiesces in certain modern liberties . . . in better times she would use her own liberty."[21]

There is little doubt that the messages of triumphalism from the bishop of Rome were not being relayed accurately by subordinates like Williams. And governmental disobedience was only one side of the coin. Rome also sensed a genuine theological heterodoxy. "We come now," *Testem Benevolentiae* persisted, "to what are [the] consequences from the [erroneous opinions] which we have touched upon . . . For, in the first place, all external guidance [individuals' acceptance of priests as spiritual directors] is rejected as superfluous, may even seem somewhat of a disadvantage for those who devote themselves to the acquisition of Christian perfection." Surely this was a paraphrase of Hecker's Emersonianism and as such accurate. But it was from latter-day enthusiasts that Rome sought recantation, not from the ghost of Hecker, a man who had died in 1888. Boston Catholic spokesmen from Louise Imogen Guiney to Father John O'Brien were guilty of such illuminism. Miss Guiney wrote that she wished the doctrine of purgatory "were away" and she commented directly on "Americanism" in a letter of 1903, explaining a casual remark as "that [remark of mine] is what the English [Catholics] would recognize as an 'Americanism' and it really is so: a sort of light-hearted, oblique, unconscious irreverence which we Catholics catch up and share, and inherit, and pass on willy-nilly." Miss Guiney's witty remark was harmless enough. However it indicated that even apart from Williams there was a substantial degree of "free-thinking" within the confines of the Boston diocese. John O'Brien, in his losing battle with the Unitarian minister, Reverend J. P. Bland, was asked in 1880 to speak to the issue raised by the Catholic Church's denial of liberty of conscience as found in the concordat with Ecuador. In reply he expressed himself as ready to dismiss whatever the diplomatic agreement implied. "I never saw the documents; and, as they do not concern me or my faith," he judged, "there is no reason why I should busy myself about them." Ironically it was the minister who was reminding O'Brien that Brownson had called for closer governance of the people "under the Pope of Rome."

Yet O'Brien's indifference to Roman regulations had popular support. Many Boston Catholics, for example, questioned such elaborate proposals as a nationwide celebration of Leo's jubilee in 1893.[22]

Father Thomas J. Conaty, already mentioned for the timeliness of his thinking, was quite open in his ecumenical activities. When he said in 1886, "This is an age of organization . . . [and] reform is the want of the hour," he could have been trying to summarize his assumptions regarding the necessary role of Roman Catholic clergymen in the United States. In accordance with this thinking, he was as eager as clergymen of other denominations in Worcester to initiate some cooperation among the churches in public charities. His consistent policy was to "join forces with other church groups" in public ventures. He felt no sense of "compromise" in maintaining this position in 1890. Yet Leo condemned as "liberalism" the same kind of *aggiornamento* aimed at by the Congress of Religions in the 1890's. Gibbons, Ireland, Feehan (of Chicago), and Keane had already identified themselves with this ecumenical endeavor. They supported the World's Parliament of Religions which met in Chicago from September 11 to 27, 1893, as a project of the World Congress' Auxiliary of the Columbian Exposition. The newly arrived apostolic delegate, Cardinal Satolli, was directed to check such activities.[23]

What Rome found most objectionable was the ideology behind such unauthorized roles. Reverend Anderson, the Baptist minister from Rochester, was convinced that the Catholic Church in America should feel herself advantaged by being "encompassed by free thought and spiritual religion [Protestantism]." Leo XIII was distraught by this very fact; he was certain that American Catholics were infected with both relativism and illuminism. For they were saying that "the Holy Ghost . . . pours greater and richer gifts into the hearts of the faithful now than in times past; and by a certain hidden instinct teaches and moves them with no one as intermediary."[24] Williams not only allowed the insurgents to express these and other views throughout the diocese in the 1890's, but, just two years before he was fired as rector of the Catholic University of America in Washington, Bishop John J. Keane was asked by the Catholic Union to be its principal speaker for a building fund drive in 1894.[25] And *Donahoe's Magazine* was also as worthy a propagandist of these revolutionary ideas as any mid-western publication. In 1887, it praised Bishop Ireland's call for increased Catholic participation in reform measures. Three years later, and when the circulation of the magazine was 42,475, the editors (one of them a Boston priest) reprinted a speech of Ireland in Baltimore which called for "a return of the gospel spirit." In the same address, Ireland warned that there was "a dreadful lesson [to be learned] from certain European countries in which, from the weight of tradition, the Church clings to thrones and classes, and loses her grasp upon the people." Priests there and more recently in America "fence themselves up within the sanctuary [caring nothing] about the untended thousands, the uncouth and unkept, the tenant of the cellar and alleyway." Like Gilbert Tennent, he attacked the style of the priests' sermons and like Walter Rauschenbusch he demanded "popularize religion." Baptized in American ways, the beads of America's language clung to him: "The time has come for 'salvation armies.' "[26]

One month later the people of Boston were invited to read in *Donahoe's Magazine* the Heckerism of which Bishop Ireland was accused in 1899. At ceremonies in which Father Walter Elliott preached, Ireland consecrated three bishops in St. Paul, Minnesota, in 1890. Addressing himself directly to the new bishops, he defined episcopal authority as that which should "serve the ends of freedom." A bishop "should show that the ritual is the casket and liberty of spirit the jewel; that the very meat of religion is the union of the individual soul with God's spirit and . . . authority its [the union's] safeguard." The Church is a sacramental religion with legitimate authority. However, "the natural virtues, personal liberty and intelligence have undeniable rights." If Ireland had concluded with his statement that "the natural virtues are preparatory to the supernatural," he would have ended in blessed orthodoxy. However, he took the occasion to

berate "Catholic political hucksters" and underlined his accusa-
tions with the dictum: "To undertake to be a Christian without
acquiring the natural virtues is like studying the higher mathematics without knowing the multiplication tables."[27]

Ireland ended the above remarks with an ambiguous admoni-
tion to the new bishops against "modest stillness." Before whom
one was to speak out fearlessly was not clear; Rome or one's
American constituents, American Protestants. But he warned
the new bishops not to "become what our enemies falsely accuse
our bishops of being, chief clerks in the Pope's ecclesiastical
employment bureau."[28]

In 1896 Bishop Keane was fired from that bureau, at least
from his position as rector of the Catholic University of America.
Keane was a popular speaker in Worcester and Boston, usually
lecturing on Christian education and generally citing the state
of education in Europe as benighted compared to that of "the
New World." He spoke in favor of religious pluralism. Even
more explicitly than Williams, he insisted that it was slanderous
for anyone to use the ploy that "the Pope holds views contrary
to our [American] institutions *which we are bound to respect"*
[my italics]. On the contrary, "the ultimate rule of every Catholic
is his conscience."[29]

Before Keane paid with his job for such independence, his
notions on "The American of the Future" appeared in *Donahoe's
Magazine* in 1891. He was again tying Christian theism to contemporary experience. In 1894, he continued this line of thinking, arguing that a successful religious pluralism could exist.
In fact, "this [pluralism would] become more and more true as
men become more independent and self-governing." He washed
his hands of Europe's obscurantism and authoritarianism, plead-
ing instead for freedom of conscience and cultural relativism.
Religion would grow in "the universal soul"—an Emersonian
term which Keane used alternately with "the spirit of the In-
carnation pouring into the lives of men."[30]

Along with the writings of Williams, Ireland, and Keane,
Donahoe's Magazine printed Charles Bonaparte's upstart pronouncements against European Catholicism. It also carried

Father John Talbot Smith's concise estimate of John Ireland as
as bishop who "now stands to the average American . . . for all
that is intelligent in the Church." For thirty years, Smith wrote,
"French churchmen have steadily closed their eyes to the spectacle of the Church in this Republic progressing fairly, independent of the state, unharassed by hostile legislation, working
out its destiny peacefully among 60,000,000 of people who
might be naturally hostile." Archbishop Ireland, on the contrary, was alert to any ghettoism and ready to maintain that
the Church must be "in harmony with its environment."[31]

If Boston may, as I think, be credited with the foremost artistic thrust of "Americanism" at the end of the nineteenth century, Boston clergymen and writers (always with the exception
of Williams) were largely only supportive in defining and describing needed theological innovations. Nothing makes this
clearer than hard-hitting articles like "The Future of the Catholic Church in America" by Father John Conway, editor of Ireland's St. Paul, Minnesota, paper, *The North-Western Chronicle*.
They were vividly optimistic and honest, and reproduced the
expectancy and experimentalism of Roddan forty years earlier
in Boston. They had the same developmental approach regarding Christian truth and the same self-conscious moral serious-
ness. The articles argued that as Americans, Catholics were
uniquely freed of doctrinal disputes with Protestants, they could
therefore "devote their energies to the more humanely generous
aspects of Christianity." American Catholics had the advantage
of bishops who were not quick to excommunicate social "devi-
ants," and they had the assurance that "the same democracy
that had blessed the American republic will bless the Church
here." Conway was expressing a revolutionary generalization in
asserting that contemporary experience was indeed a hospitable
environment for Christian belief.[32]

In Boston "Americanism" was strong but destined to make
little headway. First, the proposed pluralistic culture was choked
out by O'Connell's planting of a more dominant and—for the
general Catholic populace—a more satisfying cultural strain.

This strictly Catholic culture was to operate on two levels. There was to be a decidedly elite culture modeled on Roman sophistication and dominated by O'Connell for certain of his clergy and such socially prominent Boston Catholic families as the Bellamy Storers. For those below this group, O'Connell encouraged a kind of docile "low culture." Here he was a booster of Irish-Catholic virtues, Irish-Catholic mothers, Irish-Catholic peasants, "Celtic inheritance," and "Celto-American practicality." For the benefit of the ordinary Catholics he made subtle insinuations about Yankee greed. He also openly questioned the enthusiasms of those Catholics and Protestants who praised new developments in the Church by reminding them of the glories of the European Church, the ancient of days. Actually in this he was more American than the Catholic "Americanists." For they were repeatedly asking for integration into America just when Americans—Protestants and, in this instance, Catholics—were thrilling to their European origins.[33]

Secondly, Williams and those who promoted "Americanism" weakened it by persistently refusing to look squarely at any of the real instances of religious intolerance in the country in the 1890's. They threw dust in their own eyes in this respect and only paved the way for the more seemingly realistic measures of men like O'Connell. Finally and ironically, the outspokenness which the controversies provoked only better identified for attack those Catholic insurgents like Mary E. Blake about whose orthodoxy only vague queries would have existed earlier.

In touching up a supposedly authentic collection of his own early letters, O'Connell made it very clear in 1913 that only he and "the lower clergy" had recognized as early as 1894 the need to bring the archdiocese into the proper relationship with Rome. A letter of 1894—however tampered with it may be—reveals O'Connell's singular astuteness first in ignoring "Americanism" and then in latching onto the apostolic delegate, seeing the value of harmonizing Cardinal Satolli's interests with his own. The letter was a description of a ceremonial dinner for the cardinal in Boston in 1894. It shows a shrewd awareness of the disintegrating cordiality between the papal court and the American bishops. In the letter, O'Connell remarked knowingly that the opposition of American bishops to Rome was "expected and discounted" there. With feigned friendliness toward the American bishops and a condescending understanding of them, he went on to excuse them as, after all, "pioneers," men "used to the freedom of unlimited authority." But now, he continued, "the change had to come with the growth and needed organization of Church work and life here." "Organization" would be the key to the future. At the end of the letter he sealed off the past rhetorically, just as his own administration would seal it off in reality after 1907.

The description of the dinner for Satolli by Catholic church dignitaries had some revealing contours. "At the head table sat our venerable Archbishop and at his right the Delegate. I don't think they exchanged ten words during the whole meal, which I am sure was not the most comfortable condition possible."[34]

A DEATH—OR TWO—IN THE FAMILY

"Americanism" played like a powerful searchlight over fundamentally different groups within Boston Catholicism. These groups were especially at variance on the matter of a Catholic's right to integrate his Christian belief freely with his own personal experience. Those who reasoned that faith patterns should be imposed upon experience naturally showed a progressively sharper concern with the location and function of authority within the Church. Not that the *fact* of a shift in the seat of Church authority from Boston to Rome was under public scrutiny. To many it must have been imperceptible. Yet the introduction of the term "universal church" in popular literature and sermonology during the 1890's demonstrates that there was a new and developing concept of the church.[35] The attraction for consolidation which the term implies was commensurate with the larger attraction for corporateness in the United States at the turn of the century. In the case of "the universal church," authority was literally reduced to the person of Leo XIII, and he played in the popular mind no less a consolidator's role than

J. P. Morgan or Theodore Roosevelt. After 1907 Cardinal O'Connell assumed the role of authority, comfortingly sanctioning in his rising career the self-interested socio-economic mobility of the flock. But before that time and while the cult of Leo xiii was still growing, some Boston Catholics held to alternate views of the operations of authority over the individual in the church. These were finally rejected as was the group that held them. There then arose under the unopposed leadership of the new clergy a more monolithic Boston Catholic community. It had new social groupings, a new intellectual leadership, and a decidedly different stance toward the older Bostonians.

It would seem appropriate to make one funereal statement about Williams and the Yankee Catholics of the genteel tradition who were defeated in the controversies over "Americanism," namely, that they simply died out. Yet their writings, their mode of action, and their convictions about authority and intellectual freedom in the church still retained vitality beyond the turn of the century. Their aspirations and judgments give added clarity to those of the clergymen who supported them. They also illumine, by way of contrast, the mentality of those clergymen —the majority—who rejected the options which their thinking offered.

It is now commonly accepted that American Catholic writers, even more than their secular counterparts, have been unable to make peace with the world of sex. Jansenism, so it is held, permeated even their best writings, and continually produced a paradigm like: Intellectual Pride (usually Irreligion) has a shattering encounter with Innocent Piety (frequently a child) or the Corrupt Human Heart (the criminal, the sexual demonic) and "sees the light or dies or both." Nevertheless the circle of Catholic writers in Boston in the 1890's did have something of the range and humanity for which critics have searched vainly among Catholic writers until the appearance of Flannery O'Connor. These writers were supported by prominent Boston families, including some from whose ranks were many Catholic converts: "the Warrens, the Winthrops, the Tudors, the Wymans, the

Derbys, the Danas, the Wards, the Welches, the Whitneys, the Dwights, the Careys . . . the Tryons, the Tuckermans and countless others."[36] A number of priests like Theodore Metcalf, William Byrne, Julien Johnstone, Henry Austin Adams, Arthur Teeling, Michael Flatley, Hugh Blunt, and John J. Williams were either friends of these artists or were writers themselves.[37] The literary circle formed around *The Pilot*'s editor, John Boyle O'Reilly, until his death in 1890.[38] But they were equally capable of being adorers of Protestant writers like Louise Moulton. They were friends of Bernard Berenson and Vida Scudder. Mary E. Blake's *Youth in Twelve Centuries* was illustrated by the gifted impressionist, Childe Hassan. One young priest, Julien Johnstone, wrote poetry for Mrs. Moulton's "mail bag," hoping with other friends to dissipate for her the boredom of a European voyage.[39] Johnstone, in fact, dramatizes the elusiveness of the group. For this young Catholic priest had his collected poems printed in 1900 at the Park Street Church (Unitarian).[40] But there was nothing mysterious about Johnstone, Louise Imogen Guiney, Bliss Carman, Jeff Roche, Henry Austin Adams, Alice Brown, Michael Earls, James Riley, and Katherine E. Conway writing at an unparalleled pace in the 1890's. Everywhere America was doing so. These Boston writers presented a chapbook in the 1890's under Bliss Carman's editorship; they contributed to Herbert Clarke's imitation of the English Yellow-Book; and in 1891 Louise Guiney was editing *The Knight-Errant* for which Charles Eliot Norton "wrote the first edition."[41] They were flippant and defiant, humble and sincere, sentimental and didactic versifiers, often indistinguishable from other American writers. They were consciously Catholic but tentative. Each produced religious poems because they were immensely popular. Yet the poems were listed invariably in a book of verse that followed a very rigid, if self-imposed, pattern: "a stereotyped title, a laudatory or self-effacing preface, a moral or didactic poem, one discussing religion, nature description, a sentimental verse, one praising womanhood, a humanitarian reflection, a patriotic poem, one or more tributes to famous men."[42] These writers stood always on the fringe of the congregation looking out, as it were, at the snowfall rather than at the preacher. This was true whether "our crowd," as they called themselves, was acting as artists or articulators of social theory. For neither their roots nor membership descended from the Jesuits at Boston College. Rather, their lineage was from Holy Cross College in Worcester, through such early subjective writers as John Boyce and Charles Bullard Fairbanks, Jr.; it was also from Cambridge through Catholic writers like Rose Hawthorne and her husband George Parsons Lathrop; and it derived from Anglican Bostonians. Katherine Conway came to Boston as a news reporter from Rochester, New York, because she "wanted to write and . . . work for the intellectual life of the Church."[43]

These Catholic *literati* were relevant in Boston society only so long as that society remained optimistic that *aggiornamento* was worth the effort and could be achieved. In other words, they had to be able to convince the Yankees that nothing like dogma or arbitrary church authority would blind their personal perceptions of changes and evils in their shared society. This clarity would insure that the same data would bring Catholic leadership in Boston to the same judgments as those of non-Catholic Bostonians. John Boyle O'Reilly was able to do this.[44] He let his conviction that "authority must not forget humanity" grow out of personal experiences. *Moondyne* was an autobiographical novel written in 1883 and in which he enacted his days in Australia as a political prisoner. It was a tract on prison reform but, more widely, it was an attack on capitalists who take advantage of "the complexities of social life." Like contemporary Yankee urban reformers, O'Reilly was convinced that "human law should be founded on God's law and human right, not on the narrow interests of land and gold." His interest was in social and economic inequalities, and he contended repeatedly that social justice was an individual responsibility, that "no man who sees the truth however distant, can conscientiously go on as if it were not there." Old systems should be swept away and "every generation of men should have a fair start." In 1872, as editor of *The Pilot* at the age of twenty-seven, he was denouncing inhuman working conditions at Fall River,

Massachusetts. And in his collected poems, *In Bohemia* (1886), he was in league with Protestants like Vida Scudder and Henry James in censuring hypocritical, self-rewarding philanthropy: "The organized charity, scrimped and iced,/In the name of a cautious, statistical Christ." He reintroduced Brownson's name but only to criticize him for bringing religion into politics. He wanted reforms for "America's friendly cities," and he wanted to preserve "the intellectual renown of Boston."[45]

O'Reilly could keep pace with the liberal Yankee reformers of the 1870's. If he sometimes abandoned a particular reform measure because of his immigrant following, he never retracted either his fundamental openness or his optimism that "the world is all change. Every thinker is a changer—every discovery is a change." But, curiously, he dropped behind the Yankee reformers in the 1880's. In 1872, O'Reilly had unwelcome presentiments that preachers were "preferring . . . something undefined and dreamy" called "the Beautiful" to the more solid approaches of traditional religion. "Even the nominal reign of Christ is admitted because his life and his teaching have more of the beautiful in one lesson than all the modern professors of aesthetics have ever dreamed of." In this he saw a dangerous dichotomy that writers like Jeff Roche, Louise Guiney, and younger Catholic writers after him did not agree to. For whereas O'Reilly warned that "paganism loves the beautiful more than it loves the truth," Louise Guiney found *herself* "bed-rock pagan" because as a Catholic she had to "scrimmage" for the whole truth and yet "never [was] able to live up to the inestimable spiritual conditions to which . . . [she] was born." The "natural Christian," she wrote wistfully to a nonbeliever, had "a birthright of gladness and peace."[46]

The striving of these younger Catholic writers especially after 1885 for a glad Christianity which would emerge out of the ambiance of aesthetics convinced Yankees that a common liberal leadership of the divided city was possible and could be effective. The editor of *Time and the Hour* was not worried that "above all, [Jeff Roche's] authority was the Roman Church" simply because it did not interfere with his unusual "loving-kindness,

good humor and . . . sympathetic expression." The metaphor of
liquidity used for Roche—"He is a perfect brook, in fluent,
bubbling speech"—applied with equal aptness to the thinking
of the others. Father Henry Austin Adams' editorials and fictional writings as editor of *Donahoe's Magazine* in 1897 were
delightfully nonpolemical. His fable, "A Jesuit in Disguise," was
clearly intended to jab both Puritans and Catholics into an
awareness of their unexamined stereotypes. His sharpest weapon
was humor. To Protestant worriers he preached "Whom the
Lord would unprotestantize he first makes episcopalian," and to
Catholics who took the defense of their religion as seriously as
grim death he said that their efforts to supernaturalize the
clergy in their stories had made the priests look like "nincompoops." Miss Guiney made the same effort to introduce sprit-
liness into private and public religious discussion. She presented
the English devotional poet Henry Vaughn for imitation in *A
Little English Gallery* in 1894 especially because he "preserved
a humorous deference towards all things alive, even the levia-
than of Holy Writ."[47]

This group of essayists and poets could indeed give more
than credible proof that they were serious when they said that
"there are all sorts of types among the fellows who say Credo,"
and that Williams was going to encourage such free speech.[48]
But, as the 1890's wore on, they were less and less able to
present themselves as representing anyone beyond the Round
Table Club, the Papyrus Club, and their own circle of correspondents.[49] Their publications, even the very pious novels of Louise
Guiney, seldom sold well and never went beyond first-edition
printing without exclamations of wonder. Yet Lelia Harding
Bugg's *The Correct Thing for Catholics* had gone into its twelfth
edition by 1891. And Reverend Cornelius J. Herlihy's *The Celt
Above the Saxon* was already in its second edition by 1904,
though the young Boston priest had filled it with scurrility,
demogogery, and racism. Mary E. Blake's *The Coming Reform*
was a popular and significant pacifist contribution in the 1890's.
But she first ran it in the *Boston Journal* and it could in no way
be construed as sectarian. Louise Guiney admitted in a letter to

William Carew Hazlitt in 1891 that there was growing up a distinction between "the Church" and "the Establishment," meaning the parish system. How sharply she felt outside the parish establishment before leaving permanently for England is recorded later in a letter to her friend at the Church of the Advent, Father Harmon van Allen. "It's a fairly small parish here [at Oxford], and I have my fling in it, and am actually considered a useful lay curate."[50]

It would be a mistake to say that death came to "our group" because they took the losing side of issues over which the Catholic Church in Boston was divided into "liberals" and "conservatives." Officially there was no abuse of intellectuals, simply because the church was far from being a total institution. On the contrary, Williams wishfully promoted whatever literary talent was available.[51] The intellectuals were certainly careless in the emphasis they gave or failed to give to well-loved pieties. Mary E. Blake raised suspicions in the mind of one Jesuit reviewer in 1886 because she had not "given the prominence to the Blessed Virgin" in her verses which comparable Irish poetesses would give. Similarly Father Fulton wrote of his suspicions about Mrs. Blake in the 1890's. "I do not like it in Mrs. Blake's book," he wrote Louise Guiney, "that she says 'the Virgin Mary' [and] so effectually conceals her Catholicity . . . [and] does not exhibit sufficient hatred for our hereditary foe [England and the Yankees]." These writers did fight to maintain a free intellectuality and creative gentility among Catholic Bostonians. Jeff Roche and Louise Guiney wanted a community that would support a "philosophy of comment," or, as Miss Guiney put it in exasperation, that "appreciation of life" which was diminishing "in inverse proportion to the growing 'capacity' of ladies and gentlemen." But the crises they faced were more widely cultural just as their concerns were wider than Catholicism.[52]

In their approach to solving the problem of Boston's "third world," the Irish Catholics, the Catholic *literati* were alternately passive or hostile. Mary E. Blake made no attempt to cover her disgust with "Mrs. Struggle-hard and Mrs. Easy-money." "Haven't

you seen in driving through some of our Celtic suburbs," she
asked her readers in 1883, "two frosy-headed [sic] Irish women
with sleeves rolled above their red elbows exchanging confi-
dences over a rickety fence, while the open door of the cheer-
less cottage discloses a vista of general untidyness beyond?"
Louise Guiney objected in 1898 to "being re-born in Dublin or
to fall[ing] in line with the . . . Celtic Renaissance." Katherine
E. Conway was pleased not to be "part of the Irish language
movement" or "unmixed Kelt." Rather than proposing solutions
to Boston being "an empty little ranch" culturally, these talented
writers chose various escapes into aesthetics, "getting away
from the grim ethics of history." Mary E. Blake used her lecturing and writings to stand away from the society Boston was
becoming. Her pacifist stance in *The Coming Reform* was markedly individualistic and perhaps an embarrassing reminder that
her father had converted from Catholicism to the Quaker faith.[53]
To get the same distancing—and again quite like their Yankee
counterparts who were traipsing through Europe—Mrs. Blake
and Louise Guiney travelled out of Boston.[54] Miss Guiney eventually became an expatriate to England "from the horrible din
of new America" but not before trying other escapisms. She felt
that artistic concerns gave her leave to sing, "High above hate
I dwell: O storms, farewell." And she came to a new definition
of the church as an "enormous" organization, a concept which
eased her slide from residence in Auburndale to England. Jeff
Roche got away from history by hero-worship of Colonel David
Crockett and citing publicly the "fanaticism" of the Spanish
conquistadores.[55]

These writers never honed to a fine point their argument that
belief should be integrated with contemporary life on the basis
of one's own judgment. They left behind a tenor just disorderly
enough and certainly programless enough to present no opposition when O'Connell did begin the intellectual regimentation
of the diocese after 1907.[56] Nevertheless, by the 1910's they
were being presented as consciously loyal forerunners of an
American Catholic subculture later fossilized in textbook surveys of "Great American Catholic Authors."[57] Actually, they

enlivened the decade of the 1890's with an impetuous Christianity. They made this Christianity engaging and productive for themselves as well as for younger writers like Earls because they wrote out of a mentality that looked forward to "the Heaven where there is, in the fussy ecclesiastical sense, no church."[58] Yet Earls, for one, betrayed this decade and the artists who made it personally unforgettable. In his novels, literary essays, and lectures he classed them as voices of the institutional church.[59] There was just enough pietism and Catholic traditionalism in their writings to give validity to a later myth that they belonged nowhere but in a Catholic anthology. Thus the official archdiocesan history, which was finished in 1944, presented Louise Guiney as "essentially a champion of truths and ideals that never die." Yet Miss Guiney had seen truth "facing both ways." In a letter to the Anglican priest, Father van Allen, she championed the development of dogma. "How can countless generations keep a dogma . . . without accidental accretions? Is not the accretion . . . a proof of life in both the belief and the believers?" But the new intellectual leaders were eager to put ideas and people into rigid categories. They were men like Earls who understood O'Connell's move in employing one priest full time specifically to combat socialism.[60] Ironically they classified too the religious beliefs of the late-nineteenth-century artists and then imposed them on the experiences of later generations of Catholics.

Within thirteen months of his consecration as archbishop of Boston, O'Connell turned *The Pilot* into the official organ of the church. Katherine E. Conway, who had taken over the editorial desk after Roche, moved to the midwest in 1912, living thereafter as writer-in-residence at St. Mary's of Notre Dame College in Indiana. The *Sacred Heart Review* was closed down at the archbishop's directive in 1918. In 1908, *Donahoe's Magazine,* the only other major Catholic publication, had closed down. In 1906, J. Havens Richards' son, who had been a Jesuit scholastic at Boston College in the 1870's, wrote a biography of his father, a convert-minister. But in the swift turnover of intellectual patterns, his favorable opinion of the Puritans, namely, that "they would evolve a nation of saints," was by now totally foreign. Yankee Catholics like him were no longer the leaders in Boston Catholicism. In the 1890's, Lelia Harding Bugg was already writing of the emerging, wealthy upper-class Catholics who were promising to be as useful to O'Connell as the literary circle —or so Williams had hoped—was to have been useful to "the city of the Puritans." In her novel of 1894, Miss Bugg was pointedly creating patterns for the *nouveau riche*. Her characters in *Orchids* are women of society whose grandparents were born in Ireland but who are themselves reared in exclusive convent schools in France. They are patronizing to the poor (who must be watched as they are "ever on the alert to assert their perfect equality with the richest in the land . . ."). And "like all people accustomed all their lives to being leaders, and not the led . . . [they] regulate . . . [their] existence according to convenience and fancy, without a care as to what others are doing." Mrs. Clayton, an arrogant Catholic matron, is mildly upbraided by Miss Bugg in *Orchids* for her crass literary tastes. But there is also Marguerite, a young woman capable of "native refinement," gifted with "breadth of vision," and yearning "to be [herself] the dominant power . . . [her] money simply the machine." Through these characters, a few wealthy Boston Catholic families were being invited to take a new, self-confident and superior stance toward non-Catholic Boston. And, in fact, Yankees were already resentful of "their own impuissance" before the Irish. "They could present no equal counterforce [in the 1890's]," as Van Wyck Brooks emphasized. "They could not hold their end up any longer. They saw their glory vanishing before the invaders." Protestant Bostonians were no longer in a position to be approvingly grateful "for the lovely spirit of Louise Imogen Guiney." Now it was a matter of accepting standards of gentility not set in Boston but in fact set after 1907 in Rome.[61]

The passing away of Jeff Roche's "crowd" was not the only death in the family. The priests of the generation of '45 were also being gradually phased out. In a sense, this was the commonplace generational turnover, "the old Trojans in God's vineyard . . . fading away" before "the young men."[62] The priests of O'Connell's generation also forced into retirement the ideas of the older generation. The minds of younger clerical leaders like O'Connell, Louis S. Walsh, James Gillis, and Michael Earls were like windsocks blown by the currents of the late-nineteenth-century climate of opinion on consolidation, career mobility, and technological improvement. When the crises of the 1890's demanded that social and cultural problems be approached with new observations, skills, and accommodations, these leaders had the necessary sophistication. The older priests, on the contrary, lacked a contemporary point of view.[63] In the area of belief, both groups retained the traditional dogmatic patterns: the younger group was not about to experiment with fundamentals. The difference was one of sophistication versus crassness. Neither generation had learned to accept the validity of sectarian differences. But while the priests of the *Sacred Heart Review* lacked decorum and, as an outcome, wrote of Louise Guiney's friend, Father van Allen and the other priests at the Anglican Church of the Advent as "the pleasant gentlemen who play 'Father,' " O'Connell had the taste to manipulate "the Puritan" with masterful subtlety.[64] The goal remained the same; the methodology changed. The aim now was to wipe away the demeaning controversialism of the nineteenth century and impose an adroitly managed coexistence. Both generations appealed to a locus of authority to achieve this imposition. Predictably, the older generation reposed it in themselves; the younger leaders looked to Rome.

In erecting monuments to localism, the older pastors, like many other Americans in their own ways, were building on sand. They were as much the religious counterparts of ward bosses like Martin Lomasney as O'Connell was the counterpart of Josiah Quincy, mayor of Boston during the 1890's. O'Connell had Quincy's insight that if a larger unit could dispense as public blessings what was customarily gained through the influence of the local leader, that leader—pastor—"must lose his secret

sting and be reduced to a benign, responsible community spokesman."[65] The pastors did not see the need of consolidation. This
was true despite the fact that the parochial schools now functioned under a superintendent (a priest of O'Connell's generation), that the Sunday School teachers were holding their first
convention in 1901, and that the Massachusetts Society for the
Protection of Neglected Children now functioned under the direction of a priest. In some cases, the pastors were still victims
of overwhelming proximate needs. Father John J. McCoy of
Westboro wrote in 1892 that he was alone in his parish as well
as chaplain to "the Lyman School and the larger State Lunatic
Asylum." He paid for his own transportation to these institutions, bought catechisms, received $5.00 when he preached at
the Lyman School but got no pay at all at the asylum. He was
aware that city-wide organization was needed, but in the im-
mediacy of the need he would settle "for an additional priest."
It is difficult to estimate the number of priests who were exhausting themselves like McCoy. They were apparently numerous enough to justify Father Henry Austin Adams' remarks on
the "manliness" of the Catholic clergy.[66] In other cases, the pastors refused to abandon local hegemony or the hope of paltry
victories. Father John F. Mahan of St. Mary's parish in Everett
still refused the French-Canadians in his parish a French-speak-
ing director for the St. Vincent de Paul conference.[67] Priests
continued to rationalize building programs though they knew
that the laying of cornerstones had "long since lost its novelty"
with the people and that a number of Catholic "carpers" resented "the spending of money which could be given to the
poor."[68] They refused a dignified support to the St. Vincent de
Paul conferences, though that organization had paid out $559,-
310.35 in poor relief of various kinds since its beginnings in
Boston. Pursuing an inconsequential argument over having a
statue of Columbus (a Catholic) placed near the State House,
they made themselves look petulant to Bostonians. Ring commented privately that they were "hot-headed" and that he "heard
an appeal [for Catholics to protest openly when the priests'
plans were refused] from the pulpit . . . in a line of mis-state-

ments and prejudices that I hope never again to hear in a Catholic church." Whatever the causes, people increasingly accepted these clergymen as men with limited horizons. Some laymen tried to open the priests' avenues of information. One St. Vincent de Paul worker attempted to convince a pastor "that he would not hear everything about children and the placement of same [in homes as orphans] by hearing confessions." But there is more evidence that people had given up. Veronica Dwight wrote to Thomas Ring in 1891 asking "if you would be willing to call the attention of the parish priests . . . to the urgent necessity of opening sewing schools for girls in their respective parishes . . ." And Ring himself, addressing the St. John's seminarians in 1892, unwittingly contrasted the clergy's efforts on behalf of catechizing children and those of his own men who "by experience . . . are able to be of great assistance." Actually when he whitewashed the "holy priests" in this seminary address, he indicated that he too had given up on educating *any* generation of clergymen. Even out of the mouths of babes came a plea to the *Review* editors: "Couldn't you please tell [us boys] some more about things and don't give us so much advice about doing right." But the established clergy knew increasingly less not only about things but, more important, about relating to the wider community.[69]

The older clergy's outmoded mentality resulted in a variety of other outcomes. On the positive side, their inability to conceive of the Catholic Church as a worldwide "system" in the early 1890's did lead the *Review* editors to deal ambiguously with "modern Socialism." Wisely the editors treated it as a variety of "nationalisms," showing far more discrimination in this matter than younger men like O'Connell would do in their turn. Moreover, the *Review* editors still presumed that truth could be got at the ward level, as it were. They believed that a Catholic Truth Society made up of laymen-journalists and probably dominated by such federated groupings of clergymen as those presently publishing the *Review* could speak for the church without any direct control by the archbishop. Some of the priests had indeed helped to organize the North End Improvement Association and it was working well.[70] Certainly the pastors were aware of and grateful for the more influential role Rome was playing in the world, and, by 1900, at least Reverend Patrick Supple was aware that Catholic theology was best presented as a "system" to oppose the "system" of socialism.[71] Leo XIII was a real, if remote, hero. But, as their writings show, their interests and heroes were not in Italy but were still in Ireland.[72] Unlike the younger clergymen who were filling the pages of *Donahoe's Magazine* with articles on Ida Tarbell, the positive influence of the American drama, and the slums in Boston's Rand Court, their articles emphasized Ireland. Reverend Thomas J. Shahan's name appeared before an article entitled "The Ancient Schools of Ireland," Reverend Denis O'Callaghan wrote a piece entitled "Irish Race Convention," and Reverend Patrick A. McKenna referred to "popular reform" in the nineteenth century with data drawn exclusively from Irish history.[73]

This psychological alignment with Ireland rather than Rome was a case of being out of step. Still less shrewd and ultimately fatal was their "aloofness . . . from lay interests," or, to put it another way, disinterest or hostility toward things American. This foolhardiness is highlighted in the letters of Father Edward J. Moriarity during this period. His authoritarianism and isolationism were opposed by both Byrne, as Williams' chancellor, and a young seminarian whose request to Moriarity to work during the summer had been harshly refused and caused dispute.[74] Moriarity was not wise enough to realize that he was sandwiched in between two generations willing to establish rapport with American ways: with the older, there was a recognition of worth outside Catholicism; with the younger, a feverish desire to learn beyond the church and then embrace the techniques acquired, carrying them back into the church for her uses and improved reputation. The generation of '45, however, criticized as "a new enterprise" the Catholic Summer School set up on the model of the Chautauqua movement by such men as Father Thomas Conaty and George Parsons Lathrop at Plattsburg, New York.[75] With such an anti-intellectual attitude, they lost the genuine support of educated Catholics. And this was only one manifestation of what one contemporary Catholic layman called their "malignant spirit of distrust." In Boston, "young educated men" were "repelled by the work—this work of assisting the pastor—that so many members do about the church." "A Dialogue" written for *Donahoe's Magazine* in 1893 and structured around four men, a professor, a clergyman, a politician, and a merchant, revealed the clergyman in a far different light from the learned "Father John" of either Brownson's "Conversations of Our Club" or Boyce's *Mary Lee*. On the chosen subject of patriotism, the priest in the 1893 essay is no match for the professor whose arguments are timely and drawn from man's "accelerating" unity.[76]

Blind to the reality of "acceleration" and "unity," the older clergymen lost the support of other young Irish-Americans by preaching specifically to them on the uselessness of organizing strikes for higher wages. The *Review* ran one such editorial calling such young people "inconsiderate." Yet this came within less than a month of their own report that, with the sole exception of the South, Boston's average of wages paid to working girls was the lowest in the nation, $5.64 per week.[77] The *Review* editors were frequently unwilling to "justify the expression of a definite opinion" on labor disputes. More often they urged submission to unfair conditions because a paycheck in the *parousia* would be the reward of laborers who "dug mud faithfully . . . [and] washed clothes cleanly." This generation was aware of the "co-operative Societies" like Harmelville in France. But they appeared to believe that the Pullmantown type of existence was benevolent, that it was no different from the mediaeval organic community. In fact, milltowns like Haverhill were already scenes of gross injustices. They could read John Talbot Smith's current articles denouncing priests for their unwillingness to incur "disagreeable notoriety" by demanding just state labor legislation. But their answer was individual enterprise in a "hustling century."[78]

The priests of the generation of '45, then, were showing unhealthy signs of being old-fashioned men. One younger priest generalized about them at this time that he had "never heard or read in the United States a sermon setting forth the glorious theology of Justice and Right; . . . The American [Catholic] pulpit ignores the command, 'Thou shalt not steal' . . ." A tale by Father Charles Warren Currier of Boston called "Rest at Last" underlined a curious development in this matter of the clergyman's seemingly lapsed concern to preach an effective sermon. In substance, he presented a model of the European priest who in his sermons expressed his theology and outlined its proofs verbally—in fact, verbosely. The same author queried why the American priest had somehow come to be understood as "preaching" by his silent example and thus exempted from the same teaching posture as his European counterpart. For some reason, the necessity of intelligent preaching of any kind had been rationalized away. The young priest who had pointed out the failure to preach on the social virtues concluded that "perfervid warm oratory" had become one more "unsightly excrescence upon the intelligent corporate body of Christians."[79]

Unintentionally the priests born a generation before O'Connell paved the way for his rigid control over the church in Boston. They made straight the path by beginning to praise intemperately "the utter monolithic nature of the Church," and by trying to put the church in absolute control of education. They pushed religious segregation to its ultimate by stating that "a Catholic priest will not be present or make an address at the dedication of a Methodist Church . . . The Catholics who contribute to build Protestant churches are certainly not consistent Catholics, are not the sound timber of which the Church is composed, but rather rotten material which instead of giving strength to the building, in time of storm would be likely to be thrown off and mingle with the outside rubbish."[80] With such unfortunate metaphors, the priests who published the *Review* exposed and encouraged the mentality of an anguished group that could not accept intellectual freedom in the church. They allowed themselves to forget the contributions of John Adams and other Protestants to Cheverus' church. Instead they presented further myths to the people. An article on Father Magennis insisted that after 1880 "there was no way out of the difficulty [of providing Christian education] but by the parish school."[81] These older clergymen created a fostering environment for a more structured diocese but they were not responsible for O'Connell's understanding of authority. Nor did their paternal teachings contribute positively to his concept of how far that authority might extend.[82] In fact O'Connell was not the choice of the local clergy for the bishopric of Portland, Maine, and certainly not their choice for coadjutor of the archdiocese of Boston in 1904.[83] The evidence is that they themselves were largely responsible for their own ineffectualness before 1907; after that, they were victims of distant maneuvers as well.

THE LOWELL OFFERING

Our age has seen priests of the mind teaching that the gregarious is the praiseworthy form of thought, and that independent thought is contemptible.—JULIEN BENDA, *The Treason of the Intellectuals*

William Henry O'Connell decisively altered the intellectual life of Boston Catholicism when he became archbishop in 1907. Behind his swift and total centralization of the diocese lay the conception of an authoritarian scheme of things that was basically medieval. Fit government for the church was defined not by the specific problems of the total Boston community but by abstract and absolute prescriptions given out in Rome. Basic principles, completely antecedent to practical experience, were arbitrarily set down. Policy was not arrived at by synods or discussion. In many ways, it is difficult to account for this way of proceeding. If O'Connell and the other leading clergymen of his generation had been unduly isolated from adult personal experience or if the lasting impression of their earlier lives had been one of geographical and educational discontinuity, this authoritarianism and refusal to rely on experience could seem consistent. In fact, if the consolidation of the diocese were examined without certain of its features, it might be thought simply very American. For if O'Connell had never gone to Rome and learned there the techniques of administration, he would

177

probably have been superior in this art by being fully and willingly, as he was, a man of his times in the United States. Yet
experience did come into the lives of O'Connell and the other
clergymen in a very coherent way; they were constantly evaluat-
ing their own experiences. O'Connell was superb and visionary
in his imaginativeness, his power of organization, his courage
at taking risks, his ability to inspire confidence in businessmen,
his driving force and tireless energy. Yet he demanded the pre-
rogatives of a medieval churchman. Upon a canny awareness of
political and ecclesiastical realities of all sorts, he, Louis S.
Walsh, Michael Earls, and other church leaders of their generation superimposed a reactionary notion of authority. This imposition of one set of ideas upon another is the key to their own
mentality as well as that of the Boston Catholic priests who had
to submit to what one writer in another context called "intellectual martial law."

Even as a young man, Louis S. Walsh was in constant won-
derment at the new experiences and roles opening rather effort-
lessly to him as a member of his generation.[84] Later as bishop
of Portland, Maine, he was thrilled at his first Confirmation
ceremonies noting naïvely, "First time for me—first boy, John
Joseph White, 11 years, first girl, Anne Mary Richards, 13."[85]
His earlier life as a student at Holy Cross College, his experiences at Issy and Paris, his role as instructor at St. John's and
then particularly his appointment as superintendent of schools
in the Boston archdiocese made him different from the priests
he had known in his youth. He never dropped Williams as an
ideal; quite the contrary, the lasting thrill of his student days at
St. Sulpice was a visit from Williams and Bishop Matthew
Harkins. However, he was quick to criticize men like Healy for
their failure to realize that "times have changed." As might be
expected, he was relentless in reshaping diocesan policy when
the opportunities came to him.[86] As a boy at Holy Cross in the
late 1870's, he read the daily papers assiduously and requested
his parents to save their copies of the Sunday *Herald* so he
might read them during vacations. He was knowledgeable but

cynical about national and local politics; he was petty about grades, expecting excellence of himself and jealous of a young friend at Boston College who had received the same number of honors "tickets" as he. This characteristic weighing of experiences emerges most prominently in the 250-page diary kept while in Europe from 1879 to 1882. He was observing (and deploring) English railway equipment as "far behind the age"; with all of the bravado of John Adams when he was in Europe, Walsh *says* he would rather walk in the Boston Common than Hyde Park. He was determined to see works of art and therefore paid out much of his meager funds in admissions' fees. He put Albert Hall, as he noted it, "under . . . [his] inspection" and he was "re-inspecting" Westminster Abbey on a second day. His notations after encountering a "London bum" again reveal him as willful and wily. He writes introspectively, "Surely, it was enough to make me homesick . . . but I then considered how many others had experienced the same difficulties—how useful they might be to me should I determine . . . to overcome them."[87]

In France, Walsh continued this barrister's way of assessing both sides of his own experiences. The entries are very often summaries of his recent experiences, opportunities for him to determine why even the most ordinary experiences and events may have unusual value. At Issy he felt himself very much an American; there was a heightened "national sense" because of the knots of Boston priests travelling through Europe. To "learn about the true nature of the French people," he disobeyed the seminary rules one summer by staying with another seminarian at a hotel in Paris during the July 14 celebrations. He took time in the diary entry to reflect later on a great dancehall at Baden: "said I [to] myself, if the young Salem folks saw this place would they not go up into raptures over it." He extracted every contrast possible from the data being gathered, noting that German priests go to beer gardens, are "among the people and are quite at home." He saw this making "a great difference between the relations of Priests and people." But he was not certain that it was not "a heavy, lazy way of living." In this spectator's role, he retained the honesty of avoiding generalizations;

the method of induction was rigidly sustained, trusting "its [the tour's] many lessons will be useful . . ."[88]

Michael Earls and William Henry O'Connell were simultaneously gatherers and jugglers of experience. The "cosmopolitan air" which characterized Earls to his later students was, like Walsh's, something he came to in his seminary and preseminary days.[89] Before completing his secondary schooling, he got a full-time job at Hamilton Woollen Mills, a plant near his home in Southbridge, Massachusetts. He worked there for three years, earning money to attend Holy Cross, teaching French-Canadian children in the public evening school and working in a drugstore. His experiences at Holy Cross (1893 to 1896) were consistent with his literary aspirations. He edited the school paper, was excited about the John Boyle O'Reilly circle in Boston and began a lasting friendship with Louise Imogen Guiney in the mid-1890's. In 1896 and 1897 he did graduate studies at Georgetown. Reverend Thomas Conaty was rector of the Catholic University of America during those years. He gave Earls letters of introduction to Oliver Wendell Holmes, Jeff Roche, and Katherine E. Conway who in turn introduced him to Catholic authors like Charles W. Stoddard and Maurice Francis Egan. In 1897–1898 he saw Europe as a traveling companion, an innovation that was a characteristic of America's "younger generation." He said that he "saw the [Spanish-American] war as a European" and criticized America's war fever and belligerency. He was highly impressionable and introspective, and he was very aware that on-going experiences were "making up" his life. Astonishingly the bulk of his writings until his death are disguised and overt reminiscences of the experiences of one decade, the 1890's.[90]

William Henry O'Connell savored and gave value to experiences in the same way. In 1899 he wrote a letter to his sister from the North American College where he was rector. He was then forty. "When I look back on my own life," he wrote, "it has been one constant strain of hard, hard work with very little assistance . . . [But] young people ought to be brought to depend on themselves . . . If I had money, it might be different—but what is the use of pretending to have what we have not . . .

Some day God may give me more, but until He does I can only be satisfied . . . I have almost broken myself down straining for the impossible—now I must give it up for I see it does no good and doesn't make me any richer."[91] These remarks, callous as they may appear for a priest, reveal O'Connell's difficult life as the son of immigrants.[92] They suggest that he had always felt and resented their severe financial destitution, but that this resentment was heightened by the opulent, smartly aristocratic society into which he was working his way in the 1890's as rector of the North American College. He took material success to be an outcome of fidelity to God and a sign of God's reciprocal blessing. This appears in an address he delivered as bishop of Portland in 1902. "The strides which our people are daily making in the betterment of their social conditions and in their material prosperity . . . is to us an unmistakeable sign of God's blessing upon this faithful children."[93] For O'Connell, Rome offered both social status and material prosperity. He was eager and calculating in seizing opportunities for promotion. He had already sized up the Roman mind as "perfectly conscious of the fact that it is the norm as the true measure of Christian principles in science and faith" and he meant to imitate it. In this atmosphere "we young ecclesiastics," as he wrote much later, "soon began to feel entirely at ease."[94] Actually he did not "feel at ease" then, or later in Boston, unless he could enforce the kind of order he needed on all matters under his control. But this was possible and he brought it about first by reorganizing the North American College and then by applying to the Boston diocese the administrative techniques learned by living in Vatican City.

When they became leaders in their own respective positions, O'Connell, Walsh, and Earls appeared to formulate and enforce policies with little or no reference to the particular needs of individuals or situations. They laid down laws on Catholic behavior, Catholic belief or Catholic literary criticism. They allowed little room for exceptions. O'Connell held that *his* definition of the good and the just was universally correct and must be adopted by priests and laymen alike. This definition was translated into a detailed codification which in fact embraced a man's professional, social, recreational, and intellectual life. Walsh was more temperate than O'Connell but he also demanded absolute fidelity to detail—from himself and others. In his diary he set up a strange dissociation. He referred to himself continually as "the bishop" and watched himself as he played his role. Earls too appeared to be unconcerned about the necessarily accidental aspects of life. In his many novels, experience was made to conform to formulae.

It is especially crucial to note how and upon which groups O'Connell demanded intellectual submission to his decisions. He excepted the rich and the well-born from the obligations of blind obedience to ecclesiastical authority. His years across the Atlantic had taught him how to be an urbane churchman, how to take cognizance of social distinctions. His position at the North American College set him among churchmen and other leaders who feared popular ideas. In Rome he became like a European conservative. As late as 1919 he was still convinced that it was "monstrous for the masses to have an equal vote with men of property and education." He was frankly elitist; he compromised in his career with democracy but retained the belief throughout that little good could come of it.[95] In Rome he was surrounded by "international gentlemen," old-school aristocrats of the pre-World-War-I era who conducted diplomacy "for the welfare of Europe."[96] From this class of titles, parties, and palazzos, he received "all sorts of flattering attention." He was elated by mingling with "the best of the colony [around the Vatican and Italian courts] and [enjoying] the cosmopolitan life." He found Catholics of similar wealth and breeding in Boston. They were the Catholics "who were running the world" and because of them "the machinery of the world was working well." They were "for good morals, as well as for good manners . . . the finest thing the civilized world has ever known," and he did not exact of them an absolute intellectual obedience. They could be trusted to make sound judgments on the basis of their own experiences and their daily affairs or business.[97] In fact "by

their fine American character as well as by their wealth and social position" these compatriots were "a considerable factor in
raising up and holding very high standards of Christian social
life."[98] When O'Connell became archbishop, he set up a double
standard of morality to protect Catholics of this kind. Such
Catholic women were allowed to wear low-cut evening gowns
although the common people were not. Even Mrs. Jack Gar-
diner, one of Boston's leading socialites, knew that.[99] For the
well-bred, being "Catholic" carried few limitations. For ordinary
Catholics, however, the "distinct Catholic lives" of which O'Connell so often spoke and wrote were to be formed by strict Catholic rules of behavior, Catholic ideals, Catholic history, and Catholic institutions.[100] He set different norms for the masses while
at the some time creating a "high culture" for the socially superior Catholics. He of course adopted for himself the distinctly
wider norms. He literally moved in with this Catholic nobility
when as a result of the *first* full meeting of clergymen he was presented with a new and "suitable Episcopal Residence."[101]

The kind of intellectual controls which O'Connell exerted on
the Catholic population best exemplify how his policies operated
and how he perceived himself as supreme ecclesiastical authority in Boston. By 1900, one-half of Boston's population was
sharing a suburban environment of some kind. Nevertheless to
a "progressive" like Robert A. Woods their outlook on "politics
and life in general . . . [was] barbaric." Irish Catholics in the
1890's were reacting harshly to the pressures from newer immigrant groups. Young Irish boys still formed the city's gangs; if
one of their number were arrested, "a dance was 'run' on a raf-
fle held by the gang to bail him out." It was on this raucous and
still insecure population that O'Connell laid his prescriptions.
As he judged it, such masses "demanded . . . thought ready-
made."[102] In order to regulate it, O'Connell presented the Irish-
Catholic population with an extreme idealization of itself. Since
the ideal Irish-American type fortuitously included the component of submissiveness, this device became one of the foremost
of O'Connell's controls.

O'Connell, Earls, and Walsh promoted the idealization of the

Boston Irish, even though it was *because* of their coarse limitations. Earls, for example, was trying to set new standards for Catholic writers during this period. Yet Father Cornelius Herlihy's racist tract, *The Celt Above the Saxon,* was considered suitable for the average reader although it was considerably below the new aesthetic standards proposed by Earls. Earls cheapened his own talents by writing sentimental stories for a gullible public. His many novels twisted everything taught him by the experiences of the 1890's. Nonetheless they served his purposes. The Irishman was honored as a lyrical, untainted "dreamer" and as the builder of a "humble household . . . endeavoring to perpetuate a nation's [Ireland's] birthright in song and music, [and] fostering the Irish love of great traditions." Irish Americans were persons who could "engage seriously with the sternest realities of life . . . [but also] find it beneficial to play child at times." Above all, they were Christian idealists with "solid assurance in [their] beliefs and morals." Louis Walsh, who was also writing in the 1890's and until 1915, similarly created mythical figures for the Irish to imitate. He presented the early Catholic settlers of Salem as "merrily sawing wood," while he conveniently neglected to mention the destructive eccentricities of Salem's first priest, Father Thayer. O'Connell created these sorts of stereotypes throughout his career. One of the strong consistencies between the letters which he published in 1915 and his autobiography written in 1934 was the determination to idealize and justify the Irish American. "The Puritan atmosphere," he wrote in his *Recollections,* "may deaden but never really kill [one with a Celtic inheritance]." Elsewhere his pages are filled with "Celtic mirth," "workers with unfailing hope," faithful Catholics attending "devotions and missions," and simple folk of the 1870's and 1880's who were "joyous in their poverty," enjoying simple fiddlers' music and "entirely devoid of anything like vulgarity and impropriety."[103]

While Irish Catholics were being congratulated for their splendid Celtic particularities, at the same time their hates were being supported. Earls' stories and poems presented the Yankee as a fretful mercenary who built reform around empty churches.

His university separated students into "exclusive sets and societies" whereas Holy Cross College "appeared more like home, with simple, pleasant domesticities . . . a great happy unit filled with mental and physical health." The Puritan's social relations were "a bloodless code of conventionalities"; his novelists were "sentimental and dogmatic"; and his religious leaders could offer nothing more than "generalities . . . splendid reaches out into the realms of the indefinite." The Yankee was actually a nonintellectual, a man "kept from self-introspection and any analysis of his own character." Earls also openly encouraged popular anti-Semitism and blind scorn of "socialists." In *Marie of the House d'Anters*, he mercilessly typed the Jews, even ridiculing their physical characteristics. They were "men of medium height, generally inclining toward corpulency as they become prosperous." They were inherently villainous, likely to be socialists and generally advocates of free-love. With characteristic pretentiousness, Earls used French to describe the nose of one of his antiheroes, "Steiny." The English language, however, conveyed the intensity of his feelings more powerfully. "His nose," he wrote after portraying Steinberg as stupid, hypocritical, and traitorous to his own father, "hung down over a disgusted mouth."[104]

Two levels of learning were clearly going on within the Boston Catholic community at the same time. On the level of "high culture," men like O'Connell and Earls were forcing their way out of both the reality and the public image of themselves as curious products of a monkish, dated learning. They wished to be courted by the clever, to be like the fortunate of the world. Yet at the same time they were supplying this identical medieval learning to the populace. They knew as early as 1886 that the bulk of Boston's legislation regarding prisons and other public institutions "followed the tolerant line." Yet Earls perpetuated the image of Yankee lawmaking as "official sang-froid."[105] In their own lives, these leading clergymen continued to experience life in an unfettered way. Publicly they warned the people against materialistic ambitions or wanting to imitate the Yankee too greedily. But privately O'Connell blessed the ambitions of his friend, the industrialist William F. Draper. Earls desired nothing more than to relive his college years of the 1890's when Holy Cross and Georgetown seemed to be closing the distance between themselves and Harvard.[106] They were consciously forging considerable intellectual careers. The people and local clergymen, however, were to be blockaded from such avenues. Not only were certain experiences to be excluded but history, that safe and manageable guide to selected facts, was employed to keep the would-be romantic artist, on the one hand, and the quasi-iconoclastic scientist, on the other, out of the road entirely. Historical writing was a favorable pursuit; it was serviceable to explain the past and present.[107] So Earls presented the historical researches of his hero in *Marie* as honorable studies whereas Steiny, *lacking* a knowledge of history, merely enunciated "flat platitudes." Walsh's explanation of Protestant hostility toward Catholics in Salem was simplistically reduced to "a problem of history."[108] O'Connell most consistently used history. "The events of history," he argued, "can be explained only by going back to the origins of the principles, whether religious, philosophical or social of which they were the logical outcome." So hastening back, he found that "absolutism and individualism" came out of the Reformation and found their way into the thinking of such men as "the capitalists of Lowell" through the writings of Adam Smith, John Locke, and John Stuart Mill. The civilizing principles resided in the Catholic Church, "the mother of all the arts as well as the sciences and literature and culture," and so on. Using history, O'Connell also rewrote—and discredited—the administration of Williams.[109] The study of history also gave a sense of continuity and universality. O'Connell and Earls appreciated it as the mechanism whereby they got to eminently literate positions. For if one studied the classics and earlier civilizations, one would become adept—as Earls was— at punctuating one's writings with untranslated Latinisms, or neoscholastic mixtures like "the loom is Ignatian, the warp is Alerican." Such a show of pedantry together with the method of historical biography would inspire and move the masses. Leo XIII became the obvious hero of Earls' *Marie* and lurked behind

every fictional clergyman ("how kindly, yet how authoritatively
he spoke").[110] In three lengthy essays in *Donahoe's Magazine*
by another priest-writer, Father Mortimer E. Twomey, Leo was
cast as the embodiment of "wisdom above knowledge." Wise
men like Leo were still superior to scientists; as long as Catholic theology was in the hands of such a man, it could not be
obsolescent. Leo was visibly the ascetic and the great sufferer.
To a generation that admired strenuousness and energy, he was
also physically dynamic, especially for his years. He created
confidence in the minds of clergymen who could only remember decades when the prestige of the Church was declining. He
laid to rest earlier fears that were only now acknowledged.
Twomey acknowledged earlier times when clergymen "might
start up alarmed, and wonder if God's spirit always guides in
the choice of the Church's leaders." In a time when younger
churchmen were offering their opinions on all matters of society and politics, Leo stood as the "scholar" who "does not
confine himself to theological discipline." Clearly it was not
what Leo said on capital-and-labor that was significant but that,
in doing so, he bounded outside the fences of theology; others
could excusably do the same and, in the case of O'Connell, legislate on the widest possible range of matters.[111] On the other
hand, the biographical genre was also useful as a weapon
against Protestants and Yankees. In the late nineteenth century
in Boston Catholic writers used biography to dispose of lurking
figures like Horace Mann, one by one.[112]

Enough has been said about the romantic artists who fell by
the wayside in favor of the historical approach to truth. Their
replacements were cautious, uncreative clergymen, some of
whom set aside careers as imaginative writers for the safer and
less personal field of literary criticism.[113] Here again average
Irish Catholics were led away from the freer, more open thinking of the 1890's. They were led by principles. "Ethics," Earls
offered, "is the elder sister in the household of art. Aesthetics,
meaning sensation as the basis of the beautiful, must remain
a modest serving-girl."[114] The outcome of these efforts to give
the children of the immigrants a respectable image of them-

selves and set their social and economic sights a bit higher was
that religion remained populistic. Yet none accused O'Connell
of unleashing the masses—the case was quite the contrary.

What O'Connell and Earls envisioned for themselves and
what the Boston Catholic community produced was a particular
kind of learnedness for a number of Catholic churchmen of
Boston. O'Connell and Earls typified a conspicuous eclectic kind
of knowledge rather than intellectual depth. They esteemed
themselves insofar as they were able to demonstrate enough
knowledge to save from total fraudulency a statement like
O'Connell's that the "great world of knowledge and learning
and science and art . . . have always remained my most precious possession and have afforded me the greatest delight of
my life." Keeping oneself aware of one's role in a "universal
church" added further spread to such an already overreaching
expansiveness. The attitudes and institutions of Williams' generation were necessarily annoying anachronisms. Now there was
a new kind of "intellectual" among church leaders in Boston.
For the first time men like O'Connell laid upon themselves the
duty of forgetting such insights as might have been accumulated by living as a particular person in Boston and having
shared the hopes and qualities of precisely those people. Among
the lower clergy, O'Connell created men who appear to have
lived with a good deal of fear of his authority. Yet if these men
wished to remain in the diocese, they had to submit to what
O'Connell told them was good and just; they themselves had
to become instruments in setting up an oppressive social order
for Boston's Catholics.[115]

After serving as Rector of the North American College in
Rome from 1895 to 1900, O'Connell was chosen for the bishopric of Portland, Maine, and served there from 1901 to 1907.
He convened the second Synod of the diocese in 1904. If Boston
priests had read its proceedings and resolutions, they would
have learned a great deal about the force that could be gathered
behind O'Connell's determination to reorganize clerical life

totally, if he felt it was in order. In Portland, the changes in priestly life were laid out in details to the clergymen even before they could look at them in broad design.[116] Four years later, that is, thirteen months after Williams' death and in O'Connell's second year as archbishop of Boston, the clergy there were given evidence of O'Connell's authoritarian intentions from a chancery office circular. The archbishop had taken over *The Pilot* and now wanted it read in every Catholic home, and the pastors were to see to it. The publication was to do for his purposes what the writings of early great philosophers had achieved, namely, "stir whole States to their depths and transform even the civic life of the people." He wanted for himself as "publisher" the immense power residing in the public press. "They [newspapers] direct," he wrote enviously in this circular, "not merely the exercise of industry and the movements of diplomacy, but they sit in the cathedra [*sic*] of the philosophers offering to the millions . . . views of life, and they even climb into the pulpit and expound . . . the mysteries of religion." He made it clear that to him the "vast multitudes . . . demand their thought ready-made." Any parish priest refusing to "assist in this vital matter" of furnishing such thought to them from the hierarchy would be "grievously lacking in the performance of the essential duties of his office." In the same chancery circular, he insisted that in general the Catholic people were to begin to "call for Catholic books in public libraries." Publications by Catholic individuals would be considered "Catholic" only if they bore "some mark of ecclesiastical approval." But those were details. For the overall goal he returned to speaking of the Church and Rome. "The general public is deserving of knowing . . . what the Church is doing . . . not only in the diocese . . . but especially at Rome . . . for to the true Catholic his Church, its life, its activities, its misfortunes are all matters of burning interest." Neither the "parish libraries" nor "the pulpit" could be relied on to reach a "new reading public." So "every parish-priest . . . should procure an annual subscription [to *The Pilot*] from every head of a family in his parish." Specifically, every pastor was to send to the chancellor by December 25 "the number of copies of the diocesan paper needed for the people of his parish, which number, I repeat, ought to correspond to the number of families in it." Furthermore, in those parishes "where there already exists a parish calendar [for example *The Sacred Heart Review*] they are to be suppressed." For they will "interfere in the general good and *broader scope* which the diocesan organ can alone accomplish . . . The axiom of preferring the common good to the particular must be followed as law" [my italics].[117]

Many new concepts were taking over. "Diocese" was given an imperial context. The parish was now an agency for the chancery office, and the pastor was expected to be a willing and docile agent. Acceptance of these redefinitions was, in some cases, hesitant but in others ingratiatingly hasty. Some priests were fearful of not being submissive enough. In one instance, Father Francis Havey wrote to O'Connell from the seminary where he was rector in 1908 regarding the ordination of Jeremiah Driscoll. His changes of wording from the first to the final draft of the letter are pathetic signs of fear. He deleted "our judgment" and substituted "our opinion." He was apparently afraid that he might reveal himself too humane a rector, for he changed the clause "he [Driscoll] seemed to be at home from the first" to "he seemed to find no hardship in a life ordered by rule." Fearful of his own affirmative statements, Havey crossed out "he is pious, I think" to read "he is not without piety." When he was able to say something severely critical of the boy, Havey was secure; only when he had to praise the young man and appear lenient did he stumble.[118]

Meanwhile, O'Connell successfully created the public image which he wanted, one swept clean of fallibility. Unpublished letters reveal him still needing to learn and reacting strongly to many different experiences. They initially puzzle the reader because publicly O'Connell had created so unflaggingly the opposite impression. O'Connell, Earls and even minor fictional writers like Father Hugh Blunt generalized experience or used it as illustrative of a larger premise. With Roddan (in his earlier career) Boyce, Haskins, or Williams experiences preceded formulae. In the 1850's, Roddan was able to defend Thomas Moore's so-called defection to England because "the influences of his days were most potent to quench any feeling of nationality." But Hugh Blunt in 1905 rejected Moore's "manifestations of genius" because desertion from the faith had destroyed his character and hence his talent. Roddan felt the necessity in 1850 of revealing the earlier experiences of his life in order to explain subsequent behaviour. O'Connell falsified experiences even in his *Recollections*. Thus when Katherine E. Conway's letter to O'Connell in 1902 is read in the shadow of his 1896–1899 series of letters expressing his disproportionate concern about money, what emerges most emphatically is how fully he had concealed his real attitudes and values. "It's high time," she commended him for a speech at Boston College, "that someone spoke, and plainly, against false ideals—the worship of brute force, the deification of the dollar—which are what Teutonism or, more familiarly, the Anglo-Saxon Protestant spirit have brought to us."[119]

In the 1890's the autonomy of the parish pastors had been reduced in some respects by the experimental beginnings of organizations like the diocesan board of education. But legislation after 1907 curtailed freedom even more drastically. Undoubtedly some of this legislation rectified an unequal balance of power between the bishop and the local pastors; in this respect it corrected the misuse of ecclesiastical power on the local level.[120] It was also promoted to bring about changes that would give greater dignity to the public image of the priest. Nevertheless the all-inclusiveness of the enactments burned the wheat as well as the chaff. The diocesan administration took on the features of a competent bureaucracy. Even before 1907 and while O'Connell was still coadjutor, a letter had gone out from Granby Street asking that, for the sake of expediency, priests should avoid seeking personal interviews with the archbishop unless absolutely necessary. By November of 1907, O'Connell had tightened his personal control of the seminary. He regulated matters ranging from the details of Christmas vacations to the men's studies and conduct. In 1909, he directed that "courses of ethics, logic and metaphysics of Philosophy, and the Moral and Dogmatic Theology be taught hereafter in Latin." Two years later, the Sulpicians were removed. French spirituality was replaced by a theology exactly like that taught in Roman seminaries. Father John Peterson was chosen as rector and began the task of setting up a new curriculum and regime. He suggested to O'Connell that books "of the soundest conservatism" be used for the Scripture studies and offered as the most persuasive evidence for several of them their use "in more seminaries, even in Rome."[121] The goal was always to imitate the procedures at the North American College in Rome whenever possible. So although the gathering of bishops at the Baltimore Council in 1883 had rejected a proposal for setting up summer villas for seminarians, O'Connell established one along the shores of Lake Winnipesaukee—because the North American College in Rome had one.[122] Unlike Williams' sleight-of-hand regarding papal pronouncements, O'Connell and Peterson followed them with strict exactitude. Peterson anticipated O'Connell's disapproval of seminarians reading current periodicals. He wrote the archbishop in 1912, "For the past year or more absolutely no papers or periodicals have come into the house without the approval of the authorities. Not even *The Boston Pilot* has been excepted nor such a useful journal for our class-work as the *Ecclesiastical Review*."[123]

With O'Connell's sweeping seminary reforms and his tightened control over the parishes, it was apparent that Catholicism in Boston had taken a new direction. Henceforth the diocese would be neither wayward nor unorganized. It would be a well-ordered diocese with no room for theologians or priests of varying convictions. Harsh term though it is, thought control became a reality. Boston clergymen operated within these structures and reached the limits of their individual exertions until the 1960's when again distant maneuvers from Rome upset their lives.

EPILOGUE

"The Puritan Has Passed; the Catholic Remains"
William Henry Cardinal O'Connell,
*Sermon for the Centennial of the
Boston Diocese,* October 28, 1908.

O'Connell could not have transformed the content and context of the priests' lives in Boston had not they and the Catholic laity been receptive to some extent. Roddan might have made sense in a bygone day by stating that once nations were highly civilized they no longer needed priests as rulers. But it was O'Connell's opinion that "he who has lived in Rome [i.e., himself], he who has acquired the possession of that spiritual Romanness of that wherewith Christ is Roman, is in a position to understand the Americans better and more easily, better and more easily to educate them and train them for the attainments of that glory to which the destinies of the young nation are calling them." The appeal to spread-eagle nationalism here—"The heartbeats of America and Rome shall be heard as if they were side by side . . ."—can be set aside for the moment. More important are the possible reasons why Boston Catholics accepted a redirection of the archdiocese *away* from practices which were more inclusive of American democratic structures. Not all clergymen did accept this new orientation. But Boston's priests were in some ways more prepared to accept what Portland's clergy under O'Connell had despised and rejected.[124]

First, the church in Boston had passed through several stages of development. Lay leadership had been tried in certain areas. That it had failed was clear to the Irish-Catholic population, although the clergy's noncooperation or sabotage was not so well known. Whatever the causes, the St. Vincent de Paul Society was exhausted. President Thomas Dwight, Ring's successor, was a forgetful and unaggressive man. The society's self-analysis was, in fact, self-demeaning. Earlier men like Ring, they judged, could make truer judgments. Feeling themselves incapable of this, they succumbed more readily to clerical dominance. On the other hand, priests like Louis S. Walsh were now recognized as successful diocesan organizers. "Organization" provoked less hostility in Boston now. "Organized charities" was not so oner-ous a term; "movements" for social uplift were common; and the diocese badly needed the administrative skill which O'Con-nell brought.

In addition, O'Connell's pose as a European statesman ap-pealed widely; it was an added symbol of arrival.[125] A few wealthy Catholic families like the Wards and the Storers did have many genuine ties with Roman society. After 1910, a greater proportion of the clergy and the laity had "arrived," at least financially. Many were living comfortably, with "the poor" at least once-removed. They were as manipulable by myths as the poor, and O'Connell appears to have made capital of this susceptibility as well. The motif of the "noble aristocrat" appears as frequently in his writings as that of the "noble peasant." Just as the happy yeoman myth appealed to lower-class Irish Catho-lics so his definitions of "heaven" and "hope" in terms of prop-erty must have been equally winning.

The orientation toward Rome meant new attitudes and re-formulation of older ones. The good of the diocese was to be subordinated to the good of a universal church trying with diffi-culty to reestablish its prestige. So Williams' efforts to manipu-late the Irish-Catholic populace into Boston provincialisms were replaced by O'Connell's attempts to manipulate the same people out of whatever provincial ways were acquired and into "Ro-man" ways or modes of life. "Being poor" was no longer auto-matically a state of virtue. A curt new rhetoric taught that being "the residuum at the bottom" was in fact un-Christian.[126] Timid-ity before the Yankee librarian or socialite was a sin. In addi-tion, enemies of European Catholicism were to be taken as dangerous to all Catholics since Catholicism was now universal and seamless. One result of this was an overemphasis on the evils of socialism, an attitude which would probably not have been provoked by American socialism alone.

A new bureaucracy arose and old structures were shattered. "The mind of the Holy Father" dominated the seminary. O'Con-nell was aware that each year a greater number of wealthy

Catholics were vacationing along the East coast. He wanted suitable young priests for them. Since he had come to assume that social status and intellectual ability were inseparable, he wanted in his seminary no "men of common average" intellectually, though the boys generally continued to come from lower-middle-class homes. Beyond the seminary grounds, the setting was also ripe for shaping new and broader principles. Williams had frequently sought clarification of church-state relationships, but never felt his personal power affronted by the growing power of the state. However O'Connell felt obliged to delineate quite carefully the limits of the state in order to carry forth his contention that "the bishops are free [in the United States]; they do not depend at all on the state; they are real and great authorities." On one occasion, he brought forth charges against the governments of both the Commonwealth of Massachusetts and the United States. He accused them of "centralizing tendencies," namely, moves that threatened the expansion of *his* episcopal powers.[127]

Locally, attitudes toward the Yankees in Boston hardened and replaced any genuine ambivalence. There had been an unconscious allowance for pluralism regarding cultural values, if only because Puritan standards were accepted on the diocesan level. But now the episcopacy of Williams was played down by O'Connell as "complete disorganization." He gave credit to Rome for any intellectual movements in the American church. As he said in 1909, "to Rome was due the intellectual movement in America." Obviously this kind of thinking did a disservice to the exciting intellectual movements within and without clerical circles before 1900. Yet in the future O'Connell was to become the most powerful American Catholic churchman of the first half of the twentieth century, and his Romanism had wide ramifications for American Catholicism. This willingness to submit to Rome, for example, resulted in the assumption that young clerics of outstanding intellectual ability should be educated at the North American College in Rome whenever possible. So it happened with Francis J. Spellman and John J. Wright, both protégés of O'Connell.[128]

By 1911, Boston held the reputation among Catholic clergymen of being a wealthy and well-organized archdiocese. New
qualities were demanded of its clergy. O'Connell, in his *Recollections,* demeaned "the good Irish clergy" by writing of their
"surface defects." They were "of sound and solid virtue . . . [but]
somewhat lethargic" and clearly not to be imitated. His priests
were to exemplify, as he felt he did, "the whole man" philosophy
of Boston College. They were to be courteously, quietly obedient.
O'Connell sought the honor of "monsignor" for many of his
priests. These were marks of distinction and reflected gloriously
on the reputation of the entire Boston Catholic community.

With isolation from Yankee Boston heightened, the clergy
moved steadily away from full participation in city affairs. The
role of the laity was also further circumscribed. Even in such
parish affairs as those of his own Catholic organizations, the
layman by 1909, was cited as merely the vanguard of the clergy,
an individual capable only of opening the way for the really
professional men-of-religion. This was precisely the opposite of
the role played by John Boyle O'Reilly. Yet it accorded precisely
with Leo's desire in *Testem Benevolentiae* that laymen be submissive to the direction of their priests. St. Vincent de Paul men
saw themselves in a state of drift. They reasoned this way publicly: a seed has been planted but seems to have died. Of course,
it will germinate and flower, later.[129] Meanwhile priests moved
in to govern and enjoy the power they now held. Catholics and
Protestants confronted one another in rejection. So, unlike the
Unitarian ministers who defended the rights of private schools
in the 1880's, the Unitarian who wrote *The Priest* in 1911 presented the Church as inflexibly bureaucratic and dogmatic. The
novel seized the Achilles' heel of this totally controlled archdiocese when it portrayed the useless search of a young priest
for intellectual freedom in the face of a domineering archbishop. Most of the pastors, however, had reached the status of
"respected churchmen" and were tempted to end their careers
"on their income" as gentlemen in well-built rectories.

Notes
Bibliography
Index

INDEX TO ARCHIVAL REFERENCES

Notes

INTRODUCTION

1. Barbara Miller Solomon, *Ancestors and Immigrants: A Changing New England Tradition* (Cambridge, Mass., Harvard University Press, 1956), 11, 60.

2. BChA: Letter of Fitzpatrick to Archbishop John Hughes, February 6, 1856 (original in New York Chancery Archives, A-11); as described in Abbé Felix Klein, *In the Land of the Strenuous Life* (Chicago, A. C. McClurg and Co., 1905), 49; for details on the cardinalate, see Robert H. Lord et al., *History of the Archdiocese of Boston in the Various Stages of Its Development, 1604 to 1943*, III (Sheed and Ward, New York, 1944), 98–99; for Catholic population statistics, see ibid., III, 334.

3. Walter Muir Whitehill, *A Memorial to Bishop Cheverus with a Catalogue of the Books Given by Him to the Boston Athenæum* (Boston, Boston Athenæum, 1951), xiii, xviii, xx.

4. Lord, et al., *History*, II, 30, 35, 125, 126.

5. Lord, et al., *History*, II, 354, 406, 408.

6. [Edwin Bacon], "Sketch," *Time and the Hour*, VIII (September 10, 1898), 6; Joseph Iasigi was an outstanding Catholic layman to whose home in Lynn the nuncio, Archbishop Gaetano Bedini, was brought and feted in 1853 by Bishop Fitzpatrick. See Lord et al., *History*, III, 661. Iasigi contributed $1,000 toward building the Jesuit Church of the Immaculate Conception (*The Pilot*, January 2, 1864) and donated $5,000 for the building of the cathedral in 1866 (*The Pilot*, August 11, 1866). In *Leading Manufacturers and Merchants of the City of Boston and a Review of the Prominent Exchanges* (no author), published in 1885, the following information is given (310): "Iasigi and Co., Importers and Commission Merchants, No. 30 Kilby St." Founded in 1833, their concern is "one of the largest

commission houses in Boston, its connections extending throughout this country and even into Europe, and the facilities possessed enable it to efficiently serve the best interests of its influential clientele. Mr. Joseph A. Iasigi is a leading member of the Board of Trade and Commercial Exchange, being actively identified with the best interests of those bodies, and is Consulate General for Turkey representing many large interests."

7. Alexander V. G. Allen, *Life and Letters of Phillips Brooks*, II (New York, E. P. Dutton and Co., 1901), 85–86; for insistences that religious hostilities were sharper in the 1850's than later, see William Henry Cardinal O'Connell, *Recollections of Seventy Years* (Boston, Houghton, Mifflin and Co., 1934). He maintains that a "freer atmosphere" began in Boston between Yankees and Catholics in the 1870's, 28, and *passim*. The "Good Bishop Cheverus" appears only in the writings of "liberals" like Louis Brandeis. See Brandeis, "Life Insurance for the Wage-Earners," *Donahoe's Magazine*, 56 (January 1907), 13, 17.

See Haskins' sermon in *In Memoriam of Rt. Rev. John B. Fitzpatrick* (Boston, 1866). He refers to Fitzpatrick's schooling at one of the Boston Latin schools, cites the election of a priest to the school board of Boston, and notes the result: "the public schools became unexceptionable to the consciences of Catholics." He further characterizes the Catholics of Boston in 1866 as "poor Catholics, honored and respected, and enjoying equal rights and immunities with the wealthiest sons of the soil; the Catholic faith [is] universally respected" 38.

8. For Brownson's remarks, see Sr. M. Alphonsine Frawley, C.S.J., *Patrick Donahoe* (Washington, D.C., Catholic University Press, 1946), 65.

9. PChA: Diaries of Rt. Rev. Bishop David W. Bacon, 1859, 1862. Unfiled papers.

10. See BChA: Letter of Turpin to Fitzpatrick, January 15, 1856; see BChA: Letter of Father Early, S.J., to Father Bercard, S.J., November 28, 1850; see BChA: Letter of Father B. Pacciarini, S.J., to Fitzpatrick, February 17, 1854; see BChA: Letter of Martin Minahan, John McLoughlin, and John Black from Sandwich, Massachusetts, to Fitzpatrick, October 2, 1864; see Reverend John F. Byrne, C.SS.R., *The Glories of Mary in Boston* (Boston, Mission Church Press, 1921), for assorted revivalistic techniques used in January 1872 at one parish, 67. See also "Protestant Revivals and Catholic Retreats," *Brownson's Quarterly Review*, N.Y. Series III (July 1858), 289–322.

11. See BChA: Diary of Father Hilary Tucker, II, 1862–1864, entry for July 5, 1863; see BChA: Tucker Diary, II, entry of June 17, 1862; for early seminary training in Boston, see *The United States Catholic Almanac or Laity's Directory for the Year, 1837*. The "school" at the bishop's home is cited as "Seminary of the Holy Cross, Boston." It "adjoins the cathedral of the Holy Cross and is immediately under the direction of the bishop and two of his clergy . . . Boarders cannot exceed twenty-five; externs received also" 107.

For the problems connected with taking unknown priests into the diocese, see BChA: Letter of Bishop H. D. Juncker of Alton to Fitzpatrick, October 21, 1864. He is determined after bad experiences not "to receive any [priests] from another diocese." See also BChA: Letter of Reverend William Quinn to Williams, November 10, 1862, regarding Father P. V. Moyce. Moyce was in New York and at that time Quinn cited him as "passable" for work in the Boston diocese. Quinn reported one incident where two girls claimed that Moyce attempted kissing, nothing more." It is also reported by Quinn that Moyce struck a person in the confessional. Quinn regarded it as "not much even if it were true" and Moyce was subsequently accepted into the Boston diocese.

12. See BChA: Letter of Father Early to Father George Fenwick, S.J., October 20, 1853 (original in Fordham Archives, 221B8). "The nuncio," it reads, "has been at Boston. The priests of the diocese gave him a dinner at the Bishop's and made him an address. In his reply, he gave them some wholesome advice which it seems they did not relish much."

The same sense of frustration with the American hierarchy is apparent in the diaries of Bishop Bacon. On June 11, 1862, he and his traveling companions visited Cardinal Barnabo "who expressed himself ever ready to serve the American bishops provided they did not take him by the nose." PChA: Diaries of Bacon. Bishop Bacon records a curious debate with a Presbyterian minister while traveling to Europe in November of 1859. At issue was the question of St. Peter's lawful successor; Bacon writes of the encounter: "I answered him that the Lawful [sic] successors of St. Peter and the other apostles were the Church, and that these successors are the Pope and the bishops form [sic] this infallible Church—You, says he—being a bishop, are then infallible.—No, I answered, Infallibility is not the privilege of each one, but of the body, quoting text from Scripture." N.p.

For a similar understanding of the papacy, see "Collection for the Pope: The Boston 'Times' " by J[ohn] T. R[oddan], *The Pilot*, July 7, 1849, 6. See also Reverend John Boyce, *The Satisfying Influence of Catholicity on the Intellect and Senses; A Lecture Delivered before the Catholic Institute of New York on Friday Evening, January 24, 1851* (New York, 1851). Here, in attempting to assert the rightful powers of "the head of the Church," he argues that "the head may be a king or a president, but in either case, he can impose no law contrary to the general will of his people" 18.

I. 1848 TO 1866: "VARIETIES OF RELIGIOUS EXPERIENCE"

1. Katherine F. Mullaney, *Catholic Pittsfield and Berkshire* (Pittsfield, Press of the Sun Printing Co., 1897); Susan L. Emery, *A Catholic Stronghold and Its Making: A History of St. Peter's Parish, Dor-*

chester, Massachusetts, and Its First Rector, the Reverend Peter Ronan, P.N., (Boston, George H. Ellis, 1910); *History of Catholicity in Haverhill, Published by St. James Parish on the Occasion of the Consecration of the Church* (Haverhill, Press of the Sun Printing Co., 1900); Reverend Patrick B. Murphy, *Fifty Years of Catholic Faith, and Historical Sketch of St. George's Church, Saxonville, Massachusetts, from 1834 to 1897* (Worcester, n.p., 1897); Reverend Louis S. Walsh, *Origin of the Catholic Church in Salem and Its Growth in St. Mary's Parish and the Parish of the Immaculate Conception* (Boston, Cashman, Keating and Company, 1890).

2. As late as the 1920's, the following are typical: Reverend John F. Byrne, C.SS.R., *The Glories of Mary in Boston: A Memorial History of the Church of Our Lady of Perpetual Help (Mission Church), Roxbury, Massachusetts, 1871–1921* (Boston, Mission Church Press, 1921); Reverend Michael J. Scanlan, *An Historical Sketch of the Parish of St. Rose (Chelsea)* (Massachusetts, n.p., n.d. Marked 1924 in Preface).

James Joyce, *A Portrait of the Artist as a Young Man* Modern Library edition (New York, Random House, 1928), 39.

3. See John Bell, "Lord Acton's American Diaries: III," *The Fortnightly Review*, III, n.s. (November–December 1921) for Acton's appreciation of Fitzpatrick, namely, that "there is a completeness, rotundity and copiousness about his observations, which I have always admired" 70–71; Sr. M. Alphonsine Frawley, C.S.J., *Patrick Donahoe* (Washington, D.C., Catholic University Press, 1946), 53; John Boyce, *The Spaewife, or the Queen's Secret: A Story of the Reign of Queen Elizabeth*, I (Baltimore, Murphy and Co., 1853), 250–251.

4. BChA: Letter of O'Callaghan to Fitzpatrick, June 23, 1847. O'Callaghan's antagonist is Bishop England from whose newspaper article on "liberality" he "culled out . . . five heresies" which he "exposed and refuted along with Bishop Hopkins' and Felix Varula's errors in a treatise entitled, 'O'Callaghan on Heresies, Burlington, 1837.'" O'Callaghan sent the treatise to Bishop Fenwick at Boston and followed this with twenty-four copies for the clergy. For the personality of O'Callaghan see BChA: Letter of William Henry Holt to Fitzpatrick, May 22, 1847, or Robert H. Lord, et al., *History of the Archdiocese of Boston in the Various Stages of Its Development, 1604 to 1943*, II (New York, Sheed and Ward, 1944), 251.

5. George K. Malone, *The True Church: A Study in the Apologetics of Orestes Augustus Brownson.* (Mundelein, Ill., St. Mary of the Lake, 1957), 103, 24; see BChA: Letter of Donahoe to Brownson, January 3, 1858 (original in Notre Dame archives); see also Frawley, *Patrick Donahoe*, 76; BChA: Letter of Haskins to Bishop James Roosevelt Bayley, March 3, 1846; BChA: Letter of Brownson to Commings, September 5, 1847 (original in Notre Dame archives).

6. Arthur M. Schlesinger, Jr., *Orestes A. Brownson: A Pilgrim's Progress.* (Boston, Little, Brown and Co., 1939), 281; Malone, *The True Church*, 17, 107.

7. BChA: Letter of Haskins to Bayley, March 3, 1846; "Conversa-

tions of Our Club" (anon. article), *Brownson's Quarterly Review*, N.Y. Series III (January 1858), 1–13; BChA: Letter of Fitzpatrick to Brownson, November 22, 1852 (original in Notre Dame archives).

8. BChA: Letter of McCallion to Archbishop Purcell, September 22, 1846. [McCallion was appointed pastor of the Church of the Most Holy Redeemer, East Boston, in 1847.]

9. BChA: Letter of Haskins to Bayley, March 3, 1846; BChA: Letter of Haskins to Brownson, December 17, 1857 (original in Notre Dame archives); Schlesinger, *Brownson*, 193.

10. BChA: Letter of Brownson to Commings, September 5, 1847 (original in Notre Dame archives); Bell, "Acton's Diaries," *Fortnightly Review*, 70–71.

11. "Conversations," *Brownson's Quarterly Review*, N.Y. Series III (April 1858), 209, 194; "Conversations," *Brownson's Quarterly Review*, N.Y. Series III (January 1858), 30.

12. "Conversations," *Brownson's Quarterly Review*, N.Y. Series III (April 1858), 209.

13. O'Connell bought *The Pilot* from the Donahoe family within thirteen months of becoming archbishop of Boston. It was thereafter "owned by the Diocese, representing the interests of the Diocese, and controlled by the authority of the Diocese." Lord et al., *History*, III, 524. Contrary to this sort of control was Fitzpatrick's attitude, see *The Pilot*, July 1, 1849, for pastoral letter of Fitzpatrick against revolution, 3. See also *The Pilot*, August 4, 1849, for Roddan's editorial encouraging readers to trust in the European revolutions because "*revolution* as well as *hurricane* is an agency in the hands of God for the just regulation of the world" 6; see "The Irishman in Ireland," *The Pilot* April 20, April 27, 1850, and "The Last Days of Thomas Moore," *The Pilot*, June 9, 1849.

14. BChA: Eulalia Tuckerman, "Life of Archbishop John J. Williams" (unpub. ms., 1911), 27; "Political Priests" (unsigned editorial), *The Pilot*, June 1, 1850, 2; BChA: Letter of Shaw to Fitzpatrick, April 14, 1847, and letter of Shaw to Bishop Benedict Fenwick (Boston), October 13, 1845.

15. *The Pilot*, April 22, 1848, 6; *The Pilot*, June 1, 1850, 1.

16. *The Pilot*, July 8, 1848, 1; *The Pilot*, April 22, 1848, 6.

17. *The Pilot*, April 22, 1848, 6.

18. *The Pilot*, April 22, 1848, 6.

19. Rev. John T. Roddan, "The Appeal of Modern Science from God's Account of His Own Creation," *The Pilot*, April 6, 1850, 1.

20. *The Pilot*, March 7, 1850, 7; for stereotyping see William Henry Cardinal O'Connell, *Recollections of Seventy Years* (Boston, Houghton, Mifflin and Co., 1934), 26, 33, 91 passim; Roddan, "The Irishman in America," *The Pilot*, May 11, 1850, 2.

21. *The Pilot*, June 30, 1849, 6; *The Pilot*, July 7, 1849, 6.

22. *The Pilot*, September 15, 1849, 6.

23. *The Pilot*, April 6, 1850, 1; *The Pilot*, April 13, 1850, 1.

24. *The Pilot*, April 13, 1850, 1.

25. Roddan, "Irishman in America," *The Pilot*, May 11, 1850, 3;

The Pilot, March 30, 1850, 7; compare Roddan, "Irishman in America" with O'Connell, *Recollections,* 14, 33; *The Pilot,* May 18, 1850, 2.

26. *The Pilot,* July 27, 1850, 5.

27. Willard Thorp, "Catholic Novelists in Defense of their Faith, 1829–1865," *Proceedings of the American Antiquarian Society,* 78 (April 1968) 47; Rev. John T. Roddan, *John O'Brien, or the Orphan of Boston: a Tale of Real Life* (Boston, P. Donahoe, 1850) a, 43, 13, 7, vi.

28. Roddan, *John O'Brien,* 15, vii, 59, 150f, 154; Thorp, "Catholic Novelists," 48; Roddan, *John O'Brien,* vi, 59, vii.

29. "Foreign Anarchists" (unsigned editorial), *The Pilot,* August 24, 1850, 6.

30. For disturbances see *The New York Tribune,* July 24, 1850; July 31, 1850; August 1, 1850; August 3, 1850. On the Young Irelanders as well as the chaotic state of Catholic newspaper competition see Robert G. Athearn, *Thomas Francis Meagher: An Irish Revolutionary in America* (Boulder, Col., University of Colorado Press, 1949) and "Foreign Anarchists in America" editorial), *The Pilot,* August 24, 1850, 6; "The Function and Place of Conscience" (unsigned editorial), *The Pilot,* November 23, 1850, 6.

31. Roddan, "The Responsibilities and Rights of Catholics in America," *The Pilot,* March 29, 1851, 1, 2; "Intolerance! Religious Liberty" (unsigned editorial), *The Pilot,* May 15, 1852, 6; "Tara" (anon. review), *The Pilot,* March 29, 1851, reports on an address of Roddan's in Philadelphia: "Premises were laid down and conclusions drawn from which no reasonable being could reasonably dissent" 6; see also "Strikes" (unsigned editorial), *The Pilot,* June 18, 1853, 4; Roddan, "Responsibilities and Rights," *The Pilot,* March 29, 1853, 1; "New Converts," *The Pilot,* May 3, 1851, 5; "Intolerance," *The Pilot,* May 15, 1852, 6; "Orestes A. Brownson" (unsigned editorial), *The Pilot,* August 28, 1852, 3; see "The Protestant Propaganda" (unsigned editorial), *The Pilot,* March 13, 1858, 4; and "Evangelization Made Easy" (unsigned editorial), *The Pilot,* May 22, 1858, 4, as compared with "Protestant Revivals and Catholic Retreats" (editorial comment), *Brownson's Quarterly Review,* N.Y. Series III (July 1858), 289–322.

32. "Strikes" (unsigned editorial), *The Pilot,* April 30, 1853, 4; "Address of N. I. Bowditch in behalf of the Petition of Bishop Fitzpatrick and Father McElroy . . . before the Joint Committee on Public Lands of the City Council," *The Pilot,* April 30, 1853, 1; "Strikes," *The Pilot,* April 30, 1853, 4 [The series runs to July 2, 1853].

33. *The Pilot,* April 9, 1853, 4; "Conversations of Our Club," *Brownson's Quarterly Review,* N.Y. Series III (January 1858) 27, 30; "The Protestant Propaganda," *The Pilot,* March 13, 1858, 4.

34. "Strikes," *The Pilot,* April 30, 1853, 4. The arguments are Brownson's and the comparative approach is that of Reverend Jaime Balmes in *Protestantism and Catholicity Compared in Their Effects on the Civilization of Europe,* tr. C. J. Hanford and R. Kershaw

(London, James Burns, 1849). The translation was widely read by
Boston Catholic clergymen during this period.

35. Roddan, "Ventura's Oration," *The Pilot*, April 22, 1848, 6;
Athearn in *Meagher* quotes the *Pilot* as among the Catholic newspapers "who were to regret their enthusiasm" for Meagher. He cites
a May 15, 1852, editorial of *The Pilot* as follows: "There is not a
heart in the country but will thrill at this news [of Meagher's arrival
in America]." Athearn then states that the editors would "change
their minds before the year was out." 26; "The Protestant Propaganda," *The Pilot*, March 13, 1858, 4.

36. "Brownson's Review," *The Pilot*, July 7, 1849, 6; "Letter of
Roddan to Friend Donahoe," March 7, 1850 as printed in *The Pilot*,
March 30, 1850, 7; Joseph Wood Krutch, ed., *Thoreau: Walden and
Other Writings* (New York, Bantam Books, 1962), 413; "The Func-
tion and Place of Conscience" (unsigned editorial), *The Pilot*, No-
vember 23, 1850, 6; Roddan, "Responsibilities and Rights," *The Pilot*,
March 29, 1851, 1; "Evangelization Made Easy," *The Pilot*, May 22,
1858, 4.

37. Roddan, "Irishman in America," *The Pilot*, May 18, 1850, 2;
The Pilot, January 1, 1853, 4; "The Protestant Propaganda," *The
Pilot*, March 13, 1858, 4.

38. "Rome and the Romans" (unsigned editorial), *The Pilot*,
August 24, 1850, 1; "Effervescent Religion" (unsigned editorial),
The Pilot, June 5, 1858, 4; "The Catholic Press" (unsigned editorial),
The Pilot, March 20, 1852, 4. Roddan admits that the paper does
not have ecclesiastical approbation. "We would certainly regard it
as a great privilege to be able to announce that the paper is published with the approbation of the Rt. Rev. bishop of Boston. We
believe that the paper as at present conducted is not disapproved by
him." Roddan concludes by further explaining that Fitzpatrick may
not read it and "it is possible, even when clergymen edit a paper as
in the case of *The Pilot* there may appear sentences that he would
not recommend" 6. See also "Secret Societies," *The Pilot*, December
3, 1853, 4.

39. The first diocesan synod was held in August, 1842, and the
second in 1868, a decade after Roddan's death; BChA: Diocesan
Circular Letters, 1855–1873. Retreats were not obligatory until 1874;
Kenneth Rexroth, "Walt Whitman," *The Saturday Review*, September 3, 1966, 43. For Roddan's awareness of "the young liberals" see
his article on Orville Dewey, *The Pilot*, May 15, 1852, 6–7.

40. BChA: Letter of Turpin to Fitzpatrick, January 15, 1856. Fitzpatrick could not even elicit obedience to his insistence that marriage banns be published on Sundays; "Intolerance," *The Pilot*, May
15, 1852, 6–7.

41. BChA: Tucker Diaries, II, 1862–1864, entries of June 9, 11,
13, 18, and 19, 1863. See also Lord et al., *History*, II, 404–408, 754–
756; Roddan, "Irishman in America," *The Pilot*, May 18, 1850, 2;
"Evangelization Made Easy," *The Pilot*, May 22, 1858, 4.

42. Oscar Handlin, *Boston's Immigrants, A Study in Accultura-tion*, rev. ed. (Cambridge, Mass., Belknap Press of Harvard University Press, 1959), 185; BChA: Eulalia Tuckerman, "Life of Williams." Even Williams was indebted to Brownson, though there is slim evidence for Tuckerman's assertion that Williams knew Brownson "intimately" 88; "The Protestant Propaganda," *The Pilot*, March 13, 1858, 4.

43. The life and works of John Boyce were the study of Father Michael Earls, S.J., in *Under College Towers, A Book of Essays* written in 1926. His interpretations were both superficial and uncritical. Father William L. Lucey, S.J., has assessed Earls' works in "The Record of an American Priest: Michael Earls, S.J., 1873–1937," *The American Ecclesiastical Review*, 137 (1957) nos. 3–6. The present writer has made inquiries for information on Boyce from St. Finian's Academy and Maynooth without success.

For historians' tendency to oversimplify the immigrant mentality see Arthur Mann, *Yankee Reformers in the Urban Age: Social Reform in Boston, 1880–1900* (New York, Harper and Row, 1954), 27–28. (Mann does exclude John Boyle O'Reilly and Jeff Roche from "the mass of transplanted peasants.") See also Father Cornelius Herlihy, *The Celt Above the Saxon* (Boston, Angel Guardian Press, 1904), 66, 62, passim; Handlin, *Boston's Immigrants*, 27–51. His differentiations are limited as well.

Such works as the following offer cultic glorification of the Irish peasant: William Henry Cardinal O'Connell, *The Letters of His Eminence William Cardinal O'Connell, Archbishop of Boston*, I. (Cambridge, The Riverside Press, 1915), 2, 48; Herlihy, *Celt Above Saxon*, passim; Michael Earls, S.J. *The Wedding Bells of Glendalough* (New York, Benziger Brothers, 1913); "Honor Before Honors," *The Sacred Heart Review*, I (Cambridge, Mass.), serialized beginning December 1, 1888; "The Enchanted Lady of the Mountain Castle," *The Sacred Heart Review*, I (January 11, 1880), 3, 5; James Alexander Mowatt, "Transformed," *The Pilot*, January 3, 1874, 1; Reverend Joseph V. O'Connor, in "The Irish-American: His Merits and Defects," *Donahoe's Magazine*, 4 (July 1880), 4–5, attempted to present a more realistic appraisal.

44. Thomas N. Brown, *Irish-American Nationalism, 1870–1890* (New York, J. B. Lippincott Company, 1966), 7, 10.

45. William James, *The Varieties of Religious Experience: A Study of Human Nature, Being the Gifford Lectures on Natural Religion Delivered at Edinburgh in 1901–1902* (New York, New American Library Co., 1958), 331.

46. "Obituary," *The Pilot*, January 16, 1864, 5; John Boyce, *Mary Lee, or the Yankee in Ireland* (Baltimore, Patrick Donahoe, 1860), 19; Boyce, *Shandy McGuire: or Tricks upon Travellers, Being a Story of the North of Ireland* (New York, Edward Dunigan and Bros., 1851), 31, passim.

47. Reverend John Healy, *Maynooth College, Its Centenary His-

tory, 1795–1895 (Dublin, Browne and Nolan, 1895), 329; Thomas J. B. Flanagan, *The Irish Novelists: 1800–1850* (New York, Columbia University Press, 1959), 162.

48. John H. Whyte, "The Appointment of Catholic Bishops in Nineteenth-Century Ireland," *Catholic Historical Review*, XLVIII (April 1962), 30; Healy, *Maynooth College*, 285.

49. *The Pilot*, January 16, 1864, 5. Boyce is not among the writers of *The Nation* whose ballads and songs are collected in *The Spirit of the Nation: or Ballads and Songs by Writers of "The Nation,"* 50th ed. (Dublin, James Duffy and Sons, 1881). Nor is he mentioned by Sir Gavan Duffy in *My Life in Two Hemispheres*, I, II (London, T. Fisher Unwin, 1903); Healy, *Maynooth College*, appendix xi. See Whyte, "Appointment of Bishops," *Catholic Historical Review*, 19.

50. Flanagan, *Irish Novelists*, 172.

51. Boyce, *Shandy McGuire*, 4.

52. Boyce, *Shandy McGuire*, 217, 191–192, 215.

53. Boyce, *Shandy McGuire*, 48, 54, 56. See *The Satisfying Influence of Catholicity on the Intellect and Senses* (New York, 1851) for Boyce's insistence elsewhere that Episcopalianism in England was one of "the best representations of Protestantism" 11.

54. Boyce, *Shandy McGuire*, 91.

55. Boyce, *Shandy McGuire*, 4, 5, 334, 338.

56. As reported in *The Pilot*, March 16, 1853, 4.

57. Lord et al., *History*, II, 279, 535, 538, 545; HCA: James A. Healy: Diary, 1849, entries of December 27, 1848, February 8, 1849, March 1, 1849 and June 13, 1849; BChA: St. Joseph's Church, Worcester, 1856. Accounts of pew rent from 1848 to July, 1850, drawn up by Sexton Thomas Magennis and submitted to Mr. Boyce, 1856; "Obituary," *The Pilot*, January 16, 1864, 5; Boyce, *Mary Lee*, 222.

58. Boyce, *Spaewife*, I (Baltimore, Murphy and Co., 1853) 53; *The Pilot*, April 2, 1853, 5; Boyce, *Spaewife*, I, 4; *The Pilot*, October 8, 1853, 4.

59. Boyce, *Spaewife*, I, 104, 138, 147; James, *Varieties*, 125.

60. Boyce, *Mary Lee*, 50, 59, 203.

61. *Mary Lee* first appeared in 1860 in Archbishop Hughes' diocesan newspaper, *The Metropolitan Record* (New York). In it the name was Horseman. See Schlesinger, *Brownson*, 223–224; Abner Forbes and J. W. Greene, *The Rich Men of Massachusetts* (Boston, W. V. Spenser, 1851), 134. See also Daniel Markewich, "David Henshaw of Massachusetts, 1791–1852" (Honors Thesis, Harvard University, 1962), 7, 5, 117–118; Boyce, *Mary Lee*, 117, 325.

62. For later stories regarding conversions to Catholicism see Lelia Harding Bugg, *Orchids, A Novel* (St. Louis, B. Herder, 1894); Reverend Hugh Blunt, "On the Wings of Song," *Donahoe's Magazine*, 52 (December 1904) 575–579; Michael Earls, S.J., *Marie of the House D'Anters* (New York, Benziger Brothers, 1916), *Melchior of Boston* (New York, Benziger Brothers, 1910), *The Wedding Bells*

of Glendalough (New York, Benziger Brothers, 1913); Reverend Louis S. Gallagher, S.J., *Episode on Beacon Hill* (Boston, Benziger Brothers, 1950).

63. Boyce, *Mary Lee*, 201, 268–269; George Bernard Shaw, *John Bull's Other Island* in *The Genius of the Irish Theater,* ed. Sylvan Barnet, Morton Berman, William Burto. (New York, New American Library, 1960), 28–29; Boyce, *Mary Lee*, 207, 266, 124, 291.

64. Boyce, *Mary Lee*, 209; Boyce, *Shandy McGuire*, 55, 35; Boyce, *Spaewife*, I, 147; Boyce, *Shandy McGuire*, 336.

65. Boyce, *The Satisfying Influence of Catholicity on the Intellect and Senses: A Lecture Delivered before the Catholic Institute of New York, on Friday Evening, January 24, 1851,* 3, 26; James, *Varieties,* 330.

65. Boyce, *Satisfying Influence,* 7, 8, 13; Boyce, *Shandy McGuire,* 250.

67. Boyce, *Satisfying Influence,* 16, 17, 19; Boyce, *Mary Lee,* 125.

68. Boyce, *Shandy McGuire,* 338; Boyce, *Mary Lee,* 6, 7.

69. Boyce, *Spaewife,* I, 149; Boyce, *Mary Lee,* 165–167. For Brownson's attitude on aesthetics see Malone, *True Church,* 26.

70. Worcester became part of the Springfield, Massachusetts, diocese in 1870.

71. For Boyce's educational experiment see Lord et al., *History,* II, 621; *The Heart of the Commonwealth or Worcester as It Is, Being a Correct Guide to All the Public Buildings and Institutes and to Some of the Principal Manufactories and Shops, and Wholesale and Retail Shops, in Worcester and Vicinity* (Worcester, Henry J. Howland, 1856), 44.

72. HCA: File: Fairbanks, Charles Bullard (1827–1859); see Fairbanks [Pseud. Aguecheek], *My Unknown Chum,* 1922 ed., foreword by Henry Garrity (New York, The Devin-Adair Co., 1922). (The essays were completed in 1859.) Fairbanks was also author of a lives of the saints, *Memorials of the Blessed: A Series of Short Lives of the Saints* (Boston, 1860).

73. HCA: Shaughnessy Collection. Letter of Earls to his sister citing his delight that the family is enjoying *Shandy McGuire,* undated. (Probably written in 1902 or 1903.)
Boyce, "The Irish Exile," quoted in Earls, *Old Ireland in New England* in *Memoirs and Manuscripts* (Milwaukee, Bruce Publishing Co., 1935), 210; Boyce, *Spaewife,* I, 73.

II. 1866 TO 1880: POLARIZATION

1. Sam B. Warner, Jr., *Streetcar Suburbs: The Process of Growth in Boston, 1870–1900* (Cambridge, Mass., Harvard University Press and the M.I.T. Press, 1962), 161.

2. Frederick A. Bushee, *Ethnic Factors in the Population of Boston* in *Publications of the American Economic Association* (New York, Macmillan Company, 1903), 27.

3. Richard Foster, "The Contemporaneity of Howells," *NEQ,* 32

(March 1959), 72. For substantiation, see William J. Tucker, *My Generation: An Autobiographical Interpretation* (Boston, Houghton Mifflin Co., 1919). Speaking of 1875, this minister states that New York was "less theological but more religious than Boston" 72.

4. Van Wyck Brooks, *New England: Indian Summer* (New York, E. P. Dutton and Co., 1950), 204, 205.

5. Henry Adams, *The History of the United States,* 1, 170, as quoted in Barbara Solomon, *Ancestors and Immigrants: A Changing New England Tradition* (Cambridge, Mass., Harvard University Press, 1956), 35.

6. Edward Everett Hale et al., *Workingmen's Homes: Essays and Stories* (Boston, James R. Osgood and Co., 1874), 72.

7. BChA: Diocesan Circulars, 1855–1873. Collection for the New Cathedral, 1872. On employment, see Bushee, *Ethnic Factors,* 65–66. For details on the cathedral, see Robert Lord, John Sexton, Edward Harrington, *History of the Archdiocese of Boston in the Various Stages of its Development 1604 to 1943,* iii (New York, Sheed and Ward, 1944), 48–55.

8. VDA: Letter of William Jamme to Thomas Ring, April 12, 1869. The letter indicates that when the society did get itself incorporated it was not as a "Particular Council" of the worldwide organization lest the "equanimity" of the Puritans be disturbed.

9. VDA: Minutes of the Monthly Meeting of the Particular Council, 1865–1878.

10. BChA: Notation of Williams, June 10, 1876, which is an iou to the Lowell Five Cent Savings Bank for forty thousand dollars "at the rate of six per cent per annum . . . payable semi-annually." It is marked "Paid, July 10, 1878." A similar negotiation is made with the same bank for ten thousand dollars, again at six per cent interest, within the above two-year period. It is marked "paid" at the same date. That Williams was a good administrator seems beyond question. See BChA: Diocesan Circulars for 1877 to 1879, Address of Cardinal McCloskey and Archbishops Assembled in New York *re* Archbishop Purcell, May 26, 1879. BChA: Father Hilary Tucker's Diary ii, 1862–1864, June 15, 1862, July 7, 1862, July 23, 1863. BChA: Letter of Father Joseph Finotti to Fitzpatrick, May 7, 1855.

11. BChA: Letter of Reverend Michael Dolan to Williams, January 2, 1877.

12. BChA: Monsignor Strain's Diary Accts [*sic*] and Collections, 1856–1881, March 10, 1866. John S. Conley deposited with Strain $5,000. Including interest, Strain paid back $6,200 in 1870.

13. BChA: Bishop Williams' Agenda for the Third Diocesan Synod, 1872. The agenda proposed for the synod discussion of such abuses as speculation and "dealing in worldly affairs," owning personal property in the parish itself, etc.

14. VDA: Letter of Ring to Charles Canfield, October 18, 1879. Ring Papers i, 309.

15. Mary Elizabeth Blake, *On the Wing* (Boston, Lee and Shepard Publishers, 1883), 21.

16. See Blake, *In the Harbor of Hope* (Boston, Little, Brown and Co., 1907). A constant plea to pluck up courage is expressed here as elsewhere by Mrs. Blake who ordinarily addressed herself to Boston at-large:

No backward-sloping brow, or vacant mind
Doth mark thee from thy kind
With slavish instinct or in brutal pain,
Bearing the mark of Cain;
But pride of place, as one within whose breast
The eternal bulwarks of the nation rest. (18)

17. HCA: Sermons of James A. Healy: "Holy Purity," Cathedral, 1857. See also, VDA: Letter of Thomas Ring to Williams, December 1, 1879. Ring Papers ɪ, 316. Letter of John Boyle O'Reilly to John Devoy, February 13, 1871, as quoted in William O'Brien and Desmond Ryan, *Devoy's Post Bag, 1871–1928,* ɪ, (Dublin, C. J. Fallon, Ltd., 1948), 31.

18. VDA: Letter of W. Connolly to Ring, December 15, 1870.

19. VDA: Ring Papers, ɪ, 216.

20. Brooks, *New England: Indian Summer,* 422. For O'Reilly's awareness that he was one of the immigrants' "representative men," see Letter of O'Reilly to Devoy, February 13, 1871 in O'Brien and Ryan, *Devoy's Post Bag,* ɪ, 30.

21. BChA: Monsignor Strain's Diary Accts, Clippings. See Sr. M. Jeanne d'arc O'Hare, "The Public Career of Patrick A. Collins," (unpub. diss., Boston College, 1959) for the early settlement of the Irish in the Chelsea section and their "sense of belonging in the Hollows" 13.

22. Bushee, *Ethnic Factors,* 150–151.

23. Letter of John O'Leary to James O'Kelly, November 8, 1872, as quoted in O'Brien and Ryan, *Devoy's Post Bag,* ɪ, 63. Thomas N. Brown in "The Origins and Character of Irish-American Nationalism," *Review of Politics,* 18 (July 1956) deals with the split between the clergy and the Irish nationalists but only in general terms, 332 ff., 348.

24. See above, note 10. For an example of the confusion and/or dishonesty which could arise see Letter of Louis Tucker to Hilary Tucker, November 27, 1871. He writes of a former parishioner of Hilary's, one from whom the latter borrowed money to raise a church and to whom he still owed $550.00. On behalf of Patrick Crosby who had made the loan, Louis Tucker writes, "He desired me to drop you these lines, in order to know if you cannot make the Congregation [*sic*] of that Church [in Boston] pay the principal at least." Somehow Hilary Tucker did pay back Crosby. BChA: Letter of Louis Tucker to Hilary Tucker, February 5, 1872.

25. VDA: Letter of Ring to F. H. Churchill, June 8, 1877. Ring Papers, ɪ, 75–79.

26. VDA: Letter of Ring to Williams, December 1, 1879, tells Williams that they plan to aid the unemployed poor, setting up a special work committee with a spiritual director. When all is settled, he will

get Williams' approval. Ring Papers I, 316. Similarly, on April 5, 1866, Father William Byrne, who was working with Williams in forming the society made certain suggestions regarding Sunday schools. In the same minutes it is recorded that secretary Davis said members will consider the suggestion. VDA: Minutes of the Monthly Meeting of the Particular Council, 1865–1877, n.p. The Report of the Society of St. Vincent de Paul for 1873 describes the society's application to Williams to inaugurate a collection for the poor in the parishes, which he does.

27. VDA: Letter of Ring to Andrew Carney, November 26, 1879. He wants Carney to support Mr. John Kennealy of Boston Highlands for the school committee. Kennealy, he takes care to tell him, is a graduate of Harvard, "a physician, well-educated, a Catholic and a brother-in-law . . . You know who are the men who may be of use . . ." Ring Papers, I, 313. See also Robert A. Woods, *The City Wilderness* (Boston, 1898), 117.

28. VDA: Letter of Ring to Churchill, June 8, 1877. Ring Papers, I, 79.

29. VDA: Letter of Ring to Father Thomas Magennis, May 8, 1879, Ring Papers I, 269. For "malcontents" in numbers in the parishes, see BChA: Agreement of Rev. J. J. Healy with the Sisters of Mercy, October 22, 1886. For the dispute of Father Healy with his parishioners, see *Donahoe's Magazine*, 16 (September, 1886), 273.

30. VDA: Letter of Ring to Sr. Raymond, October 11, 1877, Ring Papers, I, 212.

31. "The Good Parish," *The Pilot*, February 2, 1867, 4.

32. VDA: Letter of Ring to the Paper Stock, Old Metals, and Woollen Rag Trade of Boston, May 2, 1879. Ring Papers I, 266–269. Letter of O'Reilly to Devoy, February 13, 1871, as quoted in O'Brien and Ryan, *Devoy's Post Bag*, I. He encourages Devoy to go into business and concludes, "I want to see you and talk to you. I am Editor [*sic*] of this paper—really a big thing for a young man—and I am studying medicine. In three years I will be a medical doctor." 32.

33. Letter of Davitt to Devoy, 1879, as quoted in O'Brien and Ryan, *Devoy's Post Bag*, I, 454. In the same volume, see letter of O'Kelly to Devoy, October 11, 1878: "That 'skirmishing' idea must be dropped if we want to get money—the well-to-do respectables won't touch it, and with a little diplomacy they may be convinced to come out handsomely, I think." 359.

34. See Conrad Arensberg and Solon Kimball, *Family and Community in Ireland* (Cambridge, Mass., Harvard University Press, 1940) for the descent of property in the average Irish farm family, 63 ff. As to that same sense of obligation in Boston, see the example cited in *The Pilot*, August 22, 1868, which is not uncommon. "I know," writes Clericus, "in the Diocese [*sic*] of Boston a poor, hardworking Irishman who, at the advanced age of fifty, braved the perils of a long sea voyage and the still greater perils of the California gold mines, in order to make his son a priest" 4.

35. PChA: See letters of O'Connell to his sister Jule, February 19, 1898, January 30, 1899, February 27, 1899 [uncatalogued letters].
36. Warner, *Streetcar Suburbs*, 166.
37. For a discussion of the Eastern Railway's participation in Josiah Quincy's scheme for extra trains for workingmen, see Hale's *Workingmen's Homes*, 56–61.
38. Rev. John F. Byrne, C.SS.R., *The Glories of Mary in Boston: A Memorial History of the Church of Our Lady of Perpetual Help (Mission Church), Roxbury, Massachusetts, 1871–1921* (Boston, Mission Church Press, 1921), 112.
39. BChA: Circular Letter of September 14, 1877, in Circular Letters, March 8, 1877, to September, 1879. Two years after Boston had been made an archdiocese, Williams is still referring to himself as "bishop."
40. Brooks, *New England: Indian Summer*, 172.
41. "American Catholic Historical Notes." Note on "The Old Holy Cross Cathedral of Boston," quoting *The Irish Pictorial*, Boston, September 29, 1860, in *The American Catholic Historical Review*, ii, 59.
42. Tuckerman, *Life of Williams*, 88.
43. BChA: Letter of Archbishop Hughes to Bishop David Bacon, February 3, 1860 [original in New York Archives, Cope A 1].
44. *The Pilot*, March 12, 1864, offered pictures of Cheverus, Fitzpatrick, McElroy, Bapst, Lyndon, Finotti, Haskins, 6; *The Pilot*, October 20, 1866, 6.
45. Williams never dictated policy on Protestant-Catholic relations directly. He asks Father Magennis or Charles F. Donnelley to represent the diocese in the school controversy. See *The Pilot*, January 2, 1871, for the early endeavors of priests on school committees, 6.
46. *Sacred Heart Review*, 12 (January 3, 1891) 12. The Sacred Heart Parish picnics were events for which the pastor, Father John O'Brien, had to cooperate with factory owners in the Cambridge area. See *Sacred Heart Review*, 6 (July 25, 1891) 14.
47. See VDA: Report of the Society of St. Vincent de Paul, 1870. The council openly acknowledges the efforts of "many of our Protestant fellow-citizens" in helping the poor. The Boston Provident Association and "a gentleman who styles himself 'a staunch Protestant'" and who was known only to one member of the society gave them a sum for destitute Irish families, 5.
48. In 1868, Haskins got a "state gratuity" of $2,000 for his House of the Angel Guardian orphanage; in 1870, $3,500; in 1871, he was refused aid. Rev. George F. Haskins, *Report, Historical, Statistical and Financial of the House of the Angel Guardian from the Beginning in 1856 to October, 1864 . . . with other Later Reports Appended* (Boston, Patrick Donahoe, 1864), 6 ff.
49. James J. Bric, S.J., "An Account of Catholicity in the Public Institutions of Boston" [summary of a paper read before the American Catholic Historical Society of Philadelphia, April 28, 1886], in

Records of the American Catholic Historical Society, I–II, (1884–1885), 162–164.

50. For the Williams-Scully controversy, see BChA: Exchange of letters between Bishop McQuaid of Rochester and Scully, December 16, 1875, January 6, 1876, and February 24, 1876. For the exchange of letters between Williams and Rome regarding the parochial schools, see Instructio de Scholis Publicis, November 24, 1875, and also a letter from the Propaganda, February 22, 1877, wherein Williams' report regarding Catholic schools is commented on.

51. Tuckerman, *Life of Williams,* 123.

52. "Sketch" (anon. editorial) in *Time and the Hour,* VIII (September 10, 1898) refers to Father Joshua Bodfish's efforts to recreate the harmonious pluralistic society of earlier Boston. "Applaud as we may the conjunction of different religionists on certain humanitarian platforms, the social life of Roman Catholics or other Christians is more separate [in 1898] than it used to be in the good old days—however Father Bodfish may struggle to keep in touch with things" 6.

53. *The Pilot,* April 22, 1871, 4

54. For Williams' urgency *re* the need to cooperate with the Yankee community, see VDA: Letter of Ring to Williams, October 4, 1879. Ring Papers, I, 302–303, 305.

55. BChA: Letter of Scully to McQuaid, February 24, 1876.

56. BChA: Special Report of the Diocese to the Propaganda, January 11, 1879.

57. See BChA: Special Report to Rome, 1879. He writes, "Les protestants ne font rien directement pour le conversion des Catholiques, mais ils [tachent] d'attiser les enfants des pauvres."

58. Even *The Pilot* stated, "There is a time and place for the enforcement of doctrinal teachings, but it is not during school hours nor in the common school house." January 21, 1865, 4. For Williams' promotion of religious teachers for boys, see Report to Rome, 1879. "Nous avons besoin de Religieux pour enseigner dans les scholes, surtout pour les garçons."

59. See "Catholic Advocates of Public Schools," (anon. editorial) *Sacred Heart Review,* 1 (December 29, 1888), 1; "Duties of Parents," (anon. editorial) *Sacred Heart Review,* 4 (October 11, 1890), 6.

60. VDA: Letter of Ring, September 11, 1871. The men are fully aware that they are being shut out of teaching. Ring admits that the men are not qualified: "Again in many parishes, the Brothers of the Christian School and the Sisters have gradually monopolized this work so that if they keep on we will be entirely shut out." Early Letters, n.p.

61. Byrne, *The Glories of Mary,* 73–74, 120–121. Regarding revivals, Byrne gives the account of January, 1872, when the great enthusiasm of the people called for the rectory "being thrown open by the Fathers and their private bedrooms used for hearing confessions" 67.

62. BChA: Letter of Sherwood Healy to Williams, October 29, 1868.

63. VDA: Letter of Ring to Sr. Raymond, Ring Papers, I, 111–112. He remarks that his paper was printed in *The Pilot*. BChA: Circular *re* Catholic Union of Boston, October 5, 1877. The aim: "to usefully organize and elevate the constituents of Church Society here and especially, it desires to bring every member of the reverend clergy into active relations with the laity . . . in order that of the clergy and laity there shall be a *solidarity* of our best religious, social and intellectual forces." Having established the socializing features, the circular continues, "Is it not now the conscientious duty of every member of the clergy, as it is of every man of education connected with our body, to contribute the fruits of his study and judgment . . . ?" The circular calls for discussions of the "historical, literary, and scientific" matters in order that "right knowledge and true Catholic culture may be promoted . . . *Neglecting this duty we shall not be abreast with the average culture of our enlightened city!*" (my italics).

64. BChA: Circular of April 4, 1873, in Boston Chancery Circulars, 1855–1873.

65. Letter of Katherine E. Conway to the Rt. Rev. Bernard J. McQuaid, April 10, 1907. "I don't often get a chance to mention his Grace's [Williams'] kindness to me during the dark days that followed Boyle O'Reilly's death . . . and when he [O'Reilly] was gone, and the earth rocked under me, His Grace defined my position, my salary, and everything else that gave me some security." Quoted in Frawley, *Patrick Donahoe*, 289. For Williams' encouragement of the authoress Mary Agnes Tincker and his relationship with O'Reilly, see Tuckerman, *Life of Williams*, 489, 446.

66. Letter of Reverend John Bapst, S.J., to Reverend Paresce, S.J., May 10, 1865, quoted in David R. Dunnigan, *A History of Boston College* (Milwaukee, Bruce Publishing Co., 1947), 82. BChA: Diary of Hilary Tucker, II, 1862–1864, entry of March 8, 1863. See *The Pilot*, September 18, 1869, for Hecker's sermon at the dedication of the cathedral in Portland, Maine. See also Joseph Havens Richards, S.J., *A Loyal Life: A Biography of Henry Livingston Richards, with Selections from His Letters and a Sketch of the Catholic Movement in America* (St. Louis, B. Herder 1913). This biography documents the fact that the Jesuit church, "The Immaculate" was a gathering-place, a haven for converts like Richards and Stone, 313, 331.

67. This is exaggeration, though he did give his library.

68. "The Late Archbishop Williams" (anon. obit.), *The Republic* (Boston), 26 (September 7, 1907) 3, 6. "Sketch," *Time and the Hour*, VIII (September 10, 1898) disagrees. "The new bishop [Williams] attended the Plenary Council in Baltimore and the Oecumenical at Rome . . . and took no share in that 'liberal' movement which was in evidence for a little while. Thus the honor of the archbishopric was not long delayed" 7.

69. "The Late Archbishop Williams" (anon. obit.), *The Republic* (Boston), 26 (September 7, 1907), 3, 6. For support of these interpretations, see Tuckerman, *Life of Williams*, 518.

70. HCA: James A. Healy's Diary for 1849, passim; O'Connell's

Recollections, 26–28, 34. For O'Brien's emphasis on history, see *Sacred Heart Review,* especially in the early 1890's.

71. Even on his return from Vatican I, Williams' understanding of the purpose of religion was most liberal and simple: "[Many] men have come to a belief in natural religion and the possibility by its aid of living a moral life. The Church cannot force these men to adopt her teachings . . ." *The Pilot,* September 3, 1870, 4.

72. "Sketch," *Time and the Hour,* VIII (September 1898) 7.

73. BChA: "Advice of the Clergy in Relation to Savings Banks Prepared and Adopted by the Undersigned, April 29, 1878" in Diocesan Circulars and Chancery Notices from September 30, 1879, to January 1, 1880. For the successful results, see BChA: Letter of Henry L. Lamb to Williams, May 14, 1878.

74. BChA: Letter of Rev. Michael Dolan to Williams, January 3, 1877. In addition, priests were expected to be the financial support of young men interested in the priesthood. See *The Pilot,* August 22, 1868, 4.

75. For the correlation between administrative success and honorary titles, see BChA: Monsignor Strain's Diary; *An Unfinished Story: The Narrative of St. Mary's School on the Occasion of Its Fiftieth Birthday* (Lynn, n.p., 1931); *The Pilot,* July 15, September 24, October 4, 1879.

76. BChA: Address to the Irish Hierarchy. Williams and the clergy adopted in January of 1881 an expressed declaration supporting the principles of the Land League Convention in Buffalo, New York. For a reprint of the letter signed by Williams and other clergymen to "The Clergy and People of Ireland," see *Donahoe's Magazine,* 5 (February 1881), 264.

77. I am considering the following priests of the generation before Williams to have got sufficient mention in archives, *The Pilot,* and elsewhere to be considered prominent: Father James Fitton (d. 1881); Father George Hamilton (d. 1872); Father George F. Haskins (d. 1872); Father Patrick F. Lyndon (d. 1878); Father Hilary Tucker (d. 1872); Father Manasses Dougherty (d. 1877). Of his own generation, the following were prominent: Father William A. Blenkinsop, Father William Byrne, Father Michael Moran, Father P. T. O'Reilly, Father Thomas Scully, Father Joshua Bodfish, Father William J. Daly, Father James Healy, Father Sherwood Healy, Father John Flatley, Father Thomas Shahan, Father Patrick Strain.

78. The bibliography for Father James Fitton, who represents a thinking similar to Williams' but whose career cannot be retold here, is comparatively full, although the Holy Cross archives and the Boston chancery have little biographical data of significance: *The Youth's Companion to the Sanctuary: Containing Prayers at Mass and Vespers Together with Instructions for Receiving Holy Communion, from the French of M. L'Abbé Rignault* (Hartford, Conn., n.p., 1833); *The Triumph of Religion: or a Choice Selection of Edifying Narratives, Compiled from Various Authors* by Reverend James Fitton (Baltimore, F. Lucas, 1833); *Palestine, or The Holy Land,*

Compiled from the Travels in 1806–7 of F. H. de Chateaubriand,
I and II (Baltimore, F. Lucas, 1835); *Familiar Instructions in the
Faith and Morality of the Catholic Church, adapted to the Use Both
of Children and Adults, Compiled from the Works of the Most Ap-
proved Catholic Writers* by the Reverend James Fitton (Boston, P.
Donahoe, 1849); *Influence of Catholic Christian Doctrine on the
Emancipation of Slaves* (Boston, P. Donahoe, 1863); *Sketches of the
Establishment of the Church in New England* (Boston, P. Donahoe,
1872); *Sketch of the Progress of Catholicity in East Boston, from
1844–1888 by the Rector of the Church of the Most Holy Redeemer*
(Boston, The Advocate Office, 1880). The only biography of Fitton
is Father Lawrence P. McCarthy's inadequate work, *Sketch of the
Life and Missionary Labors of Rev. James Fitton,* in *Publications of
the New England Catholic Historical Society,* 8 (1908). For an analysis of *Influence of Catholic Christian Doctrine on the Emancipation
of Slaves* see Merwick, "The Broken Fragments of Afro-American
History: A Study of Catholic Boston, 1850–1890," *McCormick Quarterly,* 22 (May 1969), 239–252.

79. Other factors: Fitton was at the end of his career after 1866
and would die in 1881; Scully opposed Williams openly on the school
issue; Blenkinsop involved himself demonstratively in Democratic
politics in the city, an involvement which would not have pleased
Williams. See *The Boston Daily Globe,* November 3, 1876, I, for the
decorations on Blenkinsop's rectory during the Hayes-Tilden contest
for the presidency.

80. For Bodfish's public stance against further immigration see
"Protest Against the Banishment of the Irish," *Donahoe's Magazine,*
9 (April 1883), 341.

81. Tuckerman, *Life of Williams,* 173.

82. James B. Cullen, *The Story of the Irish in Boston* (Boston,
James B. Cullen and Co., 1889).

83. BChA: Announcement of the Festival in Honor of Pius IX,
Diocesan Circulars, 1855–1873. Three of the ten speakers are converts. Of the three priests, one is a Jesuit, one a protegé of Williams,
one is James Kent Stone.

84. *The Pilot,* June 2, 1849, 4.

85. Reverend George F. Haskins, *Report, Historical, Statistical
and Financial of the House of the Angel Guardian from the Beginning in 1851 to October, 1864* (Boston, Patrick Donahoe, 1864), 6.

86. Haskins, *Report,* 18–19, passim. See Haskins' statement in the
1867 lecture on St. Ignatius: "We [Catholics living amid the Protes-
tants] are enjoying all the wealth and all the honor of the freest and
mightiest nation." Rev. George F. Haskins, *St. Ignatius and the Society of Jesus: Their Influence on Civilization and Christianity: A
Sermon Delivered in the Church of the Immaculate Conception in
Boston, on Sunday, August 4, 1867* (Boston, Bernard Corr, 1867), 18.

87. The first evidence of the proposed Emmigrant Savings Bank
is found in a letter of George F. Haskins to Charles E. Wiggin in

which he endorses the endeavor but does not wish to be "prominent or active in the affair." Quoted in Frawley, *Patrick Donahoe*, 152.
88. George F. Haskins, *Six Weeks Abroad in Ireland, England and Belgium* (Boston, Patrick Donahoe, 1872). For details of these trips, see [William Kelly], *The Life of Father Haskins by a Friend of the House of the Angel Guardian* (Boston, Angel Guardian Press, 1899).
89. Haskins, *Report*, 6.
90. BChA: Letter of Sherwood Healy to Williams, October 25, 1868.
91. The resolution reads: "Resolved: That in all the relations he had with the Board his course had been strongly marked by his disinterested efforts for the good of the public schools and for increasing their excellence and for promoting harmony among the Committee . . ." Quoted in Kelly, *Life of Haskins*, 136.
92. BChA: Letter of Bodfish to O'Connell, November 8, 1908. Letter of Chancellor M. J. Splaine to Rev. O'Connell. File: Rev. Joshua P. L. Bodfish.
93. Albert S. Foley, S.J., *Bishop Healy: Beloved Outcast: The Story of a Great Priest Whose Life Has Become a Legend* (New York, Farrar, Straus and Young, 1954).
94. HCA: James A. Healy, Copies of Two Diaries, 1849, 1891. Entries of December 9, 10, 11, 12, 1848.
95. HCA: Healy, Diaries, 1849, 1891. Entry of December 21, 1848.
96. HCA: Healy, Diaries, 1849, 1891. Entry of June 23, 1891: "Our journey was taken up in a journey to San Rafael, a beautiful valley enclosed in mountains. Eleven years ago I preempted that spot for my possession, when the millennium on earth should come. But unless the purifying fire of the last day is to clear out the Chinese, Jews, and other foreigners who have taken possession of the town, it will have lost all of its charm."
97. HCA: Healy, Diaries, 1849, 1891. Entry of June 21, 1891.
98. HCA: James A. Healy, Sermons and Lectures [uncatalogued] See Sermon on "Holy Purity," 1857.
99. Foley, *Beloved Outcast*, 88, 105.
100. HCA: Healy, Diaries, 1849, 1891. Entry of 1891. "The bishop," Healy writes of himself, "can hardly keep pace with everything so high, mighty and grand. Everyone else here dressed for dinner, the Bishop washes his hands and face and tried to brush his hair. . . . The Bishop hardly has the courage to ask a blessing. But he struggles on, making numerous blunders against the rules of etiquette."
101. HCA: Healy, Sermons and Lectures [uncatalogued box containing longhand sermons and outlines, many of the outlines in Latin, hastily done]. Others of Healy's sermons, though considerably fewer, are held in the chancery offices of both Portland, Maine, and Boston. For comparison of earlier sermons and outlines of the same sermons for later use, see sermon for the First Sunday of Advent, manuscript of 1857 and outline of 1888; sermon on "Idleness" for Septuagesima Sunday delicately written out in 1855 and outlined for

the same Sunday in 1887; sermon for Trinity Sunday, 1858 and 1886; sermon for the Feast of the Conversion of St. Paul, 1873 (outlined and in Latin) and 1885.

102. PChA: Charles McCarthy Diaries, third notebook. Entry of January 15 [smudged], 1893. The diaries run from 1880 to 1918.

103. HCA: Healy, Sermons and Lectures. Sermon on St. Joseph, December 22, 1872.

104. HCA: Healy, Sermons and Lectures. Sermon for Passion Sunday, 1859.

105. HCA: Healy, Sermons and Lectures. Sermon on St. Athenasius, 1858; sermon for Passion Sunday, 1859.

106. PChA: Healy's Uncatalogued Sermons. Undated, but evidently after 1873 and before 1880.

107. PChA: Letter of Healy to Reverend William Lonergan, April 8, 1893, on the latter's abuse of drink or taking of drugs. Letter of Healy to Lonergan, April 14, 1893, warns Lonergan not to say Mass on Sundays.

108. PChA: Healy Letters [uncatalogued]. See exchange of letters between Father Charles Egan and Healy, December 4, 1877, and December 6, 1877. Egan has been deprived of his parish after being in the diocese twenty years and asks the reason. He threatens to make Healy's injustices known, including his injustices to other clergymen. The altercation becomes completely personal. Egan asks Healy, "How would you like to be investigated as to your moral and physical condition when you were struck down some years ago at Father Blenkinsop's with a severe illness—Did that disqualify you for your parish of St. James or for holding the mitre of Portland now?"

109. VDA: General Meetings: Particular Council of Boston, 1865–1871. Meeting of July 19, 1868. Healy is "spiritual director."

110. HCA: Healy, Diaries, 1849–1891. Entries of June 11, June 12, 1891.

111. William Henry Cardinal O'Connell, *Recollections of Seventy Years*, 149. Byrne was president of St. Mary's College, Emmitsburg, Maryland, from 1880–1884, bringing its finances into order and serving successfully as president. He edited the second volume of *One Hundred Years of Progress . . .* , a history of Catholicism in New England.

112. VDA: Letter of Byrne to Ring, April 19, 1886. See also, Letter of Byrne to Ring, January 14, 1889.

113. VDA: Letters of Byrne to Ring, December 1, 1888; January 8, 14, 1889.

114. William Byrne, "The Attitude of the Catholic Church to American Public Schools," reprinted in *The Pilot*, November 15, 1879, 1.

115. Both P. T. O'Reilly and James Healy were out of the diocese as bishops elsewhere. The following men had died: Patrick Donahoe, Michael Flood, Sherwood Healy, Nicholas O'Brien, John T. Roddan.

William Byrne and Joshua Bodfish were serving as officials of the diocese.

116. The following data is compiled from *One Hundred Years of Progress: A Graphic, Historical and Pictorial Account of the Catholic Church in New England, Archdiocese of Boston, embracing Portraits and Biographical Sketches of the Bishops, Prominent Priests, Eminent Church Workers of the Past, Together with Views and Sketches of the Present Churches. Also of the Many Early Church Edifaces and Educational Institutions, I., Prepared under the Editorship of James S. Sullivan, M.D., Holy Cross College, 1889 and Harvard University, 1894, assisted by a corps of Prominent Catholic Writers* (Boston and Portland, Illustrated Publishing Company, 1894). There are factual errors which have been corrected by correlation with such sources as Lord et al., *History of the Archdiocese*, the Boston chancery archives, *The Pilot*, etc.

117. Data for six priests is incomplete.

118. Data for four priests is incomplete.

119. Data for four priests is incomplete.

120. Data for four priests is incomplete.

121. Data for one priest is incomplete.

122. Data for three priests is incomplete.

123. Data for three priests is incomplete.

124. Data for five priests is incomplete.

125. Data for four priests is incomplete.

126. The picture is presented, for example, in such novels as James Riley's *Christy of Rathglin* (Boston, C. M. Clark Publishing Co., 1907).

127. *One Hundred Years*, 749.

128. For example, within ten years of ordination, Father Thomas Norris was unable to continue as pastor at Stoughton, Massachusetts. "This inability," he wrote Williams in 1878, "arises from causes outside of what has been represented. I beg to assure you they are not to be accredited." BChA: Letter of Norris to Williams, September 3, 1878.

129. In addition, united action at the instigation of clergymen was not only rare but seldom publicized. The Diocesan Circulars of Boston of 1877–1879 contain a document whereby Williams gives permission for five clergymen to take up a subscription to defray expenses of Reverend Peter McKenna's appearance in Superior Court on behalf of inmates of the charitable institutions. It is marked "confidential." BChA: Diocesan Circulars, 1877–1879, n.d. [inserted after the late summer bulletins of 1878]. See Lord et al., *History*, III, 73–74 for the case in question.

130. BChA: Letter of Sherwood Healy to Williams, October 29, 1868.

131. Richards, *Loyal Life*, 308.

132. VDA: Ring Papers, I. Letter of Ring to Churchill, June 8, 1877; Letter of Ring to J. B. O'Reilly, January 12, 1877.

133. BChA: "Sherwood Healy's Suggestions for the Bishop's Use

in his remarks on the Statutes, Decrees, etc." Filed as November–December, 1868; and BChA: "Bishop Williams' Agenda for the Third Diocesan Synod, 1872." In addition, see BChA: Diocesan Circulars. A notice of 1876 indicated that local pastors were forcing Portuguese and Italian immigrants to support the Irish church as well as their own.

134. Sermon of Healy, May 28, 1876, as quoted in Byrne, *Glories of Mary*, 84–85. For other instances of the church as an intended retreat from reality by "flinging around the beholder a mystic spell," see Father Fitton's Dedication Sermon, April 7, 1878, in Byrne, *Glories of Mary*, 103.

135. *The Sacred Heart Review*, 1 (February 9, 1889), 6.

136. BChA: Letters of Moyce to Williams, December 14, 1868. It might be argued that Moyce was an exceptionally weak priest. See BChA: Letter of Rev. William Quinn to Williams, November 10, 1862.

137. BChA: Letters of Scully to Bishop McQuaid, December 18, 1875, January 6, 1876, February 24, 1876. See also *Donahoe's Magazine*, 3 (January 1880), 110, for awareness of Scully's position in as remote a city as St. Louis, Missouri.

138. *The Public School Question. Roman Catholicism and Americanism: A Discussion Between Rev. J. P. Bland and Rev. John O'Brien of Cambridge, Mass.* Cambridge University Press, 1880, Pamphlet reprinted from *The Boston Herald*. For Bland's misinterpretation of Williams on the matter see "Meeting of the Boston Union," (anon. article), *The Boston Daily Globe*, December 15, 1876, 5.

139. Tuckerman, *Life of Williams*, 519.

140. Charles Bullard Fairbanks, *My Unknown Chum* (New York, The Devin-Adair Co., 1922) [written in 1859], 27. Louise Imogen Guiney, *Patrins*, (Boston, printed for Copeland and Day, 1897) 113–114, 195 ff.

141. Reverend Joseph V. O'Connor, "Shall I Go West?," *Donahoe's Magazine*, 2 (December 1879), 484, 486. Vida Scudder in *A Listener in Babel* (Boston, Houghton, Mifflin and Co., 1903) quotes one Irish lady—supposed by Scudder to be typical—as saying that the country was "so horrid because you couldn't see anything but spaces" 71.

142. Emery, *A Catholic Stronghold*, passim. Abbé Felix Klein in *In the Land of the Strenuous Life* (Chicago, A. C. McClurg and Co., 1905) describes the Mission Church of Roxbury. "The parish buildings occupy an entire city square or block; so that a handsome and by no means unimportant town is thus formed by the beautiful church, the rectory, the school, and club-house . . . A private dynamo in a separate building provides steam heat and electric light in a most economical way . . . It is like a return to the Middle Ages, but with greater perfection of detail, more independence . . ." 57–58.

143. See William Byrne, "The Attitude of the Catholic Church to American Public Schools," *The Pilot*, November 15, 1879, 1.

144. BChA: Letter of Sherwood Healy to Williams, October 29, 1868.

145. Compare *The Pilot*, June 16, 1868, 4; BChA: Letter of Rev. McNeirney, secretary of the archbishop of New York, to Williams, June 12, 1868; *The Boston Daily Globe*, December 15, 1876, 5; *One Hundred Years*, 638, 639, 795.

146. Rev. Thomas J. Conaty, "The Irish Land Question," reprinted in *Donahoe's Magazine*, 5 (February 1881). In this same year, Conaty was an official representative of The National Land League of America, T. V. Powderly was elected second vice-president, and P. A. Collins of Boston, president, 172. Worcester was, of course, a separate diocese at this time.

147. Stone, "The Duties of American Catholics," *The Pilot*, November 22, 1873, 2. For further reference to Stone's thinking, see Stone, *An Awakening and What Followed* (Notre Dame, Ind., Ave Maria Press, n.d.)

148. VDA: Letter of Ring to Churchill, June 8, 1877, in Ring Papers, I, 78. BChA: Agreement of Father J. J. Healy with the Sisters of Mercy, October 22, 1886.

149. VDA: Letter of Ring to Churchill, May 14, 1877, in Ring Papers, I, 69; see letters of Ring for the year 1877, passim.

150. Richards, *Loyal Life*, 3–4, 37, 307, 313. BChA: Hilary Tucker's Diary II, entry of March 8, 1863.

151. Stone, Speech on Pope Pius IX, in Baltimore, February 16, 1878, as quoted in Walter George and Helen Grace Smith, *Fidelis of the Cross: James Kent Stone* (New York, G. P. Putnam's Sons, 1926 reprint), 264. For the same conviction on the part of Catholics, see O'Conor [*sic*], "Who are the Persecuted?" *Donahoe's Magazine*, 1 (May 1879), 392.

152. For the anti-intellectualism of the three men, see Stone, *An Awakening and What Followed*, 21, 26, 28, 48, passim; "An Address at the Dedication of the Catholic University of America," as quoted in Smith, *Fidelis*, 458, 462–463; Richards, *Loyal Life*, 55; Isaac Hecker, "The Communion of Saints and Spiritism," a sermon delivered in Providence, Rhode Island on October 29, 1868 reprinted in *The Pilot*, November 14, 1868, 31.

153. Letter of Stone to his mother, November 10, 1870, as quoted in Smith, *Fidelis*, 214.

154. HCA: Walsh, Louis S., Holy Cross Letters. Letter of Louis S. Walsh to his parents, December 15, 1846.

155. PChA: Entry book of Louis S. Walsh, September 1889 to–[*sic*] Entry of June 14, 1892, n.p.

156. O'Connell, *Recollections of Seventy Years*, 149.

157. James F. Finley, C.S.P., *James Gillis, Paulist* (New York, Hanover House, 1958), 179.

158. Louise Imogen Guiney, "Willful Sadness in Literature" in *Patrins*, passim.

159. Finley, *James Gillis*, 87, 82; PChA: Letter of William H. O'Connell to Jule [his sister], June 6, 1889, in which he admits he

would only be "a crank" if he came home from Rome so worried is he about the family's financial affairs; HCA: Letter of Louis S. Walsh to his parents, September 16, 1876, indicates a strong aggressive attitude toward his own family.

160. Rev. Lawrence P. McCarthy, *Sketch of the Life and Missionary Labors of Rev. James Fitton* in *Publications of the New England Historical Society*, 8 (Boston, 1908), 10.

161. *The Pilot*, December 6, 1873, 5. Compare with William Lawrence Sullivan, *The Priest, A Tale of Modernism in New England*, 3rd ed. (Boston, Beacon Press, 1925) [first edition in 1911]. Sullivan was a member of the Council of Unitarian Laymen, author of *From the Gospel to the Creeds, Studies in the Early History of the Christian Church* (Boston, Beacon Press, 1919).

162. O'Connor, "Who Are the Persecuted?," *Donahoe's Magazine*, 1 (May 1879), passim.

163. Stone, "The Duties of American Catholics," *The Pilot*, November 22, 1873, 2.

164. In the 1890's, Stone returned to Boston, something which was not customary for him. Attending a seminar with some of his Puerto Rican parishioners, he makes no attempt to lecture nor was his presence in the diocese adverted to with any special interest. Similarly, in 1870, Professor Leander Wetherall lectured sympathetically on Cardinal Cheverus in the Unitarian Church. *The Pilot* commented on it: "The very fact of our separated brethren desiring to hear more of Catholic views, bespeaks a growing spirit of candor and liberality which must result for good . . ." *The Pilot*, January 29, 1870, 6. But in the 1880's and 1890's, such lectures, such comments, and "Cheverus" disappear, except as consciously gratuitous.

165. Illustrative both of the inaccuracy of *The Pilot* in this matter and the determined independence of the American hierarchy from Rome is the matter of the battalion for the Pope in 1868. "Carroll," in "An American Battalion for the Pope," *The Pilot*, June 13, 1868, gives the impression that Americans wish to contribute men to the army for Pius ix. "In consequence of the many offers for service and the repeated proposals from different sectors of the United States to volunteer in the army of the Pope, his Holiness has consented to sanction the formation of an American battalion . . . provided that their Catholic fellow-countrymen will defray all the expenses." The article concludes by stating that a circular to this effect will be sent from the office of Cardinal Barnabo to the bishops, and it is assumed that the bishops will eagerly respond, 4. For a quite contrary response see BChA: Letter from Rev. McNeirney, secretary of the archbishop of New York, to Williams, June 12, 1868. The letter states that "the archbishop has made up his mind not to take any action in connection with the circular lately received from Rome in regard to the raising of men for the papal army . . . It is thought that the authorities [i.e. Barnabo, et al.] there have acted under a misapprehension. And representations have been made . . ." For the conservatism of Leo xiii, see BChA: Diocesan Circulars, 1877–1879, and

Leo's encyclical on education, instructed by Williams to be read, May 28, 1878. This view is supported by Henry Chaigne, "Catholic Church and Socialism," *Cross Currents*, 15 (Spring 1965), 151–168. Both Healy and Metcalf were "poorly treated in Rome at the hands of Monsignor Agnozzi (BChA: Letter of Healy to Williams, November 24, 1878). On the Ponsardin case, Healy was resentful of Rome's decision and sure that Williams would be receptive to his criticism (BChA: Letter of Healy to Williams, November 14, 1878).

166. BChA: Responsae Brevia et sine glossae et quaestiones, a Sacra Congregatione de Propaganda Fide propositae Circa Statum Diaecesis Bostoniensis Anno Domini, 1869. See also the report marked Special Report of the Diocese to the Propaganda, January 11, 1879. In answer to a letter from Rome, June, 1878, Williams replies on the subject of persecution of Catholics merely "La diocèse ne souffre aucune persécution" without taking advantage of any opening. In his report to Propaganda on June 1, 1877, not all fifty-five questions are answered. Those which are answered give the least possible amount of information. For Bishop McQuaid's type of answer to the same questionnaire form, see Frederick Y. Zweirlein, *Life and Letters of Bishop McQuaid Prefaced with the History of Rochester before His Episcopate*, ii, (Rochester, The Art Print Shop, 1926), 172 ff.

167. BChA: Instructio de Scholis Publicis, November 24, 1875.

168. BChA: Letter from the Office of the Propaganda to Williams, February 22, 1877.

169. BChA: Special Report of the Diocese to the Office of the Propaganda, January 11, 1879, in answer to a letter of June, 1878 [my translation in the text]. For Williams' support of Archbishop John Ireland's school plans, see Zweirlein, *Life and Letters of McQuaid*, iii, 164–165.

170. Baltimore Cathedral Archives. Letter of Bishop McQuaid to Cardinal Gibbons, December 10, 1878, in Letters to Cardinal Gibbons, No. 55, as quoted in Zweirlein, *Life and Letters of McQuaid*, ii, 179–180. For Healy's attitude toward Rome, see BChA: Letters of Healy to Williams, November 14, 1878, and November 24, 1878. Study of the archival material would lead to the conclusion that even Bishop John Wright, presently archbishop of Pittsburgh, is misleading in his interpretation of American Catholics' "spiritual" allegiance to Rome as distinct from their "political" allegiance. "American Catholicism," he writes, "has been characterized from the beginning by a profound spiritual loyalty to Rome . . . The Irish have never forgotten St. Patrick's plea that they be Romans precisely because Christians . . ." This is the writings of a priest trained under Cardinal O'Connell who, at least in this article, takes "the Irish" to be the starting point and totality of American Catholicism. *One of a Series of Interviews on the American Character, Center for the Study of Democratic Institutions. Religion. Interviews by Donald McDonald with Robert E. Fitch, John J. Wright, Louis Finkelstein* (1963), 32. For the proposal that an American be apos-

tolic delegate residing *in Rome* and that Williams' name was foremost among his fellow-bishops, see Zweirlein, *Life and Letters of McQuaid,* III, 151.

171. VDA: Letter of Ring to Churchill, June 8, 1877. Ring Papers, I, 75.

172. *The Pilot,* January 10, 1874, announces the arrival of the Sisters of St. Joseph in Father Magennis' parish in Jamaica Plain. They are obviously an unwelcome novelty in need of assessment. The public school system is the standard against which their work is measured. "Both in method and textbooks," the editors write in a persuasive manner, "they conform to the public school basis, except that anything anti-Catholic is eliminated . . ." 4. Emery in *A Catholic Stronghold* tries to be positive regarding the arrival of the Sisters at St. Peter's. "The Sisters found [as late as 1898] a strong prejudice existing against parish schools, and for a time they and their methods were closely observed by the parents and other visitors," 40. See also HCA: Louis S. Walsh File, The Early Irish-Catholic Schools of Lowell, Massachusetts, by Louis S. Walsh, Supervisor [typescript]. Although he will not actually admit it, Walsh indicates that in 1852, it was the Sisters of Notre Dame in St. Patrick's parish that raised anew "the demon of bigotry." He takes pains to explain their garb ("perhaps a bit singular to untrained eyes") as the cause. Catholics too were bewildered, 8. See also the critical article of A.J.R. [Abram J. Ryan], "Some of Our Weak Points," *Donahoe's Magazine,* 7 (February 1882), 100.

173. See James Kent Stone, "The Future of the United States," *Donahoe's Magazine,* 1 (January 1879), 136.

174. BChA: Special Report of the Diocese to the Office of the Propaganda, January 11, 1879.

175. Smith, *Fidelis,* 135.

176. BChA: Williams File. Notes from Williams to James G. Davis, August 5, 1872, May 15, 1877, October 4, 1880, requesting hats. In 1872 he wrote: "If you have a light brown soft hat, with large brim, that will fit me, please to send it up."

177. Many clergymen in Ireland, as O'Reilly well knew, were at that very time leaders of the Land League and violent supporters of the "No Rent Manifesto" of 1881. See Clifford Lloyd, *Ireland Under the Land League: A Narrative of Personal Experiences* (Edinburgh and London, William Blackwood and Sons, 1892), 63, 70, 79, 84.

III. 1880 TO 1890: DRIFT, AND SOME MASTERY

1. Eleanor Hallowell Abbott, *Being Little in Cambridge When Everyone Else Was Big* (New York, D. Appleton and Century Co., 1936), 67.

2. *Sacred Heart Review,* 2 (July 13, 1889), 1; see also VDA: 1887 Report in Report of the Particular Council, 1869–1890, 7.

3. Robert A. Woods, *Americans in Process: A Settlement Study by Residents and Associates of the South End House . . . North and*

West Ends (Boston, Houghton, Mifflin and Co., 1902), 44, 56–57; VDA: Ring Papers, II, Letters of Byrne to Ring, January 8, 1889, and January 14, 1889; Geoffrey T. Blodgett, "Josiah Quincy, Brahmin Democrat," *The New England Quarterly,* 38 (December 1965), 435.

4. Letter of O'Connell to Walter ———, December 12, 1887, in William Henry Cardinal O'Connell, *The Letters of His Eminence William Cardinal O'Connell, Archbishop of Boston,* I *(From College Days, 1876 to Bishop of Portland, 1901)* (Cambridge, The Riverside Press, 1915), 135. See Chapter IV, note 1, for author's use of this work; *Sacred Heart Review,* 2 (September 21, 1889), 6, and *Sacred Heart Review,* 2 (July 13, 1889), 10. In his obituary for John P. Squires, O'Brien wrote, "The publisher of the *Review* received from him and his estimable wife more than one generous proof of interest in the works he [publisher O'Brien] had on hand in East Cambridge." *Sacred Heart Review,* 9 (January 14, 1893), 8.

5. "250th Anniversary of Haverhill" (anon. article), *Sacred Heart Review,* 3 (April 5, 1890), 10; *Sacred Heart Review,* 2 (September 21, 1889), 6; *Sacred Heart Review,* 3 (December 14, 1889), 1, 2; William Henry Cardinal O'Connell, *Recollections of Seventy Years* (Boston, Houghton, Mifflin and Co., 1934), 26, 40, 43, 223.

6. SJSA: Record: St. John's Seminary, Boston (Brighton) Faculty Meetings: 1886 to 1905 [in French] under date of June 4, 1886, 24–25. See Susan L. Emery, *A Catholic Stronghold and Its Making: A History of St. Peter's Parish, Dorchester, and of Its First Rector, the Rev. Peter Ronan, P.R.* (Boston, George H. Ellis, 1910), 1; Hale, "Shall Church Property Be Taxed?" as quoted in Reverend Joseph V. O'Connor, "The Foreign Church," *Donahoe's Magazine,* 6 (November 1881), 393.

7. "The Enchanted Lady of the Mountain Castle" (anon. short story), *Sacred Heart Review,* 3 (January 11, 1890), 5; see Reverend Bernard O'Reilly's comments on Blanche of Castile in *Sacred Heart Review,* 1 (December 22, 1888), 1; *Donahoe's Magazine,* 16 (August 1886), 185.

8. VDA: Diary, 1888, Richard Keefe: Special Agent St. Vincent de Paul Conferences, Charity Building; Cases, 1889; VDA: Cases, 1889, Keefe: Letter of McCarthy to Keefe, December 12, 1889; VDA: Cases, 1889, Keefe: Letter of Nilan to Keefe, February 21, 1889; VDA: Cases, 1889, Keefe: Letter of Sullivan to Keefe, April 12, 1889; even at the end of 1889, Keefe was only beginning to understand the relationship between the Society for the Prevention of Cruelty to Children and the Children's Aid Society, both of which handled children brought in under the Neglect Law. See VDA: Cases, 1889, Keefe: Letter of Keefe to Ring, November 13, 1889.

9. VDA: Ring Papers, II, Letter of Ring to Byrne, November 9, 1880, 82–83; VDA: Ring Papers, II, Report of Thomas Ring to Archbishop John J. Williams, February 4, 1884, 321; VDA: Report of the Particular Council, 1869–1890: Report of 1887, 11–12, 13; for Louise Imogen Guiney's description of Boston as "an experimental . . . world" see Guiney, *Patrins* (Boston, 1897), 193.

10. See James Riley, *Christy of Rathglin* (Boston, C. M. Clark Publishing Co., 1907); see "Honor Before Honors" (anon. short story), *Sacred Heart Review*, 1 (January 12, 1889), 2.

11. "Temperance Societies" (anon. article), *Sacred Heart Review*, 1 (April 6, 1889), 7; *Sacred Heart Review*, 1 (January 26, 1889), 1; VDA: Monthly Meetings, Record #3, March, 1889, 44.

12. In 1884 the Republicans, using *The Boston Journal*, made an issue of the school board elections and women voting. There was a lull on "the school question" between 1885 and 1888 when it flared up again. The Republican Party, weakened by the growth of the Prohibition Party, decided to make an issue of the parochial schools once again in the 1887 elections. See Lois Bannister Merk, "Boston's Historic Public School Crisis," *The New England Quarterly*, 31 (June 1958), 172–199. See also A.J.R. [Abram J. Ryan], "Some of Our Weak Points," *Donahoe's Magazine*, 7 (February 1882), 100; BChA: Letter of Williams to Satolli, February 16, 1881; Byrne, "The School Question: True Attitude of the Catholic Church," *Donahoe's Magazine*, 29 (January 1893), 28.

13. McQuaid as quoted in *Donahoe's Magazine*, 50 (May 1881), 453; "The Convent Graduate" (unsigned editorial), *Donahoe's Magazine*, 10 (August 1883), 178–179; for Mrs. Blake's attitude see *The Boston Daily Globe*, December 7, 1876, 8; Donahoe's indecisiveness on the school question was typical. He took pains to inform his readers that the Boston School Board had discontinued the use of Swinton's *Outlines of the World's History* because it taught that indulgences were permits to sin. "Massachusetts," the notation ended, "is a grand old Commonwealth after all." *Donahoe's Magazine*, 20 (September 1888), 183.

14. A.J.R. [Abram J. Ryan], "Some of Our Weak Points," *Donahoe's Magazine*, 7 (February 1882), 100; Reverend Joseph V. O'Connor, "The Irish American," *Donahoe's Magazine*, 5 (January 1881), 8; *Sacred Heart Review*, 2 (October 13, 1889), 1 and *Sacred Heart Review*, 1 (December 15, 1888), 5; *Sacred Heart Review*, 1 (January 12, 1889), 4; James F. Finley C.S.P., *James Gillis, Paulist* (New York, Hanover House, 1958). Finley writes of Gillis' need to excel and his realization, later in life, that "the non-Catholic was concerned not so much with distinctly Catholic dogmas as he was with the more or less religious implications of secular affairs." "Critics said he found himself more entertaining, entertained and fascinated by topics only remotely connected with the Church" 251.

15. For Scully's part in the Civil War see Daniel McNamara, *The History of the Ninth Regiment, Massachusetts Volunteer Regiment . . . Army of the Potomac. June 1861–June 1864* (Boston, E. B. Stillings and Co., 1899), 429. See also HCA: Guiney Collection. Letters of Patrick Guiney, a Civil-War officer, imply that Scully deserted. BChA: Letters of Scully to Bishop McQuaid, December 16, 1875, January 6, 1876, February 24, 1876. (Originals in Rochester Diocesan archives.)

16. Scully, "The School Question," a lecture in the Town Hall of

Malden, September 14, 1881, reprinted in *Donahoe's Magazine*, 7 (February, 1882), 130–131; from *The Western Watchman* (St. Louis), a notation reprinted in *Donahoe's Magazine*, 3 (January 1880), 110.

17. *Sacred Heart Review*, 1 (January 12, 1889), 4.

18. Reverend John F. Byrne, C.SS.R., *The Glories of Mary in Boston: A Memorial History of the Church of Our Lady of Perpetual Help (Mission Church), Roxbury, Massachusetts, 1871–1921* (Boston, Mission Church Press, 1921), 135–137. For a more direct judgment on parents in terms of their children see Scully, "The School Question," *Donahoe's Magazine*, 7 (February 1882). "The mind of the parent," he stated, "grows only to perfection as it studies out the spiritual and temporal wants of the child" 127; "Catholic Advocates of Public Schools" (unsigned editorial), *Sacred Heart Review*, 1 (January 5, 1889), 1.

19. See "The Magnanimous Mr. Mead" (unsigned editorial), *Sacred Heart Review*, 1 (December 22, 1888), 1; Dwight, "The Attack on Freedom of Education in Massachusetts," *The American Catholic Quarterly Review*, xiii (October, 1888), 553; *Sacred Heart Review*, 2 (June 1, 1889), 8; see VDA: Ring Papers, ii, Letter of Ring to Reverend Thomas Shahan, December 22, 1880, 93. Here Ring, who was an insider in local Democratic politics, gives Shahan instructions regarding the purchase of the Savage School. He had uncovered the information before the public auction from "Mr. [Hugh] O'Brien."

20. See Guiney, "An Event on the River" in *Lovers' Saint Ruth's and Three Other Tales* (Boston, Copeland and Day, 1894), 63–93 and *Sacred Heart Review*, 8 (July 23, 1892), 7; see Roddan, "The Irishman in Ireland," *The Pilot* April 20, 1850, 1, April 27, 1850, 1. For such protestations of piety as "with the honorable exception of the Irish people, very very many Catholics coming here fall away from their ancestral faith" see *Donahoe's Magazine*, 10 (November 1883), 562. For exaggerated protestations of Irish nationalism see Martin J. Roche, "The Irish Brigade," *Sacred Heart Review*, 2 (June 15, 1889), 5; and [Martin J. Roche], "Our Irish Letter," *Sacred Heart Review*, 2 (June 1, 1889), 11. During the 1880's Roche regularly wrote the Irish Column, a presentation that progressively showed signs of irrelevance. Inconsequential letters received from individuals' relatives in Ireland replaced the reports forwarded by a regular professional correspondent. See *Sacred Heart Review*, 5 (February 7, 1891), 11.

See O'Reilly, "Ireland's New Programme," *The American Catholic Quarterly Review*, x (October 1885), 711–718; and O'Reilly, "Progress and Significance of the Parnell Commission," *The American Catholic Quarterly Review*, xiv (January 1889), 103–117.

21. Roddan, "The Irishman in Ireland," *The Pilot*, April 20, 1850, 1; O'Connor, "The Exiled People," *Donahoe's Magazine*, 3 (May 1880), 429.

22. O'Connor, "Is Catholicity Spreading in the United States,"

Donahoe's Magazine, 3 (April 1880), 331; O'Connor, "The Irish-American: His Merits and Defects," *Donahoe's Magazine*, 4 (July 1880), 5; Roche, "The Irish Brigade," *Sacred Heart Review*, 2 (June 15, 1889), 5; O'Connor, "The Irish-American," *Donahoe's Magazine*, 4 (July 1880), 5.

23. For pietism as it functioned in Irish family life see Conrad M. Arensberg and Solon T. Kimball, *Family and Community in Ireland* (Cambridge, Mass., Harvard University Press, 1940); O'Reilly, "How the Leading Classes Must Lead," *Sacred Heart Review*, 1 (March 9, 1889), 1.

24. Reverend F. H. Lieretz, "Waltzing," *Donahoe's Magazine*, 5 (January 1881), 147.

25. "Character Making," from *The Philadelphia Ledger* quoted in *Sacred Heart Review*, 2 (September 14, 1889), 2. For support of that opinion see Byrne, *Glories of Mary in Boston*, 135; and *Sacred Heart Review*, 2 (September 7, 1889), 1. *Sacred Heart Review*, to mention merely one publication, was replete with religious anecdotes. See "A Neglected Custom," *Sacred Heart Review*, 1 (March 9, 1889), 3.

26. Crowley, "The Child of the Temple" in *Carmelita, and Other Stories, in Fireside Tales by Catholic Authors, published for the Benefit of the Poor Deaf Mutes by Rev. M. M. Gerend*, ed. Anna T. Sadlier (Milwaukee, J. H. Yewdale and Son Co., n.d.), 69–116; Reverend Bernard O'Reilly, "How the Leading Classes Must Lead," *Sacred Heart Review*, 1 (March 9, 1889), 1; Hugh P. McElrone, "The Necessity of Association for Catholic Youth," *Donahoe's Magazine*, 19 (January 1888), 4.

27. Peter McCorry, "Revisiting Ireland—The Exil'd Return," *Donahoe's Magazine*, 25 (January 1891), 2; see James Riley, *Songs of Two Peoples* (Boston, Estes and Lauriat, 1898); L. W. Reilly, "On Catholic Newspapers and Why Catholic Men Don't Read Them," *Donahoe's Magazine*, 22 (November 1889), 431.

28. "Protest Against the Banishment of the Irish," *Donahoe's Magazine*, 9 (April 1883), 341; O'Connor, "The Irish-American," *Donahoe's Magazine*, 4 (July 1880), 4, 6, passim; see "Harmony and Home Rule for Ireland," *Donahoe's Magazine*, 29 (January 1893), for both openness on this issue and the contributions of clergymen. In 1897 a convert-priest, Reverend Henry Austin Adams, took over the editorship; O'Connor, "Is Catholicity Spreading," *Donahoe's Magazine*, 3 (April 1880), 331; *Sacred Heart Review*, 7 (February 13, 1892). Father O'Brien (the publisher and editor) took the occasion to thank Arthur Teeling, Peter Ronan, and other pastors who had worked to increase the paper's circulation. By 1895 the *Review* was being published by The Review Publishing Company, a corporation made up of almost one hundred clergymen of New England. Reverend Robert H. Lord, et al., *History of the Archdiocese of Boston, in the Various Stages of Its Development, 1604 to 1943*, III (New York, Sheed and Ward, 1944), 398.

29. O'Reilly, "How the Leading Classes Must Lead," *Sacred Heart Review*, 1 (March 9, 1889), 1; "Your Home" (unsigned editorial),

Sacred Heart Review, 1 (February 2, 1889), 2; *Sacred Heart Review,* 1 (December 8, 1888), 6; *Sacred Heart Review,* 1 (December 8, 1888), 5 and *Sacred Heart Review,* 2 (June 1, 1889), 8; *Sacred Heart Review,* 2 (September 7, 1888), 1; Frank Foxcroft quoted in *Sacred Heart Review,* 2 (June 1, 1889), 1.

30. L. W. Reilly, "Our Catholic Newspapers," *Donahoe's Magazine,* 22 (November 1889), 432; O'Connor, "Is Catholicity Spreading," *Donahoe's Magazine,* 3 (April 1880), 330; John D. Donavan, "The Catholic Priest: A Study in the Sociology of the Professions" [unpub. diss., Harvard University, Cambridge, 1951], 242; Reilly, "Our Catholic Newspapers," *Donahoe's Magazine,* 22 (November 1889), 432.

31. *Sacred Heart Review,* 1 (February 2, 1889), 1.

32. "Boston College: Its History and Influence," *Donahoe's Magazine,* 29 (January 1893), 70, 71, 76–77. A study of SJSA: Entrance Record St. John's Seminary, Boston: 1884–1957 indicates that a predominant number of young men entering the diocesan seminary at Brighton were students at and/or graduates of Boston College. (In the mid-1890's the record is incomplete; it is not kept from 1896 to 1908.)

Date of entrance	Number entering	Number graduated from Boston College
Sept. 21, 1884	34	16
Sept. 21, 1885	53	17
Sept. 20, 1886	17	7
Sept. 13, 1887	21	6
Sept. 11, 1888	23	10
Sept. 17, 1889	23	17
Sept. 16, 1890	20	6
Sept. 15, 1891	26	13
Sept. 13, 1892	32	14
Sept. 12, 1893	33	12
1911	21	14
1912	29	15

33. "Boston College," *Donahoe's Magazine,* 29 (January 1893), 76–77; even in 1893 the "course" with the Jesuits was still seven years: three preparatory and four college years. For the "lasting influence" of the Jesuits see SJSA: Record, St. John's Seminary, Boston (Brighton) Faculty Meetings: 1886 to 1905 [in French] under date of June 3, 1896. This is a report on the progress of the seminary to the Congregation's superiors and visitors. The Fathers refer to the Jesuit training of the boys entering the seminary. They are not satisfied with this. "Nearly all [of the boys] . . . if they had not begun their classes in a Catholic college at least finished them there; but the good religious influence which they received there [and which obviously has still to be contended with] scarcely prepared them for the work of interior formation which is proper to the seminary . . ." 69.

At a similar meeting dated January 1, 1892 unanimous displeasure is expressed at the sending of the young men to Boston College for several philosophy courses, 74–78; *One of a Series of Interviews on the American Character, Center for the Study of Democratic Institutions. Religion. Interviews by Donald McDonald with Robert E. Fitch, John J. Wright, Louis Finkelstein, January, 1963,* 39.

34. Letter of Bapst to Paresce, S.J., May 10, 1865 in Jesuit Provincial Archives, Baltimore, Maryland, quoted in David R. Dunigan, *A History of Boston College* (Milwaukee, Bruce Publishing Co., 1947), 82; *The Pilot,* March 12, 1864, 2; Joseph Havens Richards, S.J., *A Loyal Life: A Biography of Henry Livingston Richards with Selections from His Letters and a Sketch of the Catholic Movement in America* (St. Louis, Mo., B. Herder, 1913), 305; Fulton Diary, entry of 1875 quoted in Dunigan, *Boston College,* 117, 124.

35. James A. Gallivan, "Catholic Sons of Harvard," *Donahoe's Magazine,* 32 (November 1894), 499–510. Not only does Gallivan tell here of Bishop John Keane's reception of an honorary degree from Harvard in June of 1894 but he also reports that between 1863 and 1892 (reports of '65 and '73 are missing) there were eighty-four Catholics graduated. This number includes the names of men who became Catholics after graduation; it excludes those graduated from the schools of law, medicine, and business; Letter of Bapst to Billet, S.J., February 11, 1868 quoted in [A. J. McAvoy], *Father John Bapst: A Sketch* in *Woodstock Letters,* 18 (1889), 242.

36. *Sacred Heart Review,* 1 (January 19, 1889), 1; D. F. Sheehan in "The YMCA of Boston College," *Donahoe's Magazine,* 29 (January 1893), stated that the organization began in 1875 with over two hundred members, 106; *Donahoe's Magazine,* 21 (April 1889), 385; Perry Miller, *The Life of the Mind in America, from the Revolution to the Civil War* (New York, Harcourt, Brace and World, Inc., 1965), 79.

37. George E. Peterson, *The New England College in the Age of the University* (Amherst, Mass., Amherst College Press, 1964), 17, 28–29; for the Jesuits' stress upon a broader cultural foundation rather than a strictly "Catholic" one see Dunigan, *Boston College,* 50 ff.

38. "Boston College," *Donahoe's Magazine,* 29 (January 1893), 70; and Fulton, "Christian Character," a lecture reprinted in *The Pilot,* June 4, 1870, 4; WCA: *Sketch of Father Robert Fulton, S.J.* [anon. article] in *Woodstock Letters,* 25 (1896), 90–93; for an excellent discussion of the role of the college president and the symbolism of "the whole man" see Peterson, *New England College,* chapter 2; WCA: *Sketch of Fulton* in *Woodstock Letters,* 25 (1896), 95; Richards, *A Loyal Life,* 304; O'Connell, *Recollections,* 79.

39. Fulton, "Christian Character," *The Pilot,* June 4, 1870, 4; Peterson, *New England College,* 38; BChA: Baccalaureate Sermon Delivered by Rev. Wm. H. O'Connell to the Class of '94, Boston College.

40. O'Connell, "If Bendaoeed Returns," *Donahoe's Magazine*, 33 (February 1894), 174.
41. White as quoted in Peterson, *New England College*, 21; A.J.R. [Abram J. Ryan], "Give God His Place," *Donahoe's Magazine*, 9 (January 1883), 193. (This is fifth in a series in *Donahoe's Magazine* and posted from Boston College.) Reverend Timothy Brosnahan, S.J., "Are Catholics Tolerant?" *Donahoe's Magazine*, 31 (January 1894), 91.
42. See Brosnahan, "Are Catholics Tolerant?" *Donahoe's Magazine*, 31 (January 1894), 87–94. See also the writings of Michael Earls, S.J., a young man educated at Holy Cross College in the 1890's. One Jesuit scholar maintained of him that his novels were "not intended primarily to entertain" but were primarily "apologetic or polemic." See William L. Lucey, S.J., "The Record of an American Priest: Michael Earls, S.J., 1873–1937," reprinted from *The American Ecclesiastical Review*, 137 (1957), iv; HCA: Guiney Collection. Letter of Fulton to Guiney, February 26, 1891.
43. See Riley, "To Boston's Public Library," *The Weekly Bouquet* (1897), June 2; and Roche, "The V-A-S-E" in *Songs and Satires* (Boston, Ticknor and Co., 1887), 63–64, 79. Riley was born in Ireland in 1854 but educated in Massachusetts. He wrote for *The Pilot* and *Donahoe's Magazine* when both were at their literary best. His articles of the 1880's and 1890's express his growing admiration for the Yankees and New England ways. For these emphases see *Christy of Rathglin* (Boston, C. M. Clark Publishing Co., 1907). For a sketch of Roche see "Sketch: Famous People at Home—xvi: James Jeffrey Roche" [anon. article], *Time and the Hour*, 5 (June 5, 1897), 7–8. Here the author presents Roche as the delightfully fresh author and reformer upon whom had fallen the mantle of John Boyle O'Reilly. Roche was editor of *The Pilot* and a leading member of many writers' clubs. His works include *Songs and Satires, The Story of the Filibusters* (London, T. Fisher Unwin, 1891), and other collections of humorous verse. See also HCA: The Grace Guiney Collection. Letters of Roche to Guiney, March 13, 1885, August 5, 1885, December 18, 1889, and March 20, 1890.
See "Father Thomas I. Gasson, S.J." (anon. article) in *Woodstock Letters*, 35 (1905), for Gasson's principles as book reviewer for *Donahoe's Magazine* after 1905. For other examples of traditional interpretations of literature see Michael Earls, S.J., *Under College Towers* (New York, Macmillan Company, 1926); Brosnahan, "Are Catholics Tolerant?" *Donahoe's Magazine*, 31 (January 1894), 87–92; for an account of the clash between Eliot and Brosnahan see Dunigan, *Boston College*, 172ff.
44. Lucey, "Record of an American Priest," pamphlet reprinted from *The American Ecclesiastical Review*, 137 (1957), 30.
45. VDA: Ring Papers, ii, Letter of Ring to Sister Raymond, August 20, 1880, 51; SJSA: Record: St. John's Seminary, Boston (Brighton), Faculty Meetings: 1886–1905 [in French]. The Relationships of Students and Teachers, 86; SJSA: Record: St. John's

Seminary, Boston (Brighton) Faculty Meetings: 1886–1905 [in French], Third Visitation of W. A. Berriee (Visitor of the Congregation to the Seminary) and M. R. deFoville, secretary, under date of September, 1904. In this entry, the Fathers still indicate the need to express the continued exaggerated criticism of the local clergy toward them and their work. In this instance they label it frankly as "resistance" in the diocese. Two years earlier, a faculty meeting discussed the fact that local clergymen were complaining of the visiting privileges at the seminary and their abuse, that is, the allowance of too many visitors, 126, 119. Frederic H. Fay, *The Planning of a City*, in *Fifty Years of Boston: A Memorial Volume Issued in Commemoration of the Tercentenary of 1930. Compiled by the Subcommittee on Memorial History of the Boston Tercentenary Committee*, Elizabeth H. Herlihy, Chairman and Editor (Boston, Published for and by the Subcommittee, 1932), 46.

46. See *Sacred Heart Review*, 1 (January 12, 1889), 4 and "Family Prayer," *Sacred Heart Review*, 1 (July 6, 1889), 2; for an excellent example of "a well-known South Boston clergyman's" denunciation of "Catholic clubs and societies" based on external evidence and admittedly without an understanding of "where the idea [of joining clubs] is coming from" see *Sacred Heart Review*, 2 (July 13, 1889), 1; *Sacred Heart Review*, 2 (July 13, 1889), 1.

47. Ella Wheeler Wilcox, "Tact and Appreciation," *Sacred Heart Review*, 1 (January 26, 1889), 6; [Abram J. Ryan] "Anglo-Saxonism," *Donahoe's Magazine* 8 (July, 1882) 15. See also O'Connor, "Is Catholicity Spreading," *Donahoe's Magazine*, 3 (April 1880), 333. Here O'Connor states that "happily, the vast majority of Catholics are ignorant of the pernicious effects attendant upon the abuse of even the marital life, nor are they in a position to become acquainted with the grave warnings of physicians on such subjects" 333; *Sacred Heart Review*, 1 (January 26, 1889), 3; O'Connor, "No God, No Government," *Donahoe's Magazine*, 6 (September 1881). He states that "it is a wretched consequence of false ideas that they reserve their worst effects for generations subsequent to their own," 200; *Sacred Heart Review*, 3 (December 14, 1889), 5.

48. See Reverend Bernard O'Reilly's column on home life, in *Sacred Heart Review*, 1 (February 2, 1889), 1; "Family Prayer" (anon. article), *Sacred Heart Review*, 1 (July 6, 1889), 2; see Wilcox, "Tact and Appreciation," *Sacred Heart Review*, 1 (January 26, 1889), 6; see "Kitchen and Parlour" (anon. article), *Sacred Heart Review*, 2 (July 27, 1889), 2; in "Honor Before Honors" in the *Sacred Heart Review*, 1 (December 15, 1888), the prescription is given that a quiet life will preserve a woman from "strong emotions," 3; for a description of emotional tensions among young girls at this time see Robert A. Woods and Albert J. Kennedy, *Young Working Girls: A Summary of Evidence from Two Thousand Social Workers, edited for the National Federation of Settlements, introduction, by Jane Addams* (Boston, Houghton, Mifflin and Co., 1913),

25ff; White, "How to Save the Boys," *Sacred Heart Review,* (March 9, 1889), 3.
49. See Kittie F. White, "How to Save the Boys," *Sacred Heart Review,* 1 (March 9, 1889), 3; *Sacred Heart Review,* 2 (October 26, 1889), 2; see Wilcox, "Tact and Appreciation," *Sacred Heart Review,* 1 (January 26, 1889), 6; "Useless Self-Sacrifice" (anon. article), *Sacred Heart Review,* 2 (October 13, 1889), 6; Reverend Bernard O'Reilly, untitled column on the home, *Sacred Heart Review,* 1 (February 2, 1889), 1. For further reference to servants see "Your Home," *Sacred Heart Review,* 1 (February 2, 1889), 2.
50. See "Family Prayer," *Sacred Heart Review,* 2 (July 6, 1889), for fears of an "effeminate" society arising from "the novels being read," 6; for the clergy's recognition of their own irrelevance to the youth see "Editorial," *Sacred Heart Review,* 2 (July 13, 1889), 1; *Sacred Heart Review,* 1 (February 16, 1889), 5.
For evidence of the timidity which the Sulpician Fathers noted in the seminarians at St. John's Seminary (Brighton) see SJSA: Record: St. John's Seminary, Boston (Brighton) Faculty Meetings: 1886–1905 (in French) under date of June 3, 1886. See also James F. Finley, C.S.P., *James Gillis, Paulist* (New York, Hanover House, 1958). The author estimates that "excessive shyness and extreme fear were a life-long problem with Gillis" 194. In "The Provider" in *Lovers' Saint Ruth,* Louise Imogen Guiney presents the accepted image of the Irish boy vis-à-vis his mother: "he worshipped [his mother] in his shy, abstinent way" 93–123.
"Beware of the Retribution" (anon. article), *Sacred Heart Review,* 1 July 13, 1889), 4; and *Sacred Heart Review,* 1 (February 16, 1889), 5.
51. See Merk, "Public School Crisis," *The New England Quarterly,* 31 (June 1958). In 1884 the Republican *Boston Journal* quoted Father James Supple's plea from the pulpit of St. Francis De-Sales Church in Charlestown that Catholic women vote in the coming school board elections, 177–178. See also Thomas Hamilton Murry, "Municipal Suffrage for Women," *Donahoe's Magazine,* 21 (May 1889), 451–454; "Honor Before Honors" (anon. short story), *Sacred Heart Review,* 1 (December 15, 1888), 2; "Advice to Boys" (anon. article), *Sacred Heart Review,* 1 (February 16, 1889), 5; *Sacred Heart Review,* 2 (October 26, 1889), 13; *Sacred Heart Review,* 1 (January 19, 1889), 1. For other exhortations to follow the calling of the success ethic see Reverend Bernard O'Reilly, "Create Your Opportunities," *Sacred Heart Review,* 1 (February 9, 1889), 1; William E. Bridges, "Family Patterns and Social Values in America, 1825–1875," *The American Quarterly,* xvii (Spring 1965), 10.
52. *Donahoe's Magazine,* 9 (May 1883), 467; for the disinterest of "spiritual directors" in those charitable endeavors of the St. Vincent de Paul Society which embraced the entire parish see VDA: Ring Papers, ii, Letter of Ring to Williams, January 8, 1880, 349; *Interview . . . with John J. Wright,* 56.
53. "Honor Before Honors" (anon. short story), *Sacred Heart*

Review, 1 (January 12, 1889), 2; Archives of the Cleveland Diocese: Letter of Gilmour to Williams, January 23, 1874. For the loneliness experienced in choosing pastoral work among foreign peoples from city to city see BChA: Letters of Reverend Henry Hughes to Williams, 1878; see BChA: Hilary Tucker's Diary, II, 1862–1864, entry of June 18, 1863. For a criticism of the local Catholic literature on the grounds that it presented the Catholic clergy as unmanly and as "nincompoops" see Reverend Henry A. Adams, "Men and Things," *Donahoe's Magazine,* 38 (August 1897), 109; for the assumption that men of the religious orders were intellectually superior see "Father Cleveland; or The Jesuit" (anon. short story), *The Pilot,* February 1, 1868, 2. See also Reverend Henry A. Adams, "A Jesuit in Disguise: Being a New England Fable of Today," *Donahoe's Magazine,* 38 (July 1897), 29–39, Guiney, "Lovers' Saint Ruth" in *Lovers' Saint Ruth* and Guiney, *The Secret of Fougereuse* (Boston, Marlier, Callanan and Co., 1898).

It is possible with some difficulty to reconstruct a list of the prominent clergymen (excepting here Yankee-Catholic priests) of the mid-1880's: Michael Moran, John O'Brien, P. J. Hally, John Delehunty, William A. Blenkinsop, William M. O'Brien, Arthur J. Teeling, John Flatley, Richard J. Neagle, Thomas Magennis, Peter Ronan, Thomas H. Shahan. Some of these clerics—William A. Blenkinsop and Thomas Shahan—were of Williams' generation. By 1895, one can add the names of additional prominent clergymen of the generation of '45, namely, those men who were chairmen of the archbishop's jubilee celebrations. See SJSA: Seminary Folder: Archbishop and Chancery, 1883–1896.

54. See VDA: Report of the Particular Council, 1869–1890: Report of 1885; Lelia Harding Bugg, *The Correct Thing for Catholics,* 12th edition (New York, Benziger Brothers, 1891), 6; Bugg, *Correct Thing,* 84–90. See also Abbé John Hogan, *Daily Thoughts for Priests,* 3rd edition (Boston, Marlier, Callanan and Co., 1900), 88–89.

55. Hogan, *Daily Thoughts for Priests,* vi, vii, 24, 82, 100–101, 113, 181–182, 101, 201.

56. Hogan, *Daily Thoughts for Priests,* 27, 22–23, 149.

57. *Donahoe's Magazine,* 8 (July 1882), 83.

58. The term was used by Alice Stone Blackwell, an editor of the *Woman's Journal* during the school controversy in July of 1888 and is quoted by Merk in "Boston's School Crisis," *The New England Quarterly,* 31 (June 1958), 185; BChA: Letter of deGoesbriand to Williams, December 7, 1879. For Williams' letter to Simioni on the affair see Letter of Williams to Simioni, August 17, 1880; BChA: Msgr. Strain's Diary Accts and Collections, 1856–1881. For a lengthy biographical sketch on Strain see "Monsignor Patrick Strain," *Sacred Heart Review,* 3 (February 22, 1890), 1. See also *An Unfinished Story: The Narrative of St. Mary's School on the Occasion of Its Fiftieth Birthday* (Lynn, Mass., n.p., 1931); and Reverend Michael J. Scanlan, *An Historical Sketch of the Parish of St. Rose, Chelsea*

Mass. (n.p., n.d. 1924 given in the Preface). For Strain's unamicable relations with the St. Vincent de Paul Society see VDA: Ring Papers, II, Letters of Ring to Sister Raymond, August 20, 1880ff., 51, 58, 77–78, 129.

59. See VDA: Ring Papers, II, Letters of Ring to Sister Raymond, August 20, 1880ff., 51, 58, 77–78; see VDA: Ring Papers, II, Letter of Ring to Bishop James Healy, September 30, 1891 [loose letter]; and letter of Ring to F. H. Churchill, March 22, 1883, 231–233; Hogan, *Daily Thoughts for Priests,* 128; William H. O'Connell himself substantiates Sullivan's judgment in his *Recollections.* "The parish priests," he wrote of pastors in the 1880's, "had naturally assumed something of the airs and the methods of the parish priests of their native country [Ireland]. They had a way of lording it over their curates and their congregations . . . There was practically no knowledge whatever of Canon Law. Not being jurists, they ruled autocratically . . ." 151–153; Sullivan, *The Priest, A Tale of Modernism in New England,* 3rd edition (Boston, Beacon Press, 1925) [first edition in 1911], 36, 24, passim. For Sullivan's ambivalence toward Catholicism see 233.

For an example of O'Connell's negative estimate of the older pastors see *Recollections,* 153. See also O'Connell, *Letters,* Letter of O'Connell to David ————, December 20, 1883, where he commented on American prelates in Rome, especially Father Daly of St. Joseph's parish who was there wearing "three enormous emerald studs" on his white shirtfront. He agreed with Roman prelates that it was time "this sort of array" stop, 89. In the Second Synod (1905) of the Portland Diocese over which he presided as bishop, O'Connell insisted that priests wear cassocks in the parish house and church; outside, they must always wear the Roman collar. See PChA: Healy Letters, Uncatalogued, Full Account in English of the Second Synod of the Diocese of Portland.

IV. 1890 TO 1910: NEW SOURCES
AND FUNCTIONS OF AUTHORITY

1. Each of the addresses of Archbishop Williams is reproduced in *Souvenir of the Sacerdotal Golden Jubilee of the Most Reverend Jno. J. Williams, D.D. Archbishop of Boston, on Thursday and Friday, May 16 & 17, 1895, with Full Reports of Receptions and Presentations Incident to the Celebration,* ed. by Bernard Corr (Boston, 1895).

2. HCA: File: Walsh, Louis S. "Banquet on the Occasion of Consecration of Louis S. Walsh, October 18, 1906."

3. Letter of O'Connell to Henry ————, January 15, 1883, in William Cardinal O'Connell, *The Letters of His Eminence William Cardinal O'Connell, Archbishop of Boston,* I (Cambridge, Mass., The Riverside Press, 1915), 78. I have made no effort to identify the correspondents whom O'Connell frequently leaves anonymous. The let-

ters were compiled by him for the public, and it is what he wants said to them that is the concern of this study.

4. For evidence of separatism see "Pastoral Letter of the Bishops Assembled in the Third Plenary Council," *Donahoe's Magazine*, 13 (February 1885), 116. In 1886, Ireland warned the bishops that even then the pope suspected them of deceit regarding the signatures on the petition for a Catholic University of America. See BChA: Letter of Ireland and Keane to the American Bishops, December 14, 1886. Reverend Anderson is quoted in Frederick J. Zwierlein, *The Life and Letters of Bishop McQuaid, Prefaced with a History of Catholic Rochester Before His Episcopate.* III (Rochester, The Art Print Shop, 1926), 235.

5. Reverend John Conway, "The Future of the Catholic Church in America," *Donahoe's Magazine*, 30 (November 1893), 493–497.

6. Reverend James Gillis, CSP, "Foreword," in Abbé Felix Klein, *Americanism: A Phantom Heresy*, tr. author (Atchison, Kansas, Aquin Book Shop, 1950), iii.

7. See Gillis, "Foreword" in *Americanism*, vi; see also Reverend Thomas T. McAvoy, C.S.C., "Americanism, Fact and Fiction," *The Catholic Historical Review*, 31 (July 1945), 135, 149.

8. Klein, *Americanism*, 6, 5–6; Ireland, "Introduction," to *The Life of Father Hecker* as reprinted in Klein, *Americanism*, xx, xviii, xx; Ireland, "Introduction" in Klein, *Americanism*, xx, xxi, xv. For rebuttals of the Klein translation see Charles Maignen, *Etudes sur l'américanisme. Le père Hecker, est-il un saint?* (Paris, V. Retaux, 1899); A. J. Delattre, *L'américanisme: une planche de salut* (Paris, V. Retaux, 1898), and Hippolite Martin, "L'Américanisme" in *Les Etudes Religieuses* of July 4, 1898.

9. Gillis, "Foreword" in Klein, *Americanism*, iv. Maignen's purpose in seeking an English edition of his rebuttal to Klein was to acquaint the American people of "the dangers into which they were being led by their own hierarchy."

10. BChA: Letter of Ryan to Corrigan, May 20, 1890.

11. BChA: Minutes of the Meetings of the Archbishops at Philadelphia, under date of October 10, 1894. Payment for the house of the delegate was $7759.76.

12. "Apostolic Letter Testem Benevolentiae, January 22, 1899, addressed to His Eminence Cardinal Gibbons, Archbishop of Baltimore," in *The Great Encyclical Letters of Pope Leo XIII*, ed. Reverend John J. Wynne. (New York, Benziger Brothers, 1903), 452.

13. "Testem Benevolentiae" in *Great Encyclical Letters*, 452.

14. An editor of *Donahoe's Magazine* characterized the pope's awareness of America in 1883 as "the ultimate boundary of an immense European emigration." *Donahoe's Magazine*, 10 (November 1883), 562.

15. Letter of O'Connell to Bishop ———, December 20, 1896, in *Letters of O'Connell*, 215 ff.

16. BChA: Minutes of the Meetings of the Archbishops, under dates of October 10, 1894, October 2, 1895, October 22, 1896.

For the bishops' fading hope that one of their number might be a representative of the American church *in Rome* rather than having a delegate residing here, see BChA: Letter of Gilmour to McQuaid, January 28, 1887 [original in Rochester Diocesan Archives] and Letter of Corrigan to McQuaid, December 29, 1887. In both letters, Williams is mentioned as one of the most likely and deserving candidates.

17. BChA: Note of Williams regarding Holy Communion, April 6, 1899; "Testem Benevolentiae" in *Great Encyclical Letters,* 442.

18. "Testem Benevolentiae" in *Great Encyclical Letters,* 442–443; Williams' sermon as quoted in "Celebration of Thanksgiving in Boston" (anon. article), *Donahoe's Magazine,* 21 (December 10, 1888 Supplement), 98. For Leo's statements on the natural virtues see "Testem Benevolentiae" in *Great Encyclical Letters,* 446–449 ff.

19. "Testem Benevolentiae" in *Great Encyclical Letters,* 445; "Celebration," *Donahoe's Magazine,* 21 (December 10, 1888 Supplement), 100; "Testem Benevolentiae" in *Great Encyclical Letters,* 445; "Celebration," *Donahoe's Magazine,* 21 (December 10, 1888 Supplement), 101.

20. "On Human Liberty," *Donahoe's Magazine,* 21 (February 1, 1889), 219, 220, 221.

21. "On Human Liberty," *Donahoe's Magazine,* 21 (February 1, 1889), 223.

22. "Testem Benevolentiae" in *Great Encyclical Letters,* 445–446; HCA: Grace Guiney Collection. Guiney-Heuser Collection. Letter of Guiney to Heuser, January 20, 1903; *The Public School Question. Roman Catholicism and Americanism: A Discussion between Rev. J. P. Bland and Reverend John O'Brien of Cambridge, Massachusetts* [Reprinted from *The Boston Herald*] (Cambridge, 1880), 20, 26–27; *Sacred Heart Review,* 9 (February 18, 1893), 4.

23. "Address of Reverend Thomas J. Conaty at the Sixteenth Annual Convention of the Catholic Total Abstinence Union of America: Sermon During the Pontifical Mass," reprinted in *Donahoe's Magazine,* 16 (October 1886), 336; VDA: Letter of Conaty to Ring, January 22, 1890, and April 22, 1890; Letter of Leo xiii to Satolli, September 18, 1895, quoted in Zwierlein, *Life and Letters of McQuaid,* iii, 237.

24. Quoted in Zwierlein, *Life and Letters of McQuaid,* iii, 235; "Testem Benevolentiae" in *Great Encyclical Letters,* 446.

25. "Address of Bishop Keane in Worcester: The American Child and the Christian School," *Donahoe's Magazine,* 23 (January 1890), 277. Three days later Keane gave the same address in Boston. For Keane's paper to the Catholic Union see "The Future of Religion," *Donahoe's Magazine,* 31 (January 1894), 61–64.

26. "Leading Men—What They Are Doing?" (anon. article), *Donahoe's Magazine,* 17 (February 1887), 122; Luther Mott, *History of American Magazines* quoted in Reverend William L. Lucey, "Catholic Journalism in New England: 1885–1900" (Reprint from *The New England Social Studies Bulletin,* May 1953), 36; Ireland, "Care

for the People: Duty of the Hour," an address delivered in Baltimore and reprinted in *Donahoe's Magazine,* 23 (February 1890), 133.

27. Quoted in Agnes Hampton, "A Triple Consecration at St. Paul," *Donahoe's Magazine,* 23 (March 1890), 236.

28. Quoted in Hampton, "Triple Consecration," *Donahoe's Magazine,* 23 (March 1890), 236.

29. "Address of Keane in Worcester," *Donahoe's Magazine,* 23 (January 1890), 277.

30. Keane, "The American of the Future," *Donahoe's Magazine,* 26 (November 1891), 461; "The Future of Religion [by] Rt. Rev. John J. Keane . . . Three Characteristic Extracts Taken from His Lecture, 'The Future of Religion' Delivered by Him in the Boston Theater Recently in Aid of the Building Fund of the Catholic Union of Boston," *Donahoe's Magazine,* 31 (January 1894), 61–64.

31. Reverend John Talbot Smith, "Archbishop Ireland: Number 2 in a Series, 'Eminent American Prelates,'" *Donahoe's Magazine,* 32 (November 1894), 495, 491.

32. Reverend John Conway, "The Future of the Catholic Church in America," *Donahoe's Magazine,* 30 (November 1893), 493, 496.

33. Van Wyck Brooks, "Aesthetic Boston" in *New England: Indian Summer* (New York, E. P. Dutton and Co., 1950), 144ff.

34. Letter of O'Connell to Msgr. T———, April 30, 1894 in *Letters of O'Connell,* 172, 170.

35. See Joseph Bernhart, *The Vatican as a World Power* tr. George M. Schuster, rev. ed. (New York, Ginn and Co., 1939), 353. For the use of the term see Louise Imogen Guiney, *Blessed Edmund Campion* (London, McDonald and Evans, 1908), 10. The term as used by William Cardinal O'Connell, Michael Earls, and other clergymen is analysed in Chapter III.

36. Judge James Fallon offered this list as those families that supported the Catholic Union and general cultural harmony. See reprint in *Donahoe's Magazine,* 23 (February 1890), 166–170.

37. Johnstone, Adams and Blunt were members of the group. Teeling and Flatley were personal friends of O'Reilly. Byrne founded the New England Catholic Historical Society and was editing a juvenile magazine in the 1870's, *The Young Crusader.* Miss Mary Murphy wrote for *The Young Crusader* and married O'Reilly in 1872. Metcalf was a close friend of the O'Reillys, Louise Guiney and, earlier, Fairbanks. See HCA: Grace Guiney Collection. Letter of Bessie Boyle O'Reilly to Guiney, June 4, 1907, and M. Earls, *Manuscripts and Memories* (Milwaukee, Bruce Publishing Co., 1935), 135–136.

38. HCA: Grace Guiney Collection. Letter of O'Reilly to Guiney, May 10, 1889, and another dated simply December 10. In the latter, O'Reilly encourages Louise to attend a reception of Mrs. Moulton's "without me" and without fear. Lucey in "Louise Imogen Guiney," *Records of the American Catholic Historical Society of Philadelphia,* 66 (March, 1955), substantiates that her first poem appeared in *The Pilot* of 1881 and that with O'Reilly's further support she was "in

the company of Francis Parkman, George P. Lathrop, and Brooks Adams" 53–63.

39. Reverend Julien Johnstone, "Sea-Longings" in *Songs of Sun and Shadow* (Boston, W. B. Clarke Co., Park Street Church 1900), 29. Mary Elizabeth Blake was also among the contributors. See Lilian Whiting, *Louise Chandler Moulton: Poet and Friend* (Boston, Little, Brown and Co., 1910).

40. Complete information on Johnstone has been impossible to gather. The records of St. John's Seminary indicate the years he spent there but without comment. Ordained in 1896, he is simply listed as "Died March 28, 1921. Absent on leave" in John E. Sexton and Arthur Riley, *History of St. John's Seminary, Brighton* (Boston, Published by the Roman Catholic Archbishop of Boston 1945), 281. Several of his poems, none of them good ones, were originally printed in *Donahoe's Magazine*. His volume of poems is not available in the seminary library but is held in the Boston Public Library as part of the Louise Chandler Moulton bequest.

41. Letter of Guiney to Clarke, April 21, 1892 as quoted in *Letters of Louise Imogen Guiney*, I, ed. Grace Guiney (New York, Harper and Brothers, 1926), 31.

42. Carlin T. Kindilien, *American Poetry in the Eighteen Nineties* (Providence, Brown University Press, 1956), 47. See also Katherine O'Mahoney, *Famous Irishwomen* (Lawrence, Mass., Lawrence Publishing Company, 1907), 14; Kindilien, *American Poetry*, 12.

43. Sr. Mary Madeleva, CSC, *My First Seventy Years* (New York, Macmillan Company, 1959), 41.

44. O'Reilly came to Boston in 1870 at the age of twenty-six and was already famous for his nationalist activities in Ireland and his subsequent imprisonment and escape from Australia. In the same year, he became editor of *The Pilot* and the foremost "representative man" of the immigrants. He lectured and wrote extensively. *Songs, Legends and Ballads* (Boston, The Pilot Publishing Co., 1878), *The Statues in the Block* (Boston, Roberts Brothers, 1881), and *In Bohemia* (Springfield, Mass., F. and E. Mathewson, 1907), are only a few of his publications. He died suddenly in 1890. Thomas N. Brown in "The Origins and Character of Irish-American Nationalism," *Review of Politics*, 18 (July 1956), states that "each week *The Pilot* taught the displaced peasants the disciplines of toleration and fair-play necessary in a multi-racial city, thereby earning the applause of Brahmin Boston" 350. For a further study of O'Reilly's contributions see Arthur Mann, *Yankee Reformers in an Urban Age* (New York, Harper and Row, 1954).

45. *Watchwords from John Boyle O'Reilly*, ed. Katherine Conway (Boston, Joseph George Cupples, private printing, 1891), 2; O'Reilly, *Moondyne: A Story from the Under-World* (Boston, Roberts Brothers, 1883), 10. For his familiarity with Bentham's works see *Moondyne*, 89, 115–116, 142; *The Pilot*, June 1, 1872, 4; James J. Roche, *Life of John Boyle O'Reilly: Together with His Complete Poems and*

Speeches edited by Mrs. John Boyle O'Reilly (New York, Cassell Publishing Company, 1891), 134, 140, 192.

46. Roche, *O'Reilly,* 121. For O'Reilly's retreating before immigrant demands see Brown, "Irish-American Nationalism," *Review of Politics,* 18 (July 1956), 351; O'Reilly, "What Is True Knowledge," *The Pilot,* March 2, 1872, 1; quoted in Alice Brown, *Louise Imogen Guiney* (New York, Macmillan Company, 1921), 52.

47. For the subtle change from O'Reilly's type of reform enthusiasm in the 1880's to the absorption in literary expression and leadership there see "Sketch—Roche," (anon. article), *Time and the Hour,* v (June 5, 1897), 7. See also Miss Guiney's reference to herself as a "reformer," that is, one who tampers with verbs and nouns in *A Little English Gallery* (New York, Harper and Brothers, 1894), 78, 83; "Sketch—Roche," *Time and the Hour,* v (June 5, 1897), 7; Reverend Henry Austin Adams, "A Jesuit in Disguise: Being a New England Fable of Today," *Donohoe's Magazine,* 38 (August 1897), 109; for Miss Guiney's lengthiest discussions on religion see her correspondence with Father Harmon van Allen of the Church of the Advent in HCA: A Collection of Intimate Autograph Letters, 124 pages, 1899 1915 to Rev. H. van Allen; Guiney, *Little English Gallery,* 62.

48. Letter of Guiney to Clarke, January 10, 1897 in *Letters,* I, 1ᴐ F r O'Reilly's independence of Williams in editing *The Pilot* see BChA: Letter of O'Reilly to Williams, May 14, 1886.

49. See HCA: Earls: Letters, 1931. Letter of Sr. M. Pauline Finn to Earls, December 23, 1931. She refers to the 1890's as "full of significance for us." But, she adds, "poetry does not find more than a crutch-support in a Catholic atmosphere." For the literary clubs to which writers like Roche belonged see HCA: Guiney Collection. Letter of Roche to Guiney, September 13, 18— [catalogued after a letter of December 18, 1889].

50. Herlihy entered St. John's Seminary from Roxbury in 1891 at the age of twenty. He was born in Ireland and educated there until the age of twelve. After attending public schools in Boston, he attended St. Charles College for one year. SJSA: Entrance Records, 28–29; HCA: Collection of Autograph Letters. Letter of Guiney to van Allen, May 17, 18— [probably written shortly after 1904]. For another expression of her not feeling "at full value" in Catholic Boston see Letter of Guiney to van Allen, August 16, 1896, in *Letters,* I, 127.

51. For Williams' patronage of Katherine E. Conway see Letter of Conway to Bishop McQuaid, April 10, 1907, quoted in Sr. M. Alphonsine Frawley, C.S.J., *Patrick Donahoe* (Washington, D.C., Catholic University Press, 1946), 289. For Williams' patronage of Mary Agnes Tinckor see BChA: Eulalia Tuckerman, "Life of Archbishop John J. Williams" [unpublished manuscript, 1911], 489.

52. Reverend Matthew Russel, S.J., "Mary E. Blake," *Donahoe's Magazine,* 15 (February 1886), 142; HCA: Guiney Collection. Letter of Fulton to Guiney, October 29, 18— [probably after 1892]; Guiney,

"On Dying Considered as a Dramatic Situation," in *Patrins* (Boston, Copeland and Day, 1897) 88; for her remarks on "the philosophy of comment" see Guiney, *Goose-Quill Papers* (Boston, Roberts Brothers, 1885), 115.
53. Blake, *Twenty-Six Hours a Day* (Boston, D. Lathrop and Co., 1883), 35. Mrs. Blake is more sympathetic in *In the Harbor of Hope* (Boston, Little, Brown and Co., 1907); HCA: Cordon Collection of Louise Imogen Guiney Letters, Portfolio I, Letter of Guiney to Miller, March 4, 1898; HCA: File: Katherine E. Conway. Letter of Conway to Earls, January 21, 1910; Guiney, *Monsieur Henri: A Footnote to French History* (New York, Harper and Brothers, 1892), 43. For Miss Guiney's admission that she reads for "the beautiful" rather than political facts see "Preface" to *Monsieur Henri*, v, vi; Blake, *The Coming Reform: The Absurdities of Old-Fashioned Militarism at Home and Abroad in These Closing Years of the Nineteenth Century* (Boston, The American Peace Society, n.d.), passim; Blake, *Patrick McGrath* (n.p., n.d.)
54. See Blake, *On the Wing: Rambling Notes of a Trip to the Pacific*, 2nd ed. (Boston, Lee and Shepard, 1883), and Mary E. Blake and Margaret F. Sullivan, *Mexico: Picturesque, Political and Progressive* (Boston, Lee and Shepard, 1888).
55. Guiney, "Quiet London" in *Patrins*, 197; Letter of Guiney to van Allen, September 10, 1896 in *Letters*, I, 136; Roche, *The Story of the Filibusters: To Which Is Added the Life of Colonel David Crockett* (London, T. Fisher Unwin, 1891), 56.
56. George Parsons Lathrop insisted that O'Reilly's poetry did not live because his following was largely personal. See Reverend Francis J. McManimin, S.J., *The American Years of John Boyle O'Reilly, 1870–1890* [unpub. diss., Catholic University of America, 1959], 18. For Miss Guiney's regard for her own privacy see "Privacy" in *Patrins*, 9.
57. See O'Mahoney's treatment of Mrs. Blake in *Famous Irishwomen* (Lawrence, Mass., Lawrence Publishing Co., 1907), passim.
58. Letter of Guiney to van Allen, August 16, 1896, in *Letters*, I, 127.
59. See Earls, *Stuore* (New York, Benziger Brothers, 1911), passim. For Earls' friendship with Miss Guiney and her support of his career as writer see HCA: Guiney-Earls Collection (22 letters and cards), 1899–1920. For his dependence upon Roche see HCA: Shaughnessy Collection, undated letter of Earls to his parents from Issy, France [After October 22, 1897].
60. Reverend Robert H. Lord, et al., *History of the Archdiocese of Boston, in the Various Stages of Its Development, 1604 to 1943*, III (New York, Sheed and Ward, 1944), 406. Letter of Guiney to van Allen, September 12, 1896, in *Letters*, I, 136; SJSA: Folder: Archbishop and Chancery, 1913–1914. Letter of Reverend John B. Peterson to Reverend Denis F. Sullivan, February 3, 1914, acknowledging the archbishop's request that "a priest be set aside to meet Socialist propaganda."

61. J. Havens Richards, S.J., *A Loyal Life: A Biography of Henry Livingston Richards* (St. Louis, B. Herder, 1913), 4; Bugg, *Orchids, A Novel* (St. Louis, B. Herder, 1894), 53, 27, 39, 51, 99; Brooks, *New England: Indian Summer* (New York, E. P. Dutton and Co., 1950), 423, 422. See also Alexander Young [pseudo. "Taverner"], "Here in Boston—The Evil Quality of the Puritan Conscience," *Time and the Hour*, v (June 5, 1897), 3–6.

62. Joseph Noonan, "Physical Culture in Our Seminaries," *Donahoe's Magazine*, 25 (March 1891), 245.

63. For the congregations' greater sense of rapport with the younger clergymen see PChA: Louis S. Walsh, Entry Book, 1889 to [1897]. Writing as professor at the Boston seminary, he reminds himself to encourage the newly ordained men "always" to "maintain the pastor's popularity, rather than increase their own at his expense."

64. *Sacred Heart Review*, 9 (January 7, 1893), 4; see address of O'Connell at the celebration of the centennial of the Boston diocese, October 28, 1908, quoted in Lord et al., *History*, III, 508–516.

65. For the problem of the dying "good parishes" in the inner-city see William I. Cole, "Two Ancient Faiths," in *Americans in Process* ed. Robert A. Woods (Boston, Houghton, Mifflin and Co., 1902), 261–269; Geoffrey T. Blodgett, "Josiah Quincy, Brahmin Democrat," *New England Quarterly*, 38 (December 1965), 444.

66. VDA: Letter of McCoy to Ring, April 20, 1892, in Thomas Ring, Scrapbook, 9. See also Reverend Henry Austin Adams, "Men and Things," *Donahoe's Magazine*, 38 (August 1897), 199.

67. VDA: Thomas Ring: Letterpress Book, 1884–1885. Letter of Ring to Byrne, March 20, 1886.

68. *Sacred Heart Review*, 6 (August 29, 1891), 9.

69. VDA: Ring Papers, III, Letter of Ring to Sister Raymond; VDA: Reprint of a Paper Read at a Catholic Congress, September 1893 (Chicago), in Ring Scrapbook, 128; VDA: Ring Papers III, Letter of Dwight to Ring, May 1, 1891 and letter of Ring to Dwight, May 8, 1891; VDA: Transcript of an Address, November 2, 1892 at St. John's Seminary, in Ring Scrapbook, 5–6; Letter printed in full in "Our Future Men and Women," *Sacred Heart Review*, 9 (March 4, 1893), 4.

70. *Sacred Heart Review*, 4 (July 15, 1890), 1; *Sacred Heart Review*, 4 (July 26, 1890), 1; Cole, "Community of Interest" in *Americans in Process*, ed. Woods, 354.

71. Supple, "W. H. Mallock's *Doctrine and Doctrinal Description*," *Donahoe's Magazine*, 44 (October 1900), 330–332.

72. *Sacred Heart Review*, 4 (July 15, 1890), 1; see also the 130-line poem of Reverend Denis J. O'Farrell, "Leo XIII," *Donahoe's Magazine*, 49 (January 1903), 66–68.

73. Shahan, "The Ancient Schools of Ireland," *Donahoe's Magazine*, 31 (May 1894), 525–537; O'Callaghan, "Irish Race Convention," *Donahoe's Magazine*, 36 (December 1896), 585–587; McKenna, "Catholic Temperance Reform Work," *Donahoe's Magazine*, 30 (Sep-

tember 1893), 261–264. See also Supple, "The Typical Catholic Novel," *Donahoe's Magazine*, 43 (March 1900), 325–328.
74. See SJSA: Ordinandi Files. Letter of Timothy Sullivan to Reverend Francis P. Havey, July 27, 1905.
75. The dominance of New England writers and dramatists at the Champlain School (Plattsburg) was so evident that Reverend Mortimer E. Twomey, a young Boston supporter, had to defend it against charges of provincialism in 1897. See *Donahoe's Magazine*, 38 (July 1897).
76. John Talbot Smith, "Catholic Summer Schools," *Donahoe's Magazine*, 34 (July 1895), 760, 762, 763; VDA: Tenth Annual Report of the Central Council of Boston for the Year Ending December 31, 1898 (Boston, 1899), 7. In Salem, Massachusetts, when the parishioners wanted to form a committee of laymen to assist the pastor directly with finances, they were labelled "liberal Catholics" with "modern Ideas" and fault-finders. See *Sacred Heart Review*, 6 (July 18, 1891), 6; Leland Mason, "Patriotism: A Dialogue," *Donahoe's Magazine*, 29 (March 1893), 331–336.
77. "A Word to Young Employees" (unsigned editorial), *Sacred Heart Review*, 5 (April 11, 1891), 9; *Sacred Heart Review*, 5 (May 9, 1891), 14.
78. The *Review* articles on "The Co-operative Society of Harmelville in France" ran for four weeks in 1892. This was extraordinary for the editors; Smith, "The Indirect Increase of Wages," *Donahoe's Magazine*, 44 (November 1900), 431, 436; *Sacred Heart Review*, 6 (September 12, 1891), 1.
79. Reverend John Conway, "The Pulpit," *Donahoe's Magazine*, 32 (December 1894), 589; Charles Warren Currier, C.SS.P., "Rest at Last," *Donahoe's Magazine*, 23 (February 1890), 138–141; Conway, "Pulpit," *Donahoe's Magazine*, 32 (December 1894), 588.
80. *Sacred Heart Review*, 9 (February 11, 1893), 9.
81. "People in Print" (anon. article), *Donahoe's Magazine*, 57 (April 1907), 422.
82. For an example of the older generation's undefined stance on the matter of church authority see Abbé John Hogan, "Freedom of Thought in the Catholic Church," *Donahoe's Magazine*, 30 (December 1893), 640–645.
83. See Rochester (New York) Chancery Archives, Letter of Williams to McQuaid, December 30, 1904, for Williams' impatience that "Rome has not yet sent an answer to our demand for a Coadjutor— Put off for the present is the only news." On March 26, 1906, Williams was apprized that O'Connell had been nominated by the Holy Father to the appointment. Mrs. Dorothy Wayman, an authority on O'Connell's life, concedes that "there was no animosity there [between Williams and O'Connell], just that he [Williams] preferred three other men." See HCA: File: William Cardinal O'Connell. Undated letter of Wayman to Daniel E. Moran.
See also BChA: Letter of Archbishop Diomede Falconio to Williams, April 16, 1905. It indicates the three nominees for coadjutor

selected by the consultors and irremovable rectors of the Boston diocese and also those three suggested by the suffragen bishops of the diocese. Matthew Harkins, John Brady, and William Byrne were nominated by the local rectors. Matthew Harkins, Bernard McQuaid, and Richard Neagle were nominated by the bishops. For Williams' notification of Rome's decision regarding the bishopric of Portland, see BChA: Letter of Satolli to Williams, April 21, 1901.

84. Walsh was born in 1858 in Salem, Massachusetts. He was educated at Holy Cross College and trained for the priesthood at St. Sulpice near Paris. After ordination in 1882, he returned to the diocese, serving as a professor at St. John's Seminary from 1884 to 1897. In 1897 he was appointed as first supervisor of the Boston parochial school system and retained that position until his appointment as bishop of Portland in 1906. He died there in 1924.

85. PChA: Diaries: Chancery Office, Diocese of Portland, Maine. Louis S. Walsh, 1906 to 1924, entry of September 16, 1906.

86. HCA: Walsh: Letters. Letter of Walsh to his family, September 16, 1876; PChA: Walsh: Entry Book, entry of June 14, 1892.

87. HCA: Walsh: Letters. Letters of Walsh to his family, September 16 and November 10, 1876. For further remarks on national politics see PChA: Louis S. Walsh Collection [letters of Walsh to his parents from Holy Cross College, 1876–1877. Thirty-nine autographs in all]; letter of Walsh to his parents, March 2, 1877; PChA: Diaries. Louis S. Walsh: My Journey to Paris. From September 13, 1879 to [1883]; entries of September 20–27, 1879.

88. PChA: Walsh: My Journey to Paris, entry of July 24, 1881.

89. HCA: File: Earls, Rev. Michael, S.J. Bibliography of His Writings. An Album of Autographs. Letter of James A. Treanor, Jr. to Rev. William Lucey, S.J., March 31, 1957.

90. Lucey, "The Record of an American Priest, Michael Earls, S.J., 1873–1937" (reprinted from *The American Ecclesiastical Review*, 137, 1957); see Earls, "Dacey," "The Place of Purgatory," "Old Captain" in *Stuore*; Earls, *Memories and Manuscripts* 3, 8–9, 33, 39, 80; Earls, *Under College Towers*, 23, 46, 66, passim.

In 1899, Earls entered the Jesuit novitiate at Woodstock, Maryland where he remained until he took up teaching at Boston College from 1904 to 1919. He returned to Woodstock for theology (1909–1912). For the next twenty-four years he taught literature and rhetoric at Holy Cross College.

91. PChA: Uncatalogued Letters. Letter of O'Connell to his family, June 6, 1899.

92. O'Connell was born in 1859 in Lowell, Massachusetts. He attended public schools there. After graduation, he entered St. Charles College, Maryland in 1876. Because of poor health, he transferred to Boston College in 1878. In 1891, he began studies at the North American College (seminary) in Rome, returning to Boston as a curate for St. Joseph's church. In 1895, he was appointed rector of the North American College until 1901 when he was consecrated

bishop of Portland. In 1906 he was selected by Rome as coadjutor-bishop to Williams for Boston.

93. HCA: File: O'Connell, William Cardinal. Address in Portland, 1902.

94. William Henry Cardinal O'Connell, *Recollections of Seventy Years* (Boston, Houghton, Mifflin and Co., 1934), 135.

95. See HCA: File: O'Connell. "The Reasonable Limits of State Activity." (Reprint of the Catholic Educational Association, *Bulletin 15*, August, 1919), 3.

96. H. Stuart Hughes, *Contemporary Europe: A History* (Englewood Cliffs, N.J., Prentice-Hall, Inc., 1961), 14, 6. For a summary statement of O'Connell's acceptance of this mentality, see O'Connell, *Recollections*, 191.

97. Letter of O'Connell to W———, December 12, 1897, in *Letters*, 238. See also O'Connell, *Recollections*, 191–192.

98. In a later enumeration of these aristocrats, O'Connell lists: "Vice-President Levi Morton, the great Chicago merchant Potter Palmer, the rich Bostonian, Montgomery Sears accompanied by Mrs. John Burnett whose sister is now Superior of the Convent of the Sacred Heart in Newton . . . Mr. B. F. Kieth, the well-known owner of many theaters in America." O'Connell, *Recollections*, 204–205.

99. Louise Tharp, *Mrs. Jack* (Boston, Little, Brown and Co., 1965).

100. O'Connell, *Recollections*, 192; SJSA: Folder: Archbishop and Chancery, 1908–1909. Circular from Archbishop O'Connell regarding a diocesan newspaper.

101. SJSA: Folder: Archbishop and Chancery, 1907–1908. Report of the Committee of Twenty-one Priests, October 26, 1907. For his determined rejection of humble Irish-Catholic beginnings in the face of overwhelming evidence to the contrary see "Preface" to *Letters*, n.p. For the very real poverty of the O'Connell family and his acute awareness of it, see PChA: Uncatalogued Letters. Letters of O'Connell to his sister Jule, February 19, 1898, February 27, 1899, passim.

102. Woods, "Traffic in Citizenship," in *Americans in Process*, 150; Woods, *The City Wilderness* (n.p., n.d.), 221 ff; SJSA: Folder: Archbishop and Chancery, 1908–1909. Circular regarding diocesan paper. For the Irish-Catholic populace's continued insecurity in 1897 see Reverend Henry Austin Adams, "Men and Things," *Donahoe's Magazine*, 38 (October 1897), 309–312.

103. Earls, "In the Tenement District," in *From Bersabee to Dan* (Worcester, Holy Cross College, 1926), 76, *The Wedding Bells of Glendalough* (New York, Benziger Brothers, 1913), 33, 17, *Marie of the House D'Anters* (New York, Benziger Brothers, 1916), 273; Walsh, *Origins of the Catholic Church in Salem* (Boston, Cashman, Keating and Co., 1890), 102; O'Connell, *Recollections*, 13, 14, 33.

104. See Earls, *Melchior of Boston*, 17; Earls, *From Bersabee to Dan*, 76; *Marie*, 29, 7, 99, 7; *Melchior of Boston*, 17, 20; Earls, *Marie*, 38–39; Earls, *Marie*, 321.

105. For the intensity of O'Connell's striving for place see O'Connell, *Recollections*, 7, 105. For the importance of "arrival" in Earls'

life see *Melchior of Boston,* passim. In *The Wedding Bells of Glenda-lough* he notes that "in this day admission to certain Boston circles" is according to "one's prominence in some branch of art or science" 28; see Reverend James J. Bric, "An Account of Catholicity in the Public Institutions of Boston" (Summary of a Paper Read before the American Catholic Historical Association of Philadelphia, April 28, 1886) (Philadelphia, 1887).

106. For the paternalistic control which Draper maintained at his works in Hopedale, Massachusetts, and among the tenement-dwellers in his buildings near Medford see L. C. Creedon, "Ideal Industrial Conditions," *Donahoe's Magazine,* 54 (November 1905) [20, 21, 23]; Earls, *Wedding Bells of Glendalough,* 382.

107. See Abbé Felix Klein, *In the Land of the Strenuous Life* (Chicago, A. C. McClurg and Co., 1907). He makes the slip, "For nations as well as for individuals, history, or rather, Providence, very often holds . . ." x. See also Earls, "A Cleric's Literary Laboratory" in *Under College Towers,* 142.

108. Walsh, *Catholic Church in Salem,* vi.

109. O'Connell, *Recollections,* 26, 27; O'Connell, *Recollections,* 154.

110. Earls, "The Tailor of St. Botolph's," *Donahoe's Magazine,* 54 (September 1905), 277, and Earls, "Cleric's Laboratory" in *Under College Towers,* 136–137; Earls, *Melchior of Boston,* 104.

111. Twomey, "Leo XIII and the United States," *Donahoe's Magazine,* 41 (May 1891), 545.

112. Walsh, *Historical Sketch of the Growth of Catholic Parochial Schools in the Archdiocese of Boston* (Newton Heights, Mass., Press of St. John's Industrial School, 1901), 4.

113. For Twomey's rationalization of his own career in this direction see "The Priest-Novelist," *Donahoe's Magazine,* 44 (July 1900), 45–49. See also the writings and career of Father Hugh Blunt of Boston.

114. Earls, *Under College Towers,* 40.

115. O'Connell, *Recollections,* 7; for a study of the psychological effects of total institutionalization see Erving Goffman, *Asylums: Essays on the Social Situation of Mental Patients and Other Inmates* (Chicago, Aldine, 1961); for an example of restrained opposition see Springfield (Massachusetts) Diocesan Archives: Exchange of letters between O'Connell and Bishop Thomas Beaven, October 17, 1908, October 15, 1908, September 25, 1908, September 29, 1908.

116. PChA: Healy Letters, Uncatalogued. Account of the Second Synod of the Diocese of Portland, 1904.

117. SJSA: Folder: Archbishop and Chancery, 1908–1909. Circular regarding a diocesan newspaper.

118. SJSA: Ordinandi file on Jeremiah Driscoll, ordained 1908. Letter of Francis Havey to O'Connell, December 11, 1907.

119. PChA: Uncatalogued Letters. Letter of Conway to O'Connell, June 24, 1902. For O'Connell's overwrought letters regarding finances see PChA: Uncatalogued Letters. Letters of O'Connell to his family,

February 19, 1898, January 30, 1899, February 27, 1899, June 6, 1899, October 24, 1899.

120. See PChA: Untitled volume marked "From Rt. Rev. Msgr. Hurley—formerly Vicar General [of the Diocese of Portland]." This book is clearly intended only for the use of Bishop Louis S. Walsh as in-coming bishop in 1906. It contains notations on each of ninety-eight priests in the diocese, and it sheds light on the problems faced by both O'Connell and Walsh in Maine. Such comments as these on individual priests make up the bulk of the notebook: "a little odd—trustworthy"; "trouble-maker during interregnum"; "removed from Westbrook for drinking . . . fine since at Bitteford [*sic*]"; "heavy drinker at Augusta, but with Msgr. Wallace, all right"; "on testimony of pastor only, might be homosexual tendencies"; "a hypocrite—trouble with bishop"; "questionable life before coming to Maine"; "tactless but brilliant"; "trouble-maker after Healy's death"; "very active in the campaign against O'Connell . . . perhaps opium fiend"; "obliged to leave many sections because of drinking, all right now"; "Healy distrusted him"; "connected with contraband trouble in Jackman"; "a transient, not reliable"; "accused of homosexual tendencies"; "all right, but accused of misappropriating funds"; "fine, 'til O'Connell came—then aggressively disloyal—might be mentally ill"; "a strange background—Dominicans distrust him"; "Healy thinks too familiar with schoolchildren, especially girls"; "brilliant but a drunk and a slanderer"; "serviceable 'til drug addict"; "poor at finances but good"; "lonesome, drinker, then homosexual"; "tired of the French"; "talented but drinks"; "questionable finances"; "not suave enough for Bar Harbor"; "bitter tongue, foe of Healy's"; "not loyal to Healy or O'Connell"; "brilliant, disliked and disloyal"; "insubordinate to O'Connell"; "two-faced; despised O'Connell but praised him." Fifty-one of the men are "good" (with qualifications) in Hurley's estimate. For the trustworthiness of Hurley's opinions see PChA: Walsh Diary, 1907, entry of February 15, 1907.

O'Connell's presentation of his administration in Portland and the priests' faithfulness to him is quite the opposite. See *Recollections*, 218.

121. SJSA: Folder: Archbishop and Chancery, 1907–1908, passim; SJSA: Folder: Archbishop and Chancery, 1909–1910. Letter of O'Connell to Havey, September 29, 1909. Letter of Peterson to O'Connell, January 12, 1911.

122. SJSA: Letter of Peterson to O'Connell, November 23, 1912. For the Baltimore Council's rejection of the villa proposal see Stafford Poole, *Seminary in Crisis* (New York, Herder and Herder, 1965), 49–50.

123. SJSA: Folder: Seminary Miscellaneous. Letter of Peterson to Reverend James A. Walsh, February 20, 1912.

124. Roddan, "Political Priests," *The Pilot*, June 1, 1850, 1; O'Connell, "The Influence of Rome in the Formation of the American Clergy: Paper Read at the Jubilee Academia of the American College, June 12, 1909, tr. from the Italian," in Henry A. Brann, *History*

of the American College of the Roman Catholic Church of the United States, Rome, Italy (New York, Benziger Brothers, 1910), 372; PChA: Entry Book of Louis S. Walsh, entry of October 17, 1907.

125. "People in Print," *Donahoe's Magazine,* 55 (February 1906), 294.

126. The term is Robert A. Woods' in *Americans in Process,* 371.

127. O'Connell, "Influence of Rome" in Brann, *History of the American College,* 359; HCA: File: William Henry O'Connell. "The Reasonable Limits of State Activity," *The Catholic Educational Association Bulletin,* xv (August 1919), 5.

128. O'Connell, "Influence of Rome" in Brann, *History of the American College,* 364.

129. Reverend William J. Kerby, "Tribute: Thomas Maurice Mulry," *St. Vincent de Paul Quarterly,* 21 (May 1916), 89.

Bibliography

ARCHIVAL MATERIALS

BOSTON ARCHDIOCESAN CHANCERY ARCHIVES (BChA)

Vertical files of the correspondence of Bishops John B. Fitzpatrick, John J. Williams and William Henry Cardinal O'Connell. In addition to such correspondence, the files contain such items as accounts of the synods, diocesan meetings, and meetings of archbishops; letters between individual clergymen; letters of priests to the vicar general of the diocese; reports on the diocese to the Office of the Propaganda in Rome; a sparse diary kept by Williams in 1870.

Diocesan Circulars, seven volumes from 1855 to 1906.

Hilary Tucker Diaries II and III (1862–1864; 1864–1865).

Monsignor Patrick Strain's Accts and Collections, 1856–1881.

Files on individual priests—incomplete.

Eulalia Tuckerman, "Life of Archbishop John J. Williams." Typescript completed in 1911.

PORTLAND, MAINE, DIOCESAN CHANCERY ARCHIVES (PChA)

Diaries of Right Reverend Bishop David Bacon, 1859, 1862.

Miscellaneous and uncatalogued letters of Bishop James A. Healy, 1876, 1877. Letterpress books of correspondence until his death in 1900.

Diaries of Charles McCarthy, Jr., 1883–1917.

Journal of Louis S. Walsh. My Journey to Paris. From September 1879 to [1883].

Entry Book of Louis S. Walsh. September, 1889 to [1896].

Entry Books of Louis S. Walsh [1906 yearly until his death].
Untitled book of notations by Monsignor Hurley, formerly vicar general of the diocese. It was completed for Louis S. Walsh presumably in 1906.
Miscellaneous and uncatalogued letters of William Henry O'Connell to his sister and family, 1897 to 1906, many undated.

HOLY CROSS COLLEGE (WORCESTER) ARCHIVES (HCA)

REVEREND JOHN BOYCE
The Satisfying Influence of Catholicity on The Intellect and Senses; A Lecture Delivered Before the Catholic Institute of New York, on Friday Evening, January 24, 1851. (New York, 1851).

REVEREND MICHAEL EARLS, S.J.

Shaughnessy Collection: letters of Earls to his family from Europe, 1897–1898; Notebooks, 1890, 1899–1900; miscellaneous letters.
Earls—Letters, 1910–1916.

LOUISE IMOGEN GUINEY

The Grace Guiney Collection. Letters to Louise Imogen Guiney, catalogued alphabetically.
The Cordon Collection of Guiney Letters, Portfolios.
Correspondence of Guiney and Father W. Harmon van Allen.
Guiney—Earls Collection (22 letters and cards), 1899–1920.
Guiney—Heuser Collection.

REVEREND JAMES A. HEALY

File: James A. Healy, '49, Bishop of Boston.
James A. Healy: Copies of Two Diaries: 1849, 1891.
James A. Healy: Sermons, uncatalogued. From the 1850's to 1900.

REVEREND LOUIS S. WALSH

Holy Cross Letters. To his parents, 1876.
Files on Reverend Thomas J. Conaty, Katherine E. Conway, William Henry Cardinal O'Connell, Mary B. O'Reilly and letters to Michael Earls, S.J.

ST. JOHN'S SEMINARY ARCHIVES (SJSA)

Record: St. John's Seminary, Boston (Brighton) Entrance Records, from 1884.

Record: Register of Calls. St. John's Seminary, Boston, from 1884.
Record: St. John's Seminary, Boston (Brighton), Faculty Meetings, 1886–1905 [in French].
Canonical Register, St. John's Seminary, Boston. 1884–1960.
Archbishop and Chancery, 1883–1896; 1883–1906.
Seminary History, 1898–1908.
Ordinandi Files, 1908 to date.
Ordination Correspondence, 1894, passim.
Entrance Examinations: 1886, 1889, 1890, 1892–1894, 1899 to date.
Records of the House of Philosophy, 1909–1914.
Correspondence with Priests, 1882–1916.
Seminary: Miscellaneous Correspondence: 1902–1913.

ARCHIVES OF THE BOSTON OFFICE OF THE
ST. VINCENT DE PAUL SOCIETY (VDA)

Reports of the St. Vincent de Paul Society in Boston, 1869–1890.
Diary, 1888: Richard Keefe, Special Agent, St. Vincent de Paul Conferences, Charities Building; also, Cases: 1889.
Correspondence of Thomas Ring, 1860–1870 cited as "Early Letters."
Scrapbooks of the Society, cited as "Ring Scrapbooks." Valuable materials from 1892–1896.
Two volumes of Thomas Ring's correspondence: 1876–1880, 1880–1886, cited as "Ring Papers ɪ" and "Ring Papers ɪɪ." Letterpress books of Thomas Ring: 1891–1892, 1894–1897, cited as "Ring Papers ɪɪɪ" and "Ring Papers ɪᴠ."
Letterpress book marked St. Vincent de Paul Society from December 5, 1884, to 1888.
Vertical file of correspondence, 1880 to date.
Minutes of the Monthly Meetings of the Particular Council, 1865–1877, 1877–1901.

SELECTED WORKS

Abbott, Eleanor Hallowell. *Being Little in Cambridge when Everyone Else Was Big.* New York: D. Appleton and Century Co., 1936.
Allen, Alexander V. G. *Life and Letters of Phillips Brooks.* 3 vols. New York: E. P. Dutton & Company, 1901.
Arensberg, Conrad M., and Solon T. Kimball. *Family and Community in Ireland.* Cambridge, Mass.: Harvard University Press, 1940.
Athearn, Robert G. *Thomas Francis Meagher: An Irish Revolutionary in America* in University of Colorado Studies Series in History. Boulder: University of Colorado Press, 1902.
[Bacon, Edwin]. "Sketch: Archbishop John J. Williams," *Time and the Hour,* vɪɪɪ (September 10, 1898), 6–7.
Barnet, Sylvan, Morton Berman, and William Burto (eds). *The*

Genius of the Irish Theater. New York: Mentor Book, New American Library, 1960.

Bell, John. "Lord Acton's American Diaries, I, II, III," *The Fortnightly Review,* 110, n.s., 111, n.s. (November 1921; January 1922), 743–752; 917–934, 68–83.

Bernhart, Joseph. *The Vatican as a World Power,* tr. George M. Schuster, rev. ed. New York: Ginn and Co., 1939.

Blake, Mary Elizabeth. *The Coming Reform: The Absurdities of Old Fashioned Militarism at Home and Abroad in These Closing Years of the Nineteenth Century. A Woman's Word.* Boston: The American Peace Society, n.d.

———— *In the Harbour of Hope.* Boston: Little, Brown and Co , 1907.

———— *A Memoir, Patrick McGrath, 1812–1894.* Private printing, n.p., n.d.

———— and Margaret Sullivan. *Mexico: Picturesque, Political and Progressive.* Boston: Lee and Shepard Publishers, 1888.

———— *On the Wing: Rambling Notes of a Trip to the Pacific,* 2nd ed. Boston: Lee and Shepard Publishers, 1883.

———— *Twenty-Six Hours a Day.* Boston: D. Lathrop and Co., 1883.

Blodgett, Geoffrey T. "Josiah Quincy, Brahmin Democrat," *The New England Quarterly,* 38 (December 1965), 435–453.

Boyce, Reverend John [pseudo. Paul Peppergrass]. *Mary Lee, or the Yankee in Ireland.* Baltimore: Patrick Donahoe, 1860.

———— *The Satisfying Influence of Catholicity on the Intellect and Senses; A Lecture Delivered before the Catholic Institute of New York, on Friday Evening, January 24, 1851.* New York: Printed by Robert Coddington, 1851.

———— [pseudo. Paul Peppergrass]. *Shandy McGuire, or Tricks upon Travellers Being a Story of the North of Ireland.* New York: Edw. Dunigan and Bros., 1851.

———— [pseudo. Paul Peppergrass]. *The Spaewife, or the Queen's Secret; A Story of the Reign of Queen Elizabeth.* 2 vols. Baltimore: Murphy and Co., 1853.

Brann, Henry A. *History of the American College of the Roman Catholic Church of the United States, Rome, Italy.* New York: Benziger Brothers, 1910.

Bric, Reverend James J. "An Account of Catholicity in the Public Institutions of Boston," (Summary of a Paper read before the American Catholic Historical Society of Philadelphia, April 28, 1886, by Rev. James J. Bric, S.J.) in *Records of the American Catholic Historical Society,* vols. 1 and 2, 1884–1885. Philadelphia, 1887.

Bridges, William E. "Family Patterns and Social Values in America, 1825–1875," *American Quarterly,* xvII (Spring 1965), 3–11.

Brooks, Van Wyck. *New England: Indian Summer.* New York: E. P. Dutton and Co., 1950.

Brown, Alice. *Louise Imogen Guiney.* New York: Macmillan Company, 1921.

Brown, Thomas N. *Irish-American Nationalism, 1870–1890,* in *Criti-*

cal Periods of History Series, ed. by Robert D. Cross. New York: J. B. Lippincott Company, 1966.

———— "The Origins and Character of Irish-American Nationalism," *Review of Politics,* 18 (July 1956), 327–358.

Brownson's Quarterly Review, from October, 1857 to October, 1858.

Bugg, Lelia Harding. *The Correct Thing for Catholics,* 12th ed. New York: Benziger Brothers, 1891.

———— *Orchids, A Novel.* St. Louis: B. Herder, 1894.

Bushee, Frederick A. *Ethnic Factors in the Population of Boston,* Vol. 4 in *Publications of the American Economic Association,* 3rd series. New York: Macmillan Company, 1903.

Byrne, Reverend John F., C.SS.R. *The Glories of Mary in Boston: A Memorial History of the Church of Our Lady of Perpetual Help (Mission Church), Roxbury, Massachusetts, 1871–1921.* Boston: Mission Church Press, 1921.

Citizens' Association of Boston. *First Annual Report of the Executive Committee, with the Constitution, Officers and Members.* Boston, 1889.

Conway, Katherine E. (ed). *Watchwords from John Boyle O'Reilly.* Boston: Joseph George Cupples (private printing), 1891.

Corr, Bernard (ed). *Souvenir of the Sacerdotal Golden Jubilee of the Most Reverend Jno. J. Williams, D.D., Archbishop of Boston on Thurs. and Fri., May 16 and 17, 1895, With Full Reports of Receptions and Presentations Incident to the Celebration.* Boston: John L. Corr and Co., 1895.

Cross, Robert D. "The Changing Image of the City Among American Catholics," *Catholic Historical Review,* XLVIII (April 1962), 33–52.

Crowley, Mary Catherine. "The Child of the Temple" in *Carmelita and Other Stories,* ed. Anna T. Sadlier in the series *Fireside Tales by Catholic Authors.* Milwaukee: Yewdale and Sons Co., n.d.

Donahoe's Magazine, from January, 1879 to February, 1906.

Dunigan, David R. *A History of Boston College.* Milwaukee: Bruce Publishing Co., 1947.

Dwight, Thomas. "The Attack on Freedom of Education in Massachusetts," *American Catholic Quarterly Review,* XIII (October 1888), 545–555.

Earls, Michael, S.J. *From Bersabee to Dan, and Other Ballads.* Worcester: Holy Cross College, 1926.

———— *Manuscripts and Memories: Chapters in Our Literary Tradition.* Milwaukee: Bruce Publishing Co., 1935.

———— *Marie of the House D'Anters.* New York: Benziger Brothers, 1916.

———— *Melchior of Boston.* New York: Benziger Brothers, 1910.

———— *Stuore.* New York: Benziger Brothers, 1911.

———— *Under College Towers: A Book of Essays.* New York: Macmillan Company, 1926.

———— *The Wedding Bells of Glendalough.* New York: Benziger Brothers, 1913.

Emery, Susan L. *A Catholic Stronghold and Its Making: A History of St. Peter's Parish, Dorchester, Massachusetts, and of Its First Rector, the Rev. Peter Ronan, P.R.* Boston: George H. Ellis, 1910.

Fairbanks, Charles B. [pseudo. Aguecheek]. *My Unknown Chum,* 1922 ed. New York: The Devin-Adair Co., 1922.

Finley, James F., C.S.P. *James Gillis, Paulist.* New York: Hanover House, 1958.

Flanagan, Thomas J. B. *The Irish Novelists: 1800–1850.* New York: Columbia University Press, 1958.

Foley, Albert S. *Bishop Healy: Beloved Outcast: The Story of a Great Priest Whose Life Has Become a Legend.* New York: Farrar, Straus and Young, 1954.

Frawley, Sister M. Alphonsine, C.S.J. *Patrick Donahoe.* Washington, D.C.: Catholic University Press, 1946.

Gallagher, Louis J., S.J. *Episode on Beacon Hill.* Boston: Benziger Brothers, 1950.

Guiney, Grace (ed). *Letters of Louise Imogen Guiney.* 2 vols. New York: Harper and Brothers, 1926.

Guiney, Louise Imogen. *Blessed Edmund Campion.* London: MacDonald and Evans, 1908.

———— *A Little English Gallery.* New York: Harper and Brothers, 1894.

———— *Lovers' Saint Ruth's and Three Other Tales.* Boston: Copeland and Day, 1894.

———— *The Martyr's Idyl and Shorter Poems.* Boston: Houghton, Mifflin and Co., 1900.

———— *'Monsieur Henri': A Foot-note to French History.* New York: Harper and Brothers, 1892.

———— *Patrins, To Which Is Added an Inquirendo into the Wit and Other Good Parts of His Late Majesty King Charles the Second.* Boston: Printed for Copeland and Day, 1897.

———— *Robert Emmet: A Survey of His Rebellion and of His Romance.* London: David Nutt, 1904.

Hale, Edward Everett, et al. *Workingmen's Homes: Essays and Stories.* Boston: James R. Osgood and Co., 1874.

Handlin, Oscar. *Boston's Immigrants: A Study in Acculturation,* rev. and enlarged ed. Cambridge: Belknap Press of Harvard University Press, 1959.

Haskins, Reverend George F. *Report, Historical, Statistical and Financial of the House of the Angel Guardian from the Beginning in 1851 to October, 1864.* Boston: Patrick Donahoe, 1864.

———— *St. Ignatius and the Society of Jesus: Their Influence on Civilization and Christianity, A Sermon Delivered in the Church of the Immaculate Conception in Boston, on Sunday, August 4, 1867.* Boston: Bernard Corr, 1867.

———— *Six Weeks Abroad in Ireland, England and Belgium.* Boston: Patrick Donahoe, 1872.

Healy, Reverend John. *Maynooth College, Its Centenary History, 1795–1895.* Dublin: Browne and Nolan, 1895.

Herlihy, Reverend Cornelius J. *The Celt Above the Saxon, or a Comparative Sketch of the Irish and English People in War, in Peace, and in Their Character,* 2nd and rev. ed. Boston: Angel Guardian Press, 1904.

Herlihy, Elisabeth M. (ed). *Fifty Years of Boston: A Memorial Volume Issued in Commemoration of the Tercentenary of 1930. Compiled by the Subcommittee on Memorial History of the Boston Tercentenary Committee.* Boston: Published for and by the subcommittee, 1932.

Hogan, Abbé John B. *Daily Thoughts for Priests,* 3rd ed. Boston: Marlier, Callanan and Co., 1900.

Hughes, H. Stuart. *Contemporary Europe: A History.* Englewood Cliffs: Prentice-Hall, Inc., 1961.

In Memoriam of Rt. Rev. John B. Fitzpatrick. Boston: Patrick Donahoe, 1866.

James, William. *The Varieties of Religious Experience: A Study of Human Nature Being the Gifford Lectures on Natural Religion Delivered at Edinburgh in 1901–1902.* New York: Mentor Book, New American Library Co., 1958.

Johnstone, Reverend Julien E. *Songs of Sun and Shadow.* Boston: W. B. Clarke Co., Park Street Church, 1900.

[Kelly, William]. *The Life of Father Haskins by a Friend of the House of the Angel Guardian.* Boston: Angel Guardian Press, 1899.

Kindilien, Carlin T. *American Poetry in the Eighteen Nineties: A Study of American Verse, 1890–99, Based Upon the Volumes from that Period in the Harris Collection of American Poetry and Plays in the Brown University Library.* Providence: Brown University Press, 1956.

Klein, Abbé Felix. *Americanism: A Phantom Heresy. Intro. Archbishop John Ireland as Reproduced from Walter Elliott's Life of Father Hecker.* Atchison, Kansas: Aquin Book Shop, 1951.

———— *In the Land of the Strenuous Life,* tr. author. Chicago: A. C. McClurg and Co., 1905.

"The Late Archbishop Williams" (anon. article), *The Republic,* 26 (September 7, 1907), 3–6.

Lord, Reverend Robert H., Reverend John E. Sexton, Reverend Edward T. Harrington. *History of the Archdiocese of Boston, in the Various Stages of Its Development, 1604 to 1943.* 3 vols. New York: Sheed and Ward, 1944.

Lucey, Reverend William L., S.J. *Catholic Journalism in New England: 1885–1900* (Reprint from *The New England Social Studies Bulletin,* May 1953).

———— "Louise Imogen Guiney and Her 'Songs at the Start,'" *Records of the American Catholic Historical Society of Philadelphia,* 66 (March, 1955), 53–63.

———— "The Record of an American Priest: Michael Earls, S.J.,

1873–1937" (Reprint from *The American Ecclesiastical Review,* 137, 1957).

McAvoy, Reverend Thomas T., C.S.C. "Americanism, Fact and Fiction," *The Catholic Historical Review,* 31 (July 1945), 133–153.

McCarthy, Reverend Lawrence P. *Sketch of the Life and Missionary Labors of Rev. James Fitton,* in *Publications of the New England Catholic Historical Society.* Boston: George E. Crosby Co., 1908.

McManamin, Reverend Francis G., S.J. *The·American Years of John Boyle O'Reilly, 1870–1890.* (Abstract of a dissertation, Catholic University of America, Washington, D.C., 1959).

Madeleva, Sister M., CSC. *My First Seventy Years.* New York: Macmillan Company, 1959.

Malone, George K. *The True Church: A Study in the Apologetics of Orestes Augustus Brownson.* Mundelein, Illinois: St. Mary of the Lake, 1957.

Mann, Arthur. *Yankee Reformers in the Urban Age: Social Reform in Boston, 1880–1900.* New York: Harper Torchbook, Harper and Row, 1954.

Markewich, Daniel. "David Henshaw of Massachusetts, 1791–1852." (Honors Thesis, Harvard University, Cambridge, 1962).

Merk, Lois Bannister. "Boston's Historic Public School Crisis," *The New England Quarterly,* 31 (June 1958), 172–199.

Miller, Perry. *Errand into the Wilderness.* New York: Harper Torchbook, Harper and Row, 1956.

——— *The Life of the Mind in America, from the Revolution to the Civil War.* New York: Harcourt, Brace and World, Inc., 1965.

O'Brien, William and Desmond Ryan (eds). *Devoy's Post Bag, 1871–1928.* 2 vols. Dublin: C. J. Fallon, Ltd., 1948.

O'Connell, William Cardinal. *The Letters of His Eminence William Cardinal O'Connell, Archbishop of Boston, Volume I (from College Days, 1876 to Bishop of Portland, 1901).* Cambridge: The Riverside Press, 1915.

——— *Recollections of Seventy Years.* Boston: Houghton, Mifflin & Co., 1934.

O'Hare, Sister M. Jeanne d'Arc, C.S.J. "The Public Career of Patrick A. Collins." (Dissertation for Boston College, Boston, 1959).

O'Mahoney, Katherine A. O'Keefe. *Famous Irishwomen.* Lawrence, Mass.: Lawrence Publishing Co., 1907.

One of a Series of Interviews on the American Character, Center for the Study of Democratic Institutions. Religion, interviews by Donald McDonald with Robert E. Fitch, John J. Wright, Louis Finkelstein. Washington, D.C.: Printed for the Fund for the Republic, Inc., 1963.

O'Reilly, John Boyle. "An Irish Government for Ireland," *The American Catholic Quarterly Review,* 7 (April 1882), 270–278.

——— *Moondyne: A Story from the Under-World,* 4th ed. Boston: Roberts Brothers, 1883.

———— "What Had Ireland Gained by Agitation," *The American Catholic Quarterly Review*, 8 (October 1883), 710–716.

Peterson, George E. *The New England College in the Age of the University*. Amherst, Mass.: Amherst College Press, 1964.

The Pilot, from January, 1848, to July, 1873; passim.

Poole, Reverend Stafford, C. M. *Seminary in Crisis*. New York: Herder and Herder, 1965.

The Public School Question. Roman Catholicism and Americanism: A Discussion Between Rev. J. P. Bland and Rev. John O'Brien of Cambridge, Mass. Cambridge University Press, 1880. Pamphlet reprinted from *The Boston Herald*.

Rexroth, Kenneth. "Walt Whitman," *The Saturday Review*, September 3, 1966, 43.

Richards, Reverend Joseph Havens, S.J. *A Loyal Life: A Biography of Henry Livingston Richards with Speculations from His Letters and a Sketch of the Catholic Movement in America*. St. Louis: B. Herder, 1913.

Riley, James. *Christy of Rathglin: An Entertaining and Exciting Story of the Life of an Irish Lad*. Boston: C. M. Clark Publishing Co., 1907.

———— *Songs of Two Peoples*. Boston: Estes and Lauriat, 1898.

———— *To Boston's Public Library* (Reprint from *The Weekly Bouquet*, June 2, 1897).

Roche, James Jeffrey. *Life of John Boyle O'Reilly: Together with His Complete Poems and Speeches ed. by Mrs. John Boyle O'Reilly*. New York: Cassell Publishing Co., 1891.

———— *Songs and Satires*. Boston: Ticknor and Co., 1887.

———— *The Story of the Filibusters: To Which Is Added the Life of Colonel David Crockett*. London: T. Fisher Unwin, 1891.

Roddan, Reverend John T. *John O'Brien; or, The Orphan of Boston, A Tale of Real Life*. Boston: P. Donahoe, 1850.

The Sacred Heart Review, from December, 1888, to December, 1893; passim.

Scanlan, Reverend Michael J. *An Historical Sketch of the Parish of St. Rose, Chelsea, Massachusetts*. n.p., n.d.

Scudder, Vida. *A Listener in Babel*. Boston: Houghton, Mifflin and Company, 1903.

Sexton, Reverend John E. and Reverend Arthur J. Riley. *History of Saint John's Seminary, Brighton*. Boston: Publ. by the Roman Catholic Archbishop of Boston, 1945.

"Sketch: Famous People at Home—xvi: James Jeffrey Roche" (anon. article), *Time and the Hour*, v (June 5, 1897), 7–8.

"Sketch: Famous People at Home—xxvi: Josiah Quincy" (anon. article), *Time and the Hour*, viii (September 10, 1898), 6–7.

Smith, Walter George, and Helen Grace Smith. *Fidelis of the Cross: James Kent Stone*. New York: G. P. Putnam's Sons, 1926 reprint.

Solomon, Barbara Miller. *Ancestors and Immigrants: A Changing New England Tradition*. Cambridge: Harvard University Press, 1956.

Stone, James Kent. *An Awakening and What Followed*. Notre Dame, Indiana: Ave Maria Press, n.d.

Sullivan, James (ed). *One Hundred Years of Progress. A Graphic, Historical and Pictorial Account of the Catholic Church of New England, Archdiocese of Boston, embracing Portraits and Biographical Sketches of the Bishops, Prominent Priests, Eminent Church Workers of the Past, Together with Views and Sketches of the Present Churches, Also of Many Early Church Edifaces and Educational Institutions*. Boston: Illustrated Publishing Co., 1894.

Sullivan, William Lawrence. *The Priest: A Tale of Modernism in New England*, 3rd ed. Boston: Beacon Press, 1925.

Tharp, Louise Hall. *Mrs. Jack*. Boston: Little, Brown & Co., 1965.

Thorp, Willard. "Catholic Novelists in Defense of Their Faith, 1829–1865," *Proceedings of the American Antiquarian Society*, 78 (April 1968), 25–117.

Three Heroines of New England Romance: Their True Stories Herein Set Forth by Mrs. Harriet Prescott Spofford, Miss Louise Imogen Guiney, and Miss Alice Brown. Boston: Little, Brown and Co., 1895.

Tuckerman, Eulalia (Reverend Mother Augustine of the Mother of God, D.C.). "Life of Archbishop John J. Williams." (Typescript, Boston Chancery Archives, 1911).

The United States Catholic Almanac or Laity's Directory for the Year, 1837. Baltimore: James Myres, 1837.

Walsh, Reverend Louis S. *Historical Sketch of the Growth of Catholic Parochial Schools in the Archdiocese of Boston*, Newton Heights, Mass.: Press of St. John's Industrial School, 1901.

———— *Origins of the Catholic Church in Salem and Its Growth in St. Mary's Parish and the Parish of the Immaculate Conception*. Boston: Cashman, Keating and Co., 1890.

Warner, Sam B., Jr. *Streetcar Suburbs: The Process of Growth in Boston, 1870–1900*. Cambridge: Harvard University Press and the M.I.T. Press, 1962.

———— (ed). *Woods, Robert A. and Albert Kennedy. The Zone of Emergence*. Cambridge: Published by the Joint Center for Urban Studies of M.I.T. and Harvard University, 1962.

Whitehill, Walter Muir. *A Memorial to Bishop Cheverus, with a Catalogue of the Books Given by Him to the Boston Athenæum*. Boston: Boston Athenæum, 1951.

Whiting, Lilian. *Louise Chandler Moulton: Poet and Friend*. Boston: Little, Brown and Co., 1910.

Whyte, John H. "The Appointment of Catholic Bishops in Nineteenth-Century Ireland," *Catholic Historical Review*, 48 (April 1962), 12–32.

Woods, Robert A. (ed). *Americans in Process: A Settlement Study be Residents and Associates of the South End House . . . North and West Ends*. Boston: Houghton, Mifflin and Co., 1902.

Woods, Robert A., and Albert J. Kennedy (eds). *Young Working*

Girls: A Summary of Evidence from Two Thousand Social Workers, edited for the National Federation of Settlements, introduction by Jane Addams. Boston: Houghton, Mifflin and Co., 1913.

Woods, Robert A. *The City Wilderness: A Settlement Study.* Boston: n.p., 1898.

Wynne, Reverend John J. *Great Encyclical Letters of Pope Leo XIII.* New York: Benziger Brothers, 1903.

Zwierlein, Frederick J. *The Life and Letters of Bishop McQuaid, Prefaced with the History of Catholic Rochester before His Episcopate.* 3 vols. Rochester: The Art Print Shop, 1926.

Index